KINESIC
MAGIC

About the Author

Donald Tyson (Nova Scotia, Canada) is an occult scholar and the author of the popular, critically acclaimed Necronomicon series. He has written more than two dozen books on Western esoteric traditions.

DONALD TYSON

KINESIC
MAGIC

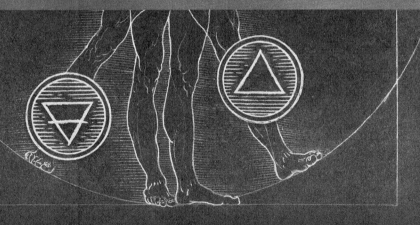

Channeling Energy with
Postures & Gestures

Llewellyn Publications
Woodbury, Minnesota

FIRST EDITION
First Printing, 2020

Cover design by Shannon McKuhen
Cover illustration by Erwin Sherman
Illustrations by Wen Hsu on pages 7, 9, 11, 13, 15, 17, 19, 21, 23, 25, 27, 29, 31, 33, 35, 37, 39, 41, 43, 45, 47, 49, 51, 53, 86, 88, 90, 92, 94, 133, 149, 151, 153, 155, 157, 158, 160,180, 209, 210, 212, 214, 215, 217, 219, 220, 222, 224, 225, 227, 270, and 271
All other illustrations by the Llewellyn Art Department on pages 66, 68, 72–74, 115, 117, 120, 122, 124, 125, 127, 129, 175, 177, 178, 181–183, 185–193, and 272

Llewellyn Publications is a registered trademark of Llewellyn Worldwide Ltd.

Library of Congress Cataloging-in-Publication Data
Names: Tyson, Donald, author.
Title: Kinesic magic : channeling energy with postures & gestures / by
  Donald Tyson.
Description: First edition. | Woodbury, Minnesota : Llewellyn Worldwide,
  Ltd, 2020. | Summary: "This is a book on using body postures and hand
  gestures in magic, with lots of planetary, qabalistic, and elemental
  associations"—Provided by publisher.
Identifiers: LCCN 2020008061 (print) | LCCN 2020008062 (ebook) | ISBN
  9780738764139 (paperback) | ISBN 9780738765266 (ebook)
Subjects: LCSH: Magic. | Yoga. | Occultism.
Classification: LCC BF1623.Y64 T97 2020 (print) | LCC BF1623.Y64 (ebook)
  | DDC 133.4/3—dc23
LC record available at https://lccn.loc.gov/2020008061
LC ebook record available at https://lccn.loc.gov/2020008062

Llewellyn Worldwide Ltd. does not participate in, endorse, or have any authority or responsibility concerning private business transactions between our authors and the public.

All mail addressed to the author is forwarded, but the publisher cannot, unless specifically instructed by the author, give out an address or phone number.

Any internet references contained in this work are current at publication time, but the publisher cannot guarantee that a specific location will continue to be maintained. Please refer to the publisher's website for links to authors' websites and other sources.

Llewellyn Publications
A Division of Llewellyn Worldwide Ltd.
2143 Wooddale Drive
Woodbury, MN 55125-2989
www.llewellyn.com

Printed in the United States of America

Other Books by Donald Tyson

Tarot Magic (2018)

Serpent of Wisdom (2013)

The Demonology of King James I (2011)

The Dream World of H. P. Lovecraft (2010)

The 13 Gates of the Necronomicon (2010)

The Fourth Book of Occult Philosophy (2009)

Runic Astrology (2009)

Grimoire of the Necronomicon (2008)

Necronomicon Tarot (with Anne Stokes) (2007)

Soul Flight (2007)

Alhazred (2006)

Portable Magic (2006)

Familiar Spirits (2004)

Necronomicon (2004)

1-2-3 Tarot (2004)

The Power of the Word (2004)

Enochian Magic for Beginners (2002)

Tetragrammaton (2002)

The Magician's Workbook (2001)

Sexual Alchemy (2000)

Forthcoming Books by Donald Tyson

Essential Tarot Writings (2020)

Disclaimer

The material in this book is not intended as a substitute for trained medical or psychological advice. Readers are advised to consult their personal health-care professionals regarding treatment. The publisher and the author assume no liability for any injuries caused to the reader that may result from the reader's use of the content contained herein and recommend common sense when contemplating the practices described in the work.

Contents

Tables

Figures

INTRODUCTION
A HANDS-ON APPROACH TO MAGIC

Kinesics: The expression of meaning through postures, gestures, and body movements.

THIS BOOK CONTAINS A COMPLETE system of practical Western magic that has been stripped to its bare essentials—divested of the unnecessary trappings of the grimoires, arcane schools, and esoteric traditions that have grown up over the centuries.

It requires no ritual temple, no special robes or jewelry, no instruments, furniture, tools, or materials of any kind. It can be performed using only your hands, your body, and your mind. It can be worked anywhere, at any time, and once you learn it nobody will ever be able to take it away from you or prevent you from using it, because it will be a part of you.

Kinesic magic may be thought of as the magic of the empty hand. If you were stripped, confined to a prison cell without light, and chained to a wall, you could still work this system of magic without any loss of its potency, because you need nothing but your own body to work it.

I've been teaching and writing about all forms of Western occultism for over three decades, and I've noticed that students of magic, especially beginners, are intimidated by two things. One is the complexity of traditional systems both ancient and modern, which require a knowledge of many obscure disciplines, among them astrology, alchemy, numerology, geomancy, the Tarot, and the Kabbalah. New students are bewildered. They don't know where to begin to study and feel overwhelmed by the sheer volume of information they are required to absorb.

The other aspect of traditional magic that intimidates students is the need to make their own ritual instruments, temple furniture, robes and other clothing, ritual jewelry, and so on, often with costly and difficult-to-obtain materials. The student is expected to craft these things personally, or at the very least to have some part in their making. Many just don't have the craft skills to make them, or for that matter the money to buy them—some of these ritual objects, when properly made, can be very expensive. Often students don't have a spare room they can set aside to serve as a consecrated ceremonial chamber, or even closet space to store their altar and other ritual furniture once they acquire them.

Kinesic magic makes it unnecessary to study complicated books on arcane subjects. You don't need to learn to read Hebrew or Latin, draw up horoscopes, or memorize the esoteric symbolism of Tarot cards. You don't need to know what the Tree of Life is, or how to cast yarrow sticks, or how to cut runes. You don't need a wand, a sword, a chalice, or an altar. You don't need virgin parchment, dragon's blood ink, the tongue of a frog, or mandrake root.

Kinesic magic is based on twenty-four hand gestures that define and embody the twenty-four most fundamental occult forces, and twenty-four body postures that channel and direct these forces. Anything you can do with conventional methods of Western magic can be achieved with kinesic magic.

What I've provided you with in this book is a completely new and original method for manipulating and channeling occult energies. Nothing like it has ever existed before, although there are antecedents for it in the ancient systems of occult philosophy of the East.

For example, the postures of yoga are today predominantly used for physical exercise, but originally they were designed to open energy pathways along the nerves and awaken occult abilities. Similarly, the ancient Chinese masters of *chi* channeled occult energy through their bodies to heal and achieve other astonishing effects, and there is no doubt that the system of movements known as *tai chi*, which today is used mainly for exercise, was originally designed for this esoteric purpose. Buddhist monks use hand positions and gestures to trigger specific spiritual states of mind during meditation— you see these gestures represented in Buddhist religious statues and paintings.

In the Western world, nothing of this nature ever arose—or if it did, it has been completely forgotten. It may be that medieval Christian monks developed a physical culture similar to yoga for controlling the flow of spiritual energies, but if so, we have no record of it, and can only speculate about what it might have been like had it existed. For the most part, Western magicians have always used external, physical instruments and objects to channel, hold, and control esoteric forces.

We see this dichotomy between East and West in the esoteric discipline of alchemy. European alchemy was done with physical furnaces, beakers, retorts, chemicals, acids, quicksilver, and so on. Chinese alchemy, on the other hand, is internal. It is done inside the body using postures, controlled breathing, visualization, and the power of the will. The lungs of the Chinese alchemist become his bellows, and his belly becomes his furnace. His saliva is his elixir of life.

Kinesic magic is the yoga of Western occultism. You can, if you wish, apply its postures and gestures to create talismans, charms, magic mirrors, and other useful physical devices, but at root nothing other than your own body and mind are needed for this work. You are not bound to the external physical world, or constrained by it, when you do this magic.

There are numerous workings in this book, each a complete meditation or magic ritual in its own right. Some of them are simple and brief, others more complex. I composed them to give you practice in manipulating the twenty-four essential forces of Western occultism—those of the five elements, the seven planets of traditional astrology, and the twelve signs of the zodiac.

Do as many or as few of these workings as you wish. Their value does not lie in the specific techniques of magic they teach, but in the way they show you how to use the whole of the system of kinesic magic creatively for your own purposes. Think of this system as a new language of magic with which you can create any ritual, any charm, any spell you need in your own life.

You may be wondering why I chose these particular twenty-four energies of the elements, the planets, and the zodiac, and not others. They were chosen because they lie at the very root of Western occultism. You encounter them again and again when studying the history of magic in Egypt, Persia, the Middle East, and Europe.

The most influential system of ceremonial magic for more than the past hundred years, that of the Hermetic Order of the Golden Dawn, is built around these three sets of esoteric energies. The First Knowledge Lecture of the Golden Dawn system, which is the very first teaching that initiates receive when they join the Order, is devoted to the elements, the planets, and the signs of the zodiac.

These twenty-four forces are building blocks. You can put them into any arrangement you choose, provided you understand how to fit them together. Eventually you will create original rituals of your own to serve your specific needs, but the wide spectrum of workings in this book will give you the initial training you require to learn how to manipulate these energies in a creative, flexible manner.

This book had its germination three decades ago, when I suggested in my book *The New Magus* (Llewellyn, 1988) that it was theoretically possible to create a complete system of magic that used only the bare hands. *Kinesic Magic* is the evolution of this basic truth, but I have expanded the concept to include the use of the entire body.

The principles that underlie kinesic magic are few in number, easy to learn, and simple to practice. But don't let the simplicity fool you—this magic is as powerful as any that has ever been devised. You can apply these principles to any existing occult system, or use them to create your own completely original personal style of magic.

Kinesic magic will free you to do magic in your own way, unburdened by the weight of centuries of tradition. It is your own body, your own mind, working in perfect harmony to channel the root energies of the universe. It is all you will ever need.

CHAPTER 1
THE TWENTY-FOUR POSTURES

IN KINESIC MAGIC, YOU WILL RELY on twenty-four hand gestures to define the occult forces of the elements, planets, and zodiac, but you will channel those forces through your body and through your environment by means of twenty-four basic postures. The postures are easy to remember because they form complementary pairs.

The following descriptions present the ideal forms of these postures. In actual use, the forms will often be modified in small ways for practical reasons. You should practice these ideal forms until you know them before using modified versions of them.

As you practice each posture, keep in mind its purpose. Be aware of how it directs and focuses occult energy.

There are four main leg-separation distances used with these postures, in addition to a number of special leg positions that will be described individually. These four leg distances are (1) *together*, with the feet touching each other; (2) *narrow*, with the feet separated by about four inches (ten centimeters); (3) *medium*, with the feet separated by about twelve inches (thirty centimeters); and (4) *wide*, with the feet separated by about thirty to thirty-six inches (seventy-five to ninety centimeters).

These distances are approximations—very tall people should use slightly wider separations, and very short people somewhat narrower separations. It is not necessary to be exact with these distances provided the four classes of together, narrow, medium, and wide are observed.

The following table will serve as a quick reference to the leg positions of the twenty-four postures.

1. medium	2. narrow	3. medium	4. medium
5. narrow	6. narrow	7. step left	8. step right
9. narrow	10. narrow	11. medium	12. medium
13. together	14. narrow	15. medium	16. together
17. medium	18. step forward	19. crossed	20. medium
21. step forward	22. step back	23. wide	24. together

Leg Positions of the Twenty-Four Postures

1. Sitting Posture

Exercises that involve intense concentration and visualization may often be done sitting down. The sitting posture is relaxing and does not require much energy to maintain for long periods of time. When the work requires that you close your eyes, the sitting posture prevents loss of balance that might occur if you were standing. It is the best posture for prolonged scrying or divination.

Sit in a chair with your back straight, your head level, and your feet planted firmly on the floor, with about twelve inches of space between them. If the chair has no arms, rest your hands on your knees. If the chair has arms, you may rest your forearms on the arms of the chair.

Find a chair to work with that you can sit in without becoming uncomfortable or restless. You can use a wooden chair from the kitchen table or a padded chair with arms, but whichever chair you choose, do not sag back in it—keep your spine straight until the exercise has been completed.

Figure 1.1: Sitting Posture

2. Standing Posture

You will use the standing posture as the start position and also the end position for most of the workings. When you begin a working, assume the standing posture to relax and calm your thoughts, so that you can mentally prepare yourself for what you are about to do. After completing the working, adopt this same posture to clear your mind of the work you have just done. It is also a good posture for breathing exercises, and is the starting position when assuming all the postures that follow.

Stand with your feet separated by about four inches and your arms at your sides, gazing straight forward at eye level, as though looking at a distant horizon. Your arms and hands should be loose and comfortable, with just a slight bit of muscle tone to keep your fingers from curling. Do not lock your elbows. Extend your fingers partially, but do not completely flatten your hands. Keep your back straight, your shoulders open and wide, and your head level. Extend upward from your spine through the top of your head, and imagine that the very center of your head is attached to a string that pulls you gently upward.

Avoid any tenseness in your knees, elbows, hands, or neck. Strive for a straight line that rises from between your feet to the top of your head. Breathe slowly and deeply. Focus your eyes on infinity, as though looking through whatever objects or walls may be in front of you to what lies beyond.

Figure 1.2: Standing Posture

3. Invoking Posture

This is the general posture of invocation. Its purpose is to call forth from the astral spheres occult forces that you will use in your magic.

From the standing posture, separate your feet so they are about twelve inches apart, and raise both arms above your head in a V-shape, with your hands upturned and fingers separated, as though to catch the falling rain. Your arms should be nearly straight at the elbows and inclined slightly forward so that your hands are a little in front of the vertical plane of your body. As you raise your arms, tilt your head back and gaze upward at an angle.

You are not trying to reach or look straight upward. There must be no tenseness in your arms or neck. Do not lock your elbows or splay your fingers forcefully. Keep your arms and hands relaxed.

Remember this general rule: what is above, or supernal, is what exists above your line of sight to the horizon; what is below, or infernal, is what exists below your line of sight to the horizon. It is enough that you incline your face upward, your eyes upward, while your arms form a V-shape over your head and somewhat forward.

Figure 1.3: Invoking Posture

4. Banishing Posture

The opposite of the invoking posture is the general banishing posture. Its purpose is to banish into the earth occult energies. This practice is sometimes called "earthing" the energies. It neutralizes them and renders them void. Think of it as pouring out a cup of liquid onto the dry ground, where it is instantly absorbed. With this posture you can empty yourself or the space around you of whatever energy or spiritual presence you may have invoked.

From the standing posture, separate your feet by about twelve inches and extend your arms downward at an angle away from your sides so that they form an A-shape with the crown of your head. Your hands should be a little in front of the vertical plane of your body. Turn your palms downward as though pushing down toward the ground, and separate your fingers. Incline your head slightly downward, and turn your gaze down at an angle.

Do not strain your body to make or hold this position. If there is strain, you are doing it incorrectly. Think of the V-shape you form with your arms in the invoking posture as a cup that fills with occult energy, and the A-shape of the banishing posture as that same cup turned upside down to empty it.

Figure 1.4: Banishing Posture

5. Spiral Invoking Posture

Energy is drawn into your body and projected from your body by means of spirals, even if you are unaware of it. A contracting inward spiral is used to draw occult energy from outside and concentrate it inside your body.

Adopt the standing posture, with your gaze directed forward at the distant, unseen horizon. Maintain the position of your feet. Raise your left hand high above your head, with the palm turned upward and the fingers separated a bit and angled upward. Your wrist should be rotated so that your fingers are turned to point a little toward the front. Keep your elbow slightly bent. Press your right palm, fingers together, to the center of your chest so that your right wrist remains straight. Your left arm should be angled a bit out to the side and also slightly forward. As you raise your left hand, turn your face and roll your eyes upward to look at it. Holding your left hand a little in front of the plane of your body makes it easier to see it without straining your neck.

The line of the energy spiral created by this posture runs from your left hand down along your left arm, across your shoulders, and in a loop down your right arm to your right hand, where it passes from your right palm through your chest and into your heart-center. Of course it is not a perfect spiral, but it has a spiral tendency of motion. This contracting spiral serves to concentrate the occult energy that you draw into your left hand. The left is your receptive hand in an esoteric sense—the left side of the body attracts, and the right side projects.

Figure 1.5: Spiral Invoking Posture

6. Spiral Banishing Posture

In this posture, an expanding spiral is used to channel energy out from your body to banish or earth it. It is the opposite of the contracting spiral.

From a standing position with arms at your sides and feet four inches apart, your gaze directed forward at the horizon, press your left palm flat over the center of your chest, with your fingers together. Do not bend your left wrist up or down—a more or less straight line should run from your elbow to the tip of your middle finger. Extend your right arm downward at your side at a slight outward angle, with the right palm turned downward, the fingers separated, as though you were releasing a fistful of sand. Your right wrist should be just a little bit rotated so that your fingers point somewhat behind you. This rotation is very small—just enough to incline your fingers behind the plane of your body. As you lower your right hand, turn your face and eyes toward it and look at it. Keeping your right hand a little in front of your body plane makes it easier to see without straining your neck.

The energy channeled by this posture will flow from your heart-center into your receptive left hand, and from there in an expanding spiral up your left arm, across your shoulders, and down your right arm, where it will exit your body from your projective right hand. Don't worry too much about the energy stream at this stage. Just concentrate on learning the posture.

Figure 1.6: Spiral Banishing Posture

7. Receiving Posture

This is similar to the spiral invoking posture, but instead of attracting energy from one of the astral spheres above your head into yourself, you draw energy out of a place, a person, or an object and concentrate it in your own heart-center. This posture is useful when you wish to drain something of a particular esoteric energy, or when you need to charge yourself with that energy.

Extend your receptive left hand out to the left side slightly below shoulder level, with the palm turned upward and your elbow almost straight. At the same time, press the palm of your right hand over the middle of your chest, keeping your right wrist straight. In this posture, both hands are held flat, with fingers together. As you extend your left hand out to the side, turn your left foot so that its toes point to the left, and take a short step to the left with it. Do not move your right foot. There should be about twelve inches or a little more between your left heel and the arch of your right foot. If you are a tall person, the distance will be more. As you take this step, turn your head to the left and look over the top of your left palm at the unseen horizon beyond. All these movements should be done smoothly, in a flowing manner.

The energy is drawn from the object of your focus into the fingertips of your left hand, and flows along your left arm, across your shoulders, down your right arm, and from your right palm into your heart-center in the middle of your chest.

It is possible to draw energy in this way from a distance, but the working of this posture is stronger when you can actually touch your left hand to the thing from which you are receiving the energy. When you touch an object in this pose, the position of your left hand is modified—you lay your left palm flat upon the object and draw its energy into your palm.

Figure 1.7: Receiving Posture

8. Projecting Posture

The opposite of the previous posture, the projecting posture is used to project occult energy from your own body into a place, person, or object, thereby charging it with the energy.

Start in the usual way in the standing posture, arms at your sides, feet four inches apart, your gaze directed straight ahead. Press your flattened left palm, fingers together, to the center of your chest and extend your flattened right hand directly out to your right side a bit below shoulder level, its fingers touching, the palm turned downward. As you extend your right hand, turn your right foot so that its toes points to the right, and take a short step to the right. Do not move your left foot. There should be a space of about twelve inches between your right heel and the instep of your left foot. If you are tall, it will be a bit more. Simultaneously, turn your head to the right and look over the back of your right hand at the unseen horizon beyond.

By means of this posture, energy can be drawn from your heart-center into your left hand and sent in an expanding spiral up your left arm, across your shoulders, along your right arm, and out in a stream from your right hand.

It is possible to project occult energies into things from a distance, but a shorter distance yields a better result, and the best result is obtained when you actually touch with your right hand the thing you wish to charge with energy. When you are able to touch the object, lay your palm upon it and project the energy through the middle of your palm.

Figure 1.8: Projecting Posture

9. Magician Posture

This posture derives its name from the Tarot card known as the Magician. In the traditional Marseilles Tarot, the figure of the magician stands with his left hand raised high above his head and his right hand lowered. In a symbolic sense, he draws celestial fire down from the heavens and concentrates it in a place, person, or object on the material plane. This posture may also be used to invoke or evoke spirits that have their dwellings above the plane of the horizon (supernal spirits).

To assume this posture from the standing position, raise your left hand high above your head, with your palm turned upward and your separated fingers angled upward and somewhat forward, as though receiving something into your palm from above. At the same time, lower your right hand toward the floor by your right side, with its palm turned downward, fingers separated, and rotated at the wrist to point very slightly behind the plane of your body. There should be no strain in these turns of the hands— the left is just slightly rotated forward, and the right slightly rotated backward. Do not move your feet. Continue to gaze straight ahead at the unseen horizon. Both arms should be held at a slight angle away from the vertical line of your body, and both hands should be a bit in front of the plane of your body. Your arms should be fairly straight, but you do not need to lock your elbows.

This posture is used to channel and direct celestial energies through your body to concentrate them in something outside you, without accumulating those energies within yourself. In effect, you become a kind of lightning rod for energies from the higher spheres, which flow through you to the lower earthly plane. By this posture you draw down the potency of the heavens and manifest it on the Earth.

Figure 1.9: Magician Posture

10. Baphomet Posture

The opposite of the Magician posture is the Baphomet posture, so named for the pose of the famous figure of Baphomet that was drawn in 1854 by the French occultist Eliphas Levi for his book *Dogme et Rituel de la Haute Magie*. Levi's Baphomet was based upon the figure of the Devil in the Marseilles Tarot. Like this Devil, Baphomet sits looking straight forward, with his left hand lowered and his right hand raised above his head. This is the opposite of the posture of the Magician in the Marseilles Tarot. The Baphomet posture symbolizes the drawing up of infernal energies or spirits from the depths of the earth and their release or expression on our material plane of reality. It has particular application in rites of necromancy and spirit evocation.

Start in the standing posture, with your arms at your sides, your feet separated by four inches, and your eyes directed straight forward. Do not move your feet. Raise your right hand high above your head, palm turned up and fingers spread slightly—your fingers should point to the right and slightly forward. At the same time lower your left hand toward the floor beside your left leg, palm turned downward and fingers separated and turned to point to the left and slightly backward. Hold both hands a bit in front of the vertical plane of your body. Continue to gaze straight ahead at the unseen horizon.

This posture can be used to drain a person or object of infernal energies and disperse them harmlessly into the air, or to exorcise a possessing spirit. When modified, it can be used to draw energies or infernal spirits up from below the plane of the horizon for the purpose of concentrating or manifesting them in the material world. The energies are channeled through your body without being accumulated within you, so that they may be focused directly into a place, person, or object that you point at or touch with your right hand.

Figure 1.10: Baphomet Posture

11. Channeling Posture

Begin as usual in the standing posture. Widen your stance so that your feet are separated by about twelve inches, and at the same time raise both forearms to the sides by bending your elbows until your hands are roughly level with your waist. Your hands are held flat, with your palms turned downward and fingers slightly separated. Your hands should be in front of the plane of your body, with your forearms extended at approximately a forty-five-degree angle from that plane. That is to say, your forearms are midway between pointing forward and pointing to the sides. Keep your gaze directed straight ahead at the horizon.

In a broad sense, all twenty-four of the postures are channeling postures because they all channel energy. Use this posture specifically to channel occult energy through your body from one thing to another thing without accumulating the energy within your body. The energy flows into your receptive left hand, up your left arm, and through your upper body, where it circles once counterclockwise around your heart-center, then flows down your right arm and out your projective right hand to the person or object you are charging.

This is a good posture for transferring potency from one charm to another, or from an old garment or instrument to a new garment or instrument. It can also be used to transfer occult energy from one person to another person.

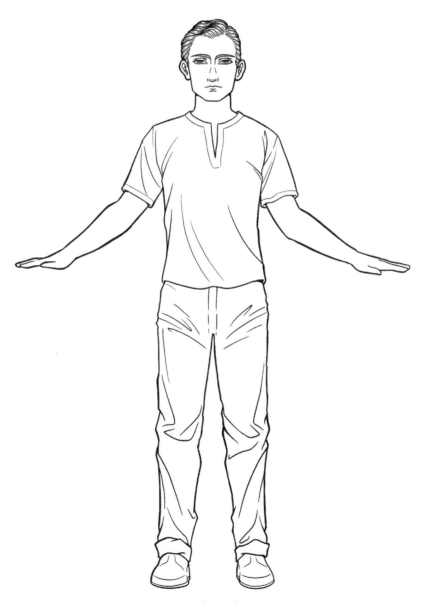

Figure 1.11: Channeling Posture

12. Balancing Posture

From the standing posture, widen your stance so that your feet are separated by about twelve inches. Bend your elbows and hold your flattened hands in front of your solar plexus, with your palms touching. Keep your wrists straight. The left hand is on top and turned downward; the right hand is beneath it and turned upward. Maintain your gaze straight ahead.

This is the basic resting hand position for this posture, which is used to balance energies within the body by moving them from one occult center to another. There are many possible variant hand positions that depend on the purpose for which the posture is used. In general terms, the left hand is placed over the energy center of the body from which you wish to draw energy out, and the right hand is placed over the energy center into which you wish this energy to flow. The seven primary energy centers will be examined at length in chapter 4.

Figure 1.12: Balancing Posture

13. Ankh Posture

From the standing posture, bring your feet together so they touch. Raise both your arms out to the sides at the level of your shoulders, with your palms flat and turned forward, your fingers together. Continue to look straight ahead at the unseen horizon. Your body will form the shape of an Egyptian ankh, a symbol of life. Your round head defines the loop at the top of the ankh, your arms are its beam, and your torso and legs are its pillar.

This is a useful posture for receiving impressions or energies, especially from a specific direction or quarter of the compass. Your body opened wide in this way acts as a kind of receptive antenna to occult energies. This posture also may be used to meditate facing the Sun to absorb solar energies or facing the Moon to absorb lunar energies.

Figure 1.13: Ankh Posture

14. Prayer Posture

From the standing posture, press your flattened palms vertically together in front of your breast bone in a gesture of prayer. Your thumbs should touch your chest. As you do this, incline your head downward and gaze down at a slight angle, keeping your eyes open. Your feet remain four inches apart.

You can use this posture for prayers, for speaking incantations, or for concentrating your mind. It is a good posture for going into yourself, for searching your memory, or for communicating with your guardian spirit.

Figure 1.14: Prayer Posture

15. Opening Posture

From the standing posture, separate your feet by about twelve inches. As you do so, extend your arms to the front at shoulder level, with your palms pressed together, and rotate your hands so that the backs of your hands touch, as though you were preparing to do the breaststroke. Slowly push your hands apart as though opening the two sides of a curtain. Keep spreading your hands while rotating your wrists to point your fingers upward until your arms are extended out to your sides at shoulder level. Your stiffly flattened palms are turned outward with the fingers pointing up, as though holding the two sides of an elevator door apart. As you spread your hands, continue to gaze directly forward.

When you wish to open an astral gateway by expanding a spiral, when you wish to expand your aura, or when you seek to dispel confusion, tension, or depression from your mind and achieve clarity, this posture should be used. In a general sense, it is good for all acts of opening.

Figure 1.15: Opening Posture

16. Closing Posture

From the standing posture, bring your feet together so they touch, and raise your forearms to your chest by crossing your right wrist in front of your left wrist, with your hands gently closed into fists. As you make this crossing motion, which resembles the arm position of an Egyptian mummy, close your eyes.

Use this posture when you wish to seal an astral gateway or cut off the flow of occult energy. It is one of the postures used for ending ritual procedures. In a symbolic sense, it is equivalent to shutting and locking a door.

Figure 1.16: Closing Posture

17. Scrying Posture

This posture may be performed standing or sitting. If standing, begin in the standing posture and widen your stance so that your feet are separated by about twelve inches. Flatten your hands and raise them in front of your face, with the palms turned forward, your fingers together but your thumbs extended out so that an L-shape is formed with the thumb and index finger of each hand. Your hands should be about twelve inches away from your face.

Touch together the tips of your index fingers and the tips of your extended thumbs, keeping both thumbs in a straight line, so that a perfect upright equilateral triangle is defined by the space between your thumbs and index fingers. Look through the center of this triangle. This upright triangle is the triangle of scrying.

This posture can be used to open an astral window through which to scry the astral planes or to perceive the presence of spirits. It is also useful for opening the third eye, a psychic energy center that corresponds with the spot between and behind the eyebrows. This posture is useful when inviting or initiating psychic perception in ritual. It can reveal things hidden.

Figure 1.17: Scrying Posture

18. Manifesting Posture

From the standing posture, take a step forward with your right foot so that there are about twelve inches between your right heel and your left toe, and lean slightly forward. At the same time, raise and extend your arms forward in front of you at the level of your heart. Your palms are flat and turned downward, with the fingers of each hand touching but the thumbs extended to the side. Bring the tips of your index fingers and the tips of your thumbs together to form a perfect equilateral triangle between them that points away from your body. This prone triangle is the triangle of manifestation. Your gaze should be directed straight ahead over the backs of your hands.

Use this posture to manifest occult forces on the material level for works that involve tangible transformations. It is also used to evoke spiritual beings, or to compel evoked spirits to render themselves perceptible to the senses.

Figure 1.18: Manifesting Posture

19. Binding Posture

Begin in the standing posture. Flatten your hands, with the fingers together, and cross them at the wrists in front of your lower belly, with your right hand in front of your left hand. At the same time, cross your right shin in front of your left shin, with your legs touching, elevating the heel of your right foot to make this position easier to maintain. Incline your head forward slightly and turn your gaze downward at an angle.

This posture is used to bind a spirit to a person, place, or object so that the spirit cannot depart without your permission. It can also be used to bind a spirit in the performance of a specific task. When bound in this way, the spirit cannot find release from that task until it is accomplished or you release it. In a more general sense, the binding posture can be used to retard or stop the progress of a plan, procedure, operation, business dealing, agreement, or other action.

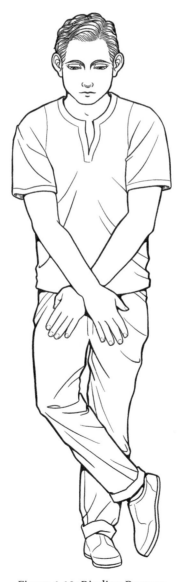

Figure 1.19: Binding Posture

20. Loosing Posture

From the standing posture, separate your feet so that they are about twelve inches apart. Raise your hands above your head, with your elbows bent, and turn your flattened palms upward at an angle. There should be a space of about twelve inches between the heels of your hands, and your elbows should be roughly in line with your ears. As you make this motion, turn your gaze upward.

Use this posture to release energies or spirits from charms or other objects to which they are bound, or from places where they reside, or from human beings to whom they are attached. Use it to release spirits that have previously been bound by you to a particular task, object, person, or location. Use it to release or set into motion any work, operation, or action that has been hindered, stopped, or delayed.

Figure 1.20: Loosing Posture

21. Commanding Posture

Begin in the standing posture, with your feet four inches apart and your arms at your sides, gazing forward. Advance your right foot about twelve inches in front of your left foot, and at the same time raise your arms and throw your hands forward with a slight bend in your elbows. Lean forward as you do so. The greater part of your weight should be on your right foot. Spread your fingers slightly, with your palms turned downward. Your wrists should be straight—do not tilt your hands at the wrists. There will be a separation of around twelve inches between your hands. Cast your gaze strongly forward between your hands, with your head inclined forward and downward.

This is a posture of great force. It is used to project the will, and also to command spiritual beings or human beings, either when they are present before you or at a distance. In particular, it is used to command and give direction to spirits you have already evoked, when they are reluctant to attend to your words.

Figure 1.21: Commanding Posture

22. Warding Posture

Begin in the standing posture, with feet four inches apart and arms at your sides, your gaze directed forward at the unseen horizon. Take a short step backward with your right foot, shifting your weight onto your right foot as you do so and leaning your body slightly backward. Your right toe should be about four inches farther back than the heel of your left foot. As you do this, bend your elbows and raise your hands at the sides until they are a little above shoulder level, your palms turned forward, with your fingers together. Keep your wrists straight. Your hands should be about twelve inches in front of the plane of your body and held somewhat wider than your shoulders so that your forearms are at a slight outward angle. Your arms will form a rough W-shape. This is the position of your hands relative to your shoulders when you do a push-up.

Use this posture to ward off unwanted astral intrusions, magic attacks, or psychic probing of your mind. You can also use it to ward off malicious or dangerous spirits. It creates an invisible wall in front of you that acts as an astral barrier.

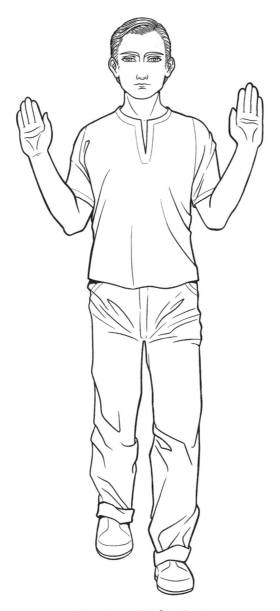

Figure 1.22: Warding Posture

23. Microcosm Posture

From the standing posture, spread your legs wide by stepping to the side with your right leg so that your feet are separated by around thirty to thirty-six inches. At the same time, raise your arms to the sides in one smooth motion, palms flat and turned forward, with fingers touching, so that your body forms roughly the shape of an upright penta-gram. Your head defines the uppermost point, your hands and feet the other four points. Continue to look straight ahead at the unseen horizon, focusing your gaze on infinity.

This posture embodies your humanity—the perfect balance of mind and body. Five is the number of humankind. Your feet, hands, and head define a star with five points, just as each of your hands defines a star with five points when you spread your fingers.

Use this posture for self-integration, to balance your thoughts and emotions with your physical needs and urges. It has a calming, centering effect. Use it to restore your confidence and gather your reserves of willpower.

Figure 1.23: Microcosm Posture

24. Macrocosm Posture

Begin in the standing posture, with feet four inches apart, arms at your sides, gazing straight forward. Bring your feet together so they touch. Raise your hands about six inches above the top of your head and press your palms flat together in a prayer gesture. Keep your elbows bent and spread them wide so that your arms form a diamond-shaped frame around your head. Your fingers should point straight up. As you bring your hands together, roll your eyes to look upward without tilting your head.

The macrocosm is the universe, the greater world around you, the spiritual realm that encloses our limited material plane of existence, the omniscient intelligence that pervades all things.

The macrocosm posture is used to invite communication and guidance from your higher self, your guardian angel, or a deity. It is used to draw down energy from above, or to send it upward. It is a connection between you and the highest agents of creation.

Figure 1.24: Macrocosm Posture

Meditation on the Postures

In this kinetic meditation, you will form all twenty-four postures one after another. As you make each pose, hold it without straining your body for the duration of a single slow inhalation and exhalation before shifting into the next pose. Move directly from one posture to the next with a single smooth transition of your entire body. Find the transition between postures that requires the least movement and smallest effort. Strive for a balance between relaxation and firm muscle tone. You may find this meditation tiring at first, but your body will soon become accustomed to it.

Before attempting the meditation, you should practice each individual posture until you understand it completely and can form it without having to think about it. Then begin joining the postures together in pairs and practice the transitions between poses. It's best to learn the postures in their related pairs—this makes them easier to remember. You should then practice the sets of postures that are described in workings 5–9 at the end of this chapter (Invoking, Channeling, Centering, Spirit, Cosmic) before finally attempting to do all twenty-four postures in a continuous sequence.

Use the illustrations in the appendix as a general reference guide while memorizing the postures. You may find it useful to scan and print out an enlargement of it that you can attach to the wall in front of you where you practice.

When you do begin to perform the full meditation, you should do it once a day at the same hour and in the same location until the postures and their transitions become second nature to you. As you shape each pose with your body, it is good practice to speak the name of the posture, either aloud or in your own mind, so that you establish a strong link between the posture and its function. It may also be helpful to do this meditation in front of a full-length mirror at least a few times so that you can see the angles of your arms and hands.

Once you gain some skill with the meditation, you can extend the period of time you hold each posture. This is best done by counting your breaths. For example, instead of holding each posture for one breath, you may wish to hold it for five or ten breaths.

In the beginning, concern yourself only with physically forming the postures and making smooth, accurate transitions between them. When you gain some practice with channeling and manipulating esoteric energies, as you will when you do the workings connected with the hand gestures that are given later in this book, you should visualize the movement of energy into and through your body as you hold each posture and count your breaths.

If you begin this meditation with the sitting posture, as indicated below, then end it with the sitting posture. If you don't have a chair or seat readily available, you may wish to begin the meditation from the standing posture. If so, end it with the standing posture and omit the sitting posture.

As a general rule, it is best to do your exercises and meditations facing east, unless you have a reason to face a different direction. The east is the usual starting point for rituals in magic, because the day begins in the east with the rising of the Sun. It is considered auspicious to do rituals facing the quarter associated with the coming of light. In a symbolic sense, light represents clarity and realization.

———

P1 (Sitting). Begin from a sitting position, with your back straight and your hands resting lightly on your knees, feet about twelve inches apart. It is best to use a simple kitchen chair without arms, but if you find this too uncomfortable, you can use an armchair.

Gaze straight forward at the unseen horizon. You cannot see it because of the walls of the room and other obstructions, but you can imagine yourself gazing through these obstacles straight ahead into the infinite distance. Take a deep breath and then let it out slowly to calm your mind.

P2 (Standing). Stand up and take a step forward to clear the chair, then assume the standing posture, with your feet four inches apart and arms at your sides. Breathe.

P3 (Invoking). Separate your feet until they are around twelve inches apart, and raise both arms up above your head as you tilt your face upward. Breathe.

P4 (Banishing). Do not move your legs. Lower your arms at an angle to your sides and tilt your face downward. Breathe.

P5 (Spiral Invoking). Bring your feet back to a narrow stance. Press the palm of your right hand over the center of your chest, and raise your left arm high above your head while looking up at your left hand. Breathe.

P6 (Spiral Banishing). Without moving your feet, lower your right hand and press your left palm over the center of your chest while turning your face to look downward at your right hand. Breathe.

P7 (Receiving). Extend your left arm out to the side just a little below shoulder level, palm upward, and press your right hand over your heart. Turn your left foot so that your toes point to the left as you step to the left. Breathe.

P8 (Projecting). Draw your left foot back and resume the narrow stance. Smoothly turn your right foot to the right and take a step to the right. As you do so, extend your right arm out to the side just below shoulder level, with the palm turned downward, and press your left palm over the center of your chest. Breathe.

P9 (Magician). Step in with your right foot and resume the narrow stance. Raise your left hand high above your head, palm turned upward. At the same time, lower your right hand to your right side, with the palm turned down. Continue to gaze straight ahead. Breathe.

P10 (Baphomet). Without shifting your feet, smoothly invert your hand positions. Raise your right hand heavenward, with the palm turned up, and lower your left hand, with your palm toward the earth. Continue to gaze straight ahead. Breathe.

P11 (Channeling). Step into the medium stance, and lower your right hand and raise your left hand until both are at the level of your waist, with palms turned downward. Continue to gaze straight forward at the horizon. Breathe.

P12 (Balancing). Without moving your feet or changing the direction of your gaze, in a single smooth motion bring your hands together, left hand on top of the right hand, with palms touching just in front of your solar plexus. Breathe.

P13 (Ankh). Bring your feet together so they touch. Stretch your arms wide apart at shoulder level, with your flattened palms turned forward, and continue to gaze forward at the horizon. Breathe.

P14 (Prayer). Open your feet to the narrow stance as you bring your flattened hands slowly together in front of your chest and press them vertically, palm to palm, in the traditional gesture of prayer. Your thumbs should touch your chest. Incline your head slightly downward and lower your gaze. Breathe.

P15 (Opening). Spread your feet to the medium stance. Extend your arms forward, with your palms still pressed together, then rotate your hands so that the backs touch. Look directly forward over your hands, then separate and open your arms outward to the sides in a swimming motion until you hold them straight out to the sides at shoulder level, fingers turned upward and palms facing outward to the sides. Breathe.

P16 (**Closing**). Close up the space between your feet so they touch, and bring your hands slowly together in front of your chest. Cross your right wrist in front of your left wrist, and clench your hands lightly into fists. As you do this, close your eyes, but keep your head level and your face turned forward. Breathe.

P17 (**Scrying**). Spread your feet to the medium stance as you open your eyes and flatten your hands. Uncross your wrists and turn your palms forward. Raise your hands to the level of your face and make an upright equilateral triangle in the space between your thumbs and forefingers. Gaze forward through this triangle at the horizon. Breathe.

P18 (**Manifesting**). Slowly extend your joined hands forward and lower them to the level of your heart as you turn your palms downward, so that the triangle between your hands points away from you. As you do this, take a step forward on your right foot. Maintain the perfect equilateral triangle between your thumbs and index fingers. Gaze straight ahead over the backs of your hands. Breathe.

P19 (**Binding**). Lower your arms and cross them at the wrists in front of your navel, hands held flat, with the fingers together. Your right wrist should be in front of your left wrist. As you do this, cross your right shin in front of your left shin. Most of your weight will be on your left leg. Lift the heel of your right foot from the floor as you cross your legs to make it easier to hold this posture. Incline your head downward and lower your gaze. Breathe.

P20 (**Loosing**). Uncross your legs and open them to the medium stance. Raise your arms above your head, with your elbows bent and your flattened palms angled upward, as though releasing a bird into the air above your head. Tilt your head and turn your gaze upward as you raise your hands. Breathe.

P21 (**Commanding**). Lower your arms until your elbows are at the height of your shoulders. Take a step forward with your right foot and thrust your hands forward at the level of your face, with the fingers slightly separated and the palms turned downward. Your head should be lowered and your gaze directed strongly forward between your hands. Breathe.

P22 (**Warding**). Step back with your right foot so that it is behind you. As you do this, lean back slightly and transfer the greater part of your weight to your right foot. Simultaneously draw your arms back and hold your flattened hands up at the level of your shoulders and a little in front of the plane of your body, palms facing forward. Gaze forward as you do this. Breathe.

P23 (Microcosm). Bring your feet together, then open them into a wide stance. As you do so, spread your arms wide, your flattened palms turned forward and held around shoulder level so that the five points of your body—crown of your head, right hand, right foot, left foot, left hand—form an irregular star shape. Gaze forward at the horizon. Breathe.

P24 (Macrocosm). Bring your right foot in close to press against your left foot, and raise your hands directly over your head. Press your palms together some six inches or so above your head, with your fingers pointing straight up. Keep your elbows spread wide. As you make this motion, roll your eyes to look upward without tilting your head. Breathe.

To end this moving meditation on the postures, lower your arms to your sides and assume the standing posture. If you began the meditation from a seated position, step back and resume your position upon the chair in the sitting posture, with your hands on your knees. Take a few slow, silent breaths to relax and clear your mind.

Workings: The Twenty-Four Postures

Your body must become accustomed to adopting these postures at a moment's notice and holding them without strain for at least several minutes. In the practical exercises below, you can begin to get a feel for the postures and how energy is directed through each of them to accomplish different purposes. As you take up each posture, strive to be completely aware of the angles of your limbs. Find a way of holding it that is comfortable, but energized with a slight tension. Avoid anything that feels strained or awkward, while taking care to sustain your body in the essential pattern of the posture.

All of us are different, so there will be minor differences in the way each of us adopts a particular posture. The goal should be to find a way of holding yourself that is dynamic, yet balanced and relaxed. Be fully aware of your body, and feel the energy within it.

Working 1: Sitting Posture

The posture is for meditation, concentration, and other mental exercises, so it is important that you be able to hold it for extended periods. Experiment until you find the best chair to use and the best place to practice where you will not be disturbed, and gradually lengthen the duration over successive sessions.

Sit in a wooden chair facing the east, with your feet flat on the floor and about twelve inches apart. Lean slightly forward, with your back straight, and put your hands on your knees. This should be a very stable position that you can hold without discomfort or fatigue.

Close your eyes. Take slow, regular breaths and be aware of your body. Extend your spine and neck upward. The best way to do this is to imagine that an invisible string is attached to the center of your skull and is stretching you gently upward.

Hold this posture for five minutes or so, then relax. Estimate the duration; don't time yourself.

Working 2: Standing Posture

Stand facing east, with your feet about four inches apart. Keep your weight evenly balanced between your toes and heels. Look straight ahead at the unseen horizon that marks the dividing plane between what is above and what is below.

Close your eyes. Feel your body as you stretch yourself from your heels upward through the top of your head. Imagine that an invisible string attached to the top of your skull is pulling you straight up. Do not raise your heels from the floor, and keep your shoulders and legs relaxed. Avoid locking your knees. If you find yourself tensing up, deliberately relax.

Always avoid strain in this posture. Your shoulders should be squared but not strongly thrown back. Your chin should be tucked in slightly, and your pelvic girdle should be rotated a very small amount so that your stomach is drawn in and your groin thrust outward.

Hold this posture for several minutes, then relax.

Working 3: Individual Postures

Find a full-length or half-length mirror in front of which you can practice your postures. Form each individual posture and study the angles of your arms and body. You should strive for graceful, relaxed angles. Imagine a stream of energy flowing through you, and try to eliminate the points at which it is blocked while maintaining the posture as described.

Work on several separate postures at a time in this way. Spend a few minutes on each, experimenting with small changes to see what difference they make in the flow of energy through your body. Become intensely aware of what is taking place inside you as you hold each position.

Working 4: Natural Pairs of Postures

The postures are designed in pairs. You should practice them in pairs before trying to practice larger sets or the full meditation of twenty-four postures.

Form the first posture of a pair and hold it for about a minute or so while taking slow, regular breaths. Then shift into the second posture of the pair, and hold it for a minute. Make the transition slow and smooth, as if you are moving in slow motion, and if possible, watch yourself in a mirror as you move from one to the other.

To practice the first pair (postures 1 and 2), which may be referred to as the earth set because they ground and provide a firm foundation, you must begin in the sitting posture and move into the standing posture, then return to the sitting posture.

For all the other pairs, begin in the standing posture, move into the first posture of the pair, then transition into the second posture of the pair, and finish in the standing posture.

For example, if you wish to practice the magician–Baphomet pair, begin in the standing posture, then move into the magician posture and hold it for a minute. Then slowly and smoothly transition into the Baphomet posture and hold it for a minute before returning to the standing posture.

Working 5: Invoking Set of Postures

The six invoking postures (postures 3–8) may be practiced as a set. Stand in front of a mirror in the standing posture, and form successively the invoking, banishing, spiral invoking, spiral banishing, receiving, and projecting postures, holding each for about a minute and transitioning smoothly from one to the next. Return to the standing posture at the end of your practice, so that you begin and end the exercise in the same posture.

Working 6: Channeling Set of Postures

There are four postures that may be referred to collectively as the channeling postures (postures 9–12). These are the magician, Baphomet, channeling, and balancing postures. In these body positions, energy is directed through the body in a balanced flow without being accumulated within the body or drawn together in one place.

Practice them one after the other in front of a mirror, holding each for about a minute and striving for a smooth transition between postures. Try to be aware of the energy dynamic within your body as you hold each posture, and how it changes when you make the transition from one to another. You should begin and end this exercise in the standing posture.

Working 7: Centering Set of Postures

The next four postures form a set that is difficult to put a name on, but they all involve defining the center point, which is why I call them centering postures (postures 13–16). The ankh posture defines the center at the intersection of the lines formed by the horizontal arms and vertical body; the prayer posture has its focal point between the joined palms; the opening posture defines the center by expanding a circle; and the closing posture has its center at the point where the forearms cross.

Practice them in front of a mirror, holding each posture for about a minute before smoothly transitioning into the next. Begin and end this set in the standing posture.

Working 8: Spirit Set of Postures

The set of six spirit postures (postures 17–22) has a particular function in dealing with spiritual beings, although these postures are also used to manipulate occult energies. By the scrying posture, spirits may be observed, and by the manifesting posture, they may be made tangibly present; the binding and loosing postures are self-explanatory, as are the commanding and warding postures.

Practice this set in front of a mirror. Hold each posture for a minute or so while feeling what it does to the energy flow inside your body, then transition smoothly to the next. Begin and end in the standing posture.

Working 9: Cosmic Set of Postures

The final pair of postures (postures 23–24), like the first pair (postures 1–2), stands apart. The sitting and standing postures that form the earth set give you the foundation for all those that follow, and the microcosm and macrocosm postures of the cosmic set represent the two universes of human and God, self and other, inside and outside, here and beyond.

Begin as usual in the standing posture. Form the microcosm posture and hold it for a minute, then move smoothly into the macrocosm posture. End the exercise in the standing posture.

Working 10: Free-Form Pairs of Postures

Select any two postures at random. From the standing posture, enter into the first posture and hold it for a minute while breathing slowly and regularly. Transition into the second posture and hold it for a minute, then return to the standing posture.

Now do the same two postures, but this time reverse their order, beginning with the second posture and transitioning into the first.

Continue in this way for half a dozen randomly selected free-form pairs.

You don't need to do all the possible combinations—there are a great many of them—but you should become comfortable with moving smoothly from posture to posture so that they can be linked into dynamic free-form sets when you reach the stage in your studies where you are composing your own original rituals.

CHAPTER 2
THE FIVE ELEMENTS

TO WORK MODERN WESTERN MAGIC, you need to understand the concept of the elements developed by the ancient Greeks centuries before the birth of Christ. They are poorly described in most books on magic, even though the Greek philosophers Aristotle (384–322 BCE) and Plato (c. 424–328 BCE) both wrote about them extensively. It was Empedocles (c. 450 BCE) who first gave the lower four elements the names we currently use for them—Fire, Water, Air, and Earth.

The basic understanding of the ancient Greeks was that these four elements, although they are not physical substances in themselves, form the basis for all types of physical substances by combining together in different proportions. A small amount of all four elements is in every physical thing, but the one element that predominates gives that thing its nature tendency. Everything in the world may be said to be fiery, watery, airy, or earthy in its nature.

There is also a fifth, higher element known as Spirit that was added to the original four by Aristotle. This fifth element is sometimes called Light, or the Quintessence (fifth essence). The four lower elements compose the dense lower sphere of matter upon which we live, while the fifth element predominates in the substance of the heavens. Spirit is what energizes living things, because the life in us comes from the heavens and not from the lower earth, which composes our bodies. Yet to some degree all things in the universe are alive, all infused with a portion of Spirit.

The element Spirit is at the root of the twenty-four occult forces examined in this book. It is the *chi* of Chinese magicians with which they are reputed to work such extraordinary marvels of healing and the martial arts. This fifth element energizes the lower four elements, the planets, and the signs of the zodiac that collectively represent the occult forces we use in kinesic magic. When Spirit is undifferentiated, it is ineffective, because it has no specific focus. It is like an arrow lying on the ground—it has no force and cannot penetrate. Its usefulness in magic arises only when it is directed in various ways. Then it becomes like an arrow fired from a bow at a specific target.

Spirit constitutes and underlies everything. It is always present in the four lower elements, embodying and energizing them, but when the expression of its watery, airy, and fiery properties are veiled or suppressed, the result is the element Earth. Similarly, when the airy, fiery, and earthy aspects of Spirit are veiled, the result is the element Water; and so on for the other two lower elements.

Think of this fifth element as white light, which contains all colors. It is effectively colorless when it is unfiltered. Only by restricting all the other colors in white light in varying degrees can we get blue, or red, or green, to manifest. Which color comes forth depends on how we restrict the colors inherent in white light that are not seen.

By restricting the totality of the Quintessence, we can obtain specific forces that may be applied to individual tasks. This is what the chi masters of China do when they channel and direct chi to one purpose or another. We do the same thing in Western magic through the use of the basic sets of occult energies that have been defined by magicians as the elements, the planets, and the zodiac signs. Each is a set of filters through which the pure white light of Spirit shines and is colored.

The pure whiteness with which we visualize Spirit must be distinguished from the whiteness associated in kinesic magic with the planet Mercury, which is a soft white with a hint of yellow in it, and also from the white light of the stars, which is a bright white with a hint of blue in it. The white of Spirit may be said to be intermediate between these two—the white of Mercury is warmer and the white of the stars cooler than the neutral white of Spirit.

In modern Western magic, the energy of Fire is visualized as bright red, the energy of Air as clear yellow, the energy of Water as deep blue, and the energy of Earth as black or an earthy olive green. Earth energy is black when it is inanimate but green when it relates to living things.

It is important to remember that the elements are not the physical things after which they are named, but are present in those things. The element Fire is not the common fire that burns wood, but the predominating essence that underlies physical fire and gives fire its properties. Similarly, elemental Water is not the water that flows in rivers, but the essence that defines flowing water; Air is not the air we breathe, but the dominant underlying quality of air; Earth is not the earth of the ground, but the essence of that earth.

Understanding this, what else can we say about the four lower elements? We can make a table that shows their defining natures, according to Aristotle and Proclus (412–485 CE). The opinions of these two philosophers do not contradict each other, but are complementary. Aristotle divided the elements according to how they affect the sense of touch, and Proclus chose to divide them according to their active qualities.

The elements are arranged in the table in descending order of density, or heaviness. Fire is the most rarefied and energetic of the four elements, followed by Air, and then Water, and finally Earth, which is inactive and dense.

Element	Aristotle	Proclus
Fire	warm and dry	sharp, subtle, and mobile
Air	warm and moist	blunt, subtle, and mobile
Water	cool and moist	blunt, dense, and mobile
Earth	cool and dry	blunt, dense, and immobile

The Elements According to Aristotle and Proclus

Aristotle observed that Fire is warm and dry, while its opposite, Water, is cool and moist. Between Fire and Water you have Air, which is both warm and moist, and Earth, which is cool and dry. This is best shown by means of a diagram (figure 2.1).

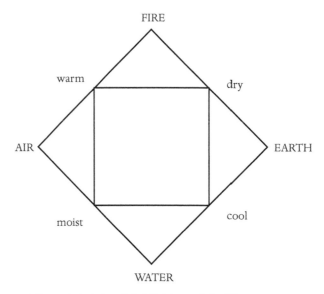

Figure 2.1: Aristotle's Division of the Elements

If you think about the physical nature of fire, you will at once agree that it is both warm and dry. When water is poured on fire, if the heat of the fire prevails over the coolness of water, then the water is transformed into steam, a kind of moist air; but if the moistness of water prevails over the dryness of the fire, then what remains are the cold, unburned cinders.

Fire, according to Proclus, is sharp, subtle, and mobile. It is sharp in the sense that it penetrates into things, subtle in that it seems to have no weight or substance, and mobile because it never stops dancing around. By contrast, Earth is blunt, dense, and immobile. It is blunt in the sense that it is thick and does not penetrate, dense in its heaviness, and immobile because it remains where it is placed, unlike the other elements which must be contained in some way.

Between them we have Air, which partakes of two qualities from Fire and one from Earth; and Water, which takes two of its qualities from Earth and only one from Fire. Water imitates Earth in that it lies on the ground, although it must be contained in a vessel. Air imitates Fire in that it expands and rises, even though it is not so aggressively penetrating as Fire.

According to Proclus, the quality of sharpness belongs to Fire alone and is not shared with any other element, and the quality of immobility belongs to Earth alone and is not shared with any other element.

Air partakes of two qualities of Fire, Water partakes of only a single quality from Fire, and Earth has no Fire qualities. Conversely, Water partakes of two qualities of Earth, Air partakes of only one of the Earth qualities, and Fire has no Earth qualities at all. It is in this sense that Air and Water are the intermediate elements between Fire at one extreme and Earth at the other.

As alluded to above, elemental Fire has two opposites. It is opposite Water because earthly water and fire are natural enemies—water tends to extinguish fire. It is also opposite Earth based on the way the elements arrange themselves naturally from lightest to heaviest. Fire rises and expands, but Earth falls and remains contracted into itself.

This arrangement from lightest to heaviest was used to define the elemental associations of the earthly spheres, four concentric spheres that were conceived to lie below the sphere of the Moon, the lowest of the wandering bodies in the heavens. The Moon was understood to be the gatekeeper between the realm of Earth and the realm of heaven. Above the Moon are the spheres of the planets and the fixed stars; below the Moon are the spheres of the four lower elements.

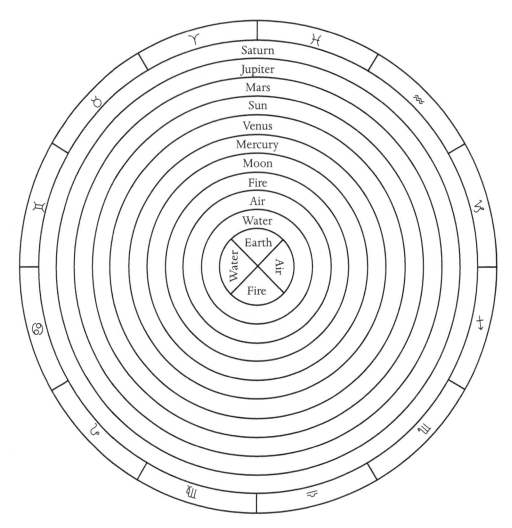

Figure 2.2: The Earthly and Heavenly Spheres

As you can see in figure 2.2, the highest elemental sphere beneath the Moon is that of Fire, the lightest of the elements, which tends to rise up vigorously. Below the earthly sphere of Fire lies the sphere of Air, which expands but does not rise as forcefully as Fire. Below the sphere of Air is that of Water, where the rain clouds float and send down their rain into the rivers and oceans. Lowest of all is the sphere of Earth, which lies at the center of creation, according to the cosmology of the ancients. The sphere of elemental Earth is what we walk upon, and in itself is composed of all four lower elements, as the cross through the smallest circle in the figure illustrates.

Plato gave a three-dimensional geometric explanation of the four elements in his dialogue *Timaeus*, which is based on the teachings of the Pythagoreans. In this work he assigned Fire to the tetrahedron (four sides), Air to the octahedron (eight sides), Water to the icosahedron (twenty sides), and Earth to the cube (six sides). Plato also alluded to the fifth element, the Quintessence, which he assigned what he believed to be the most perfect of all regular solid bodies, the dodecahedron (twelve sides). These five regular geometric forms are known today as the Platonic solids.

The common symbols for the elements that are used in magic probably derive from alchemy. Fire is represented by an upright equilateral triangle ($\triangle$), Water by a similar triangle inverted (∇), Air by the upright triangle with a horizontal line through its center ($\triangle$), and Earth by an inverted triangle with a horizontal line through its center (∇). The triangles of Fire and Air point upward because these elements rise, whereas the triangles of Water and Earth point downward because these elements tend to fall.

Spirit is usually symbolized by a circle with four radial lines crossing through its center ($\circledast$), giving it the appearance of a wheel with eight spokes. The four lines may be understood to represent the four lower elements that exist in potential within the Quintessence, which is represented by the perfect circle that surrounds and contains them.

The Four Humours

During the Middle Ages and the Renaissance, the four lower elements were best known by their effects on the human body and emotions. The elements acting inside the body were called *humours*, and their excess produced four temperaments. When these humours became unbalanced, the result was disease, which might show itself in a physical, emotional, or mental manner.

The older English spelling of the word *humour* is used here to distinguish the action of the elements inside the body from the usual modern meaning of mirth or amusement that is attached to this word.

A man with an excess of elemental Fire in his disposition suffered from too much of the humour known as yellow bile, and was called *choleric*, especially if he had a flushed face and red hair. The excess of Fire within him made it difficult for him to control his temper. He was assumed to be hot-headed and apt to fly into a rage.

A man with too much elemental Water abounding was said to have an excess of the humour called phlegm, which made his temperament *phlegmatic*. He was apathetic, listless, and easily swayed one way or the other.

A man with too much elemental Air was said to have an excess of the humour blood, which gave him a *sanguine* temperament. He was enthusiastic, talkative, impulsive, and social.

A man with too much elemental Earth suffered from an excess of the humour called black bile, which produced the temperament known as *melancholic*. He was depressed in spirits and avoided the company of others. His disposition was sour and his outlook on life pessimistic.

By manipulating the elemental energies, it is possible to restore a balance of the humours, and in this way cure many conditions that arise when there is an excess or a lack of a particular element in the body. Those who are able to see auras can determine an elemental imbalance by studying the colors in the aura of the afflicted individual; those who cannot see auras can achieve the same understanding by considering the behavior and speech of the person. The way an individual moves and speaks, as well as the expressions that pass over their face, may be read as accurately as aura colors.

For example, an excess of the fiery humour will result in a person who is very impulsive and quick to take offense, who jumps to conclusions that are unwarranted, and who finds it difficult to control their anger. This condition can be temporarily addressed either by drawing out the excess of Fire from the person's aura or by infusing the aura with the energy of Water, the elemental opposite of Fire, to balance the fiery tendency.

In order to effect a full cure, however, it is necessary to determine why the imbalance exists, and to eliminate the underlying cause so that the imbalance in the humours does not return in the future. Bear in mind that the humours are never perfectly balanced even in healthy human beings. One humour always predominates to some degree over the others.

Elementals

These humours and their resultant temperaments give insight into the natures of the four classes of elemental spirits—spiritual beings composed almost entirely of a single element. The names that Paracelsus (1493–1541) gave them are commonly used in modern magic, and I will use them here.

Salamanders are composed almost wholly of the element Fire. Consequently, they have a choleric temperament. They are dangerously unpredictable, aggressive, violent, and quick to take offense. They live in fire and are not burned by it. Most of them are male when they appear in humanoid form, but they often manifest as dancing balls of flame. They are the least social of the elementals, being the furthest removed from the sphere of the Earth where humans dwell. They dislike being summoned and are impatient to depart. When they appear, the temperature of the air rises.

Undines are composed predominately of the element Water and have a phlegmatic temperament. They are dreamy, listless, lax, lazy, sensual, self-indulgent, and self-absorbed. The only thing that rouses them in part from this listless state is sexual desire. They dwell in water. Most appear as females when they adopt humanoid form, but there are also male Undines. These spirits are beautiful and graceful. They tend to have dark hair and pale white skin that is always moist and cool.

Sylphs are made up mostly of the element Air and have a sanguine temperament. They are eager to interact with human beings and are bright, quick-witted, light in their movements, expansive, argumentative, unpredictable, and undependable. According to Paracelsus, their nature is closest of all the elementals to human nature, perhaps because they live in the air, surrounded by it, as humans are. They appear mostly in male form, but tend to be androgynous in appearance—slender, having blond or brown hair, light of step, with quick dancing movements and high voices.

Gnomes appear most often as short and stocky little humanoids in whom an excess of the element Earth abides. This gives them a melancholic temperament. They are antisocial, abrupt, gruff, impolite, scoffing, judgmental, and gloomy, and enjoy playing tricks on humans. They can move through rock and earth the way we walk through the air and are said to dwell in caves and mines. They appear as both males and females. Their voices are deep and earthy, their speech rough and vulgar, their complexions swarthy. Most often their hair is red or dark brown.

Practical Uses of the Elements

Each of the elemental energies can be applied to a different area of human experience.

Spirit

This element stands alone yet at the same time permeates and underlies all things. Spirit can be used to cleanse and purify, to drive away base or perverse energies of a sexual or emotional nature, and to enlighten and expand consciousness. For these purposes it can be applied on all three occult energy levels—elemental, planetary, and zodiacal.

Figure 2.3: Symbol for Spirit

Fire

The humour yellow bile, which gives rise to the choleric temperament in the human body, is hot and dry. It influences hot-headedness, annoyance, rage, impulsiveness, and violent actions arising from sudden anger; or, in a healthier and more balanced expression, physical courage and the courage of conviction, along with zeal of purpose and a general enthusiasm.

Figure 2.4: Symbol for Fire

An excess of Fire in the body produces sweating, fevers, and inflammations.

Material actions provoked by this energy involve violence, whether for good or evil purposes, as well as anger, bravery, resolve, and enthusiasm.

This element is applicable in matters that concern fighting, warfare, leadership, sports competition, or domination of others or the environment.

Water

The humour phlegm, which gives rise to the phlegmatic temperament in the human body, is cold and moist. It influences lassitude, dreaminess, sleepiness, visions, fantasies, imaginary fears, insanity, hysteria, emotional instability, fixations, and obsessions; or, in a healthier and more balanced expression, creativity of an emotional type, artistry, poetry, seership, channeling, empathy, and psychic abilities of the passive kind, such as clairvoyance and mediumship.

Figure 2.5: Symbol for Water

An excess of Water in the body provokes addictions, obsessive-compulsive behavior, poor digestion, diarrhea, excessive mucus from the nose, and phlegm in the throat and lungs.

Material actions provoked by this energy involve obsessive and manic behavior, irrational compulsions such as shoplifting or exhibitionism, artistic creations of the lyrical or emotional type, occult works of the mediumistic or passive kind, and spirit communications.

This element is applicable in such matters as travel by water, boating, fishing, scrying into crystals and mirrors or water-scrying, modeling and the fashion industry, and things pertaining to style or appearance.

Air

The humour blood, which gives rise to the sanguine temperament in the human body, is moist and warm. It influences social interaction, communication, restlessness, boredom, fickleness, changeability, betrayal of trust and failure of duty, talkativeness, involuntary movements, and flightiness; or, in a healthier and more balanced expression, friendliness, openness to others, social skills, organizational abilities, speaking ability, eloquence, elegance of manner, charm, and grace.

Figure 2.6: Symbol for Air

An excess of Air in the body provokes such complaints as an inability to concentrate, intestinal gas, bloating, asthma, facial twitches, restless leg syndrome, and smoking addiction.

Material actions prompted by this energy are socializing, organizing groups, hosting parties and partygoing, lecturing, teaching, journalism, acting, performing, juggling, acrobatics, dancing, telling jokes, entertaining, and social interactions.

The element is applicable in communications, the media, advertising, coordinated events, group activities, introductions, and meetings.

Earth

The humour black bile, which gives rise to the melancholic temperament in the human body, is dry and cold. It influences sadness, depression, sardonic humor, cynicism, inertness, indifference, immobility, aversion to change, dislike of travel, unsociable behavior, withdrawal, hermitism, and thoughts of suicide; or, in a healthier and more balanced expression, seriousness, steadfastness, determination, reliability, dependability, and practicality.

Figure 2.7: Symbol for Earth

An excess of Earth in the body provokes insomnia, joint problems, constipation, muscle cramps, dry skin, dandruff, kidney stones, and gallstones and other problems with the gallbladder.

Material actions provoked by this energy are collecting, saving money and other things, restoring antiques, works of art or construction, guarding, caretaking, conserving, monitoring, building and repairing, writing nonfiction, occult studies, and solitary amusements and recreations.

This element is applicable in dealing with such things as retreats, hermitages, monasteries, nunneries, remote places, distant travel, pilgrimages, constructions, environmentalism, farming, ranching, wildlife management, and forestry.

The Four Quarters

The way the quarters of the world are attributed varies from one occult system to another. The most important association with the quarters is to the lower four ancient elements that make up, in an esoteric sense, the substances underlying the physical universe, but there are many other attributions as well. I will list here a few of the more important occult correspondences that are used in the magical system of the Hermetic Order of the Golden Dawn. These are based on tradition and are the most widely accepted attributions for the quarters in modern magic.

Air is yellow, the light of the rising Sun and the airy east, which is the natural quarter of the elemental spirits known as Sylphs, and the quarter under the rule of the archangel Raphael. Fire is red and gives forth the heat of the south, the quarter associated with the elementals known as the Salamanders, and is under the rule of Michael. Water is blue in the great Atlantic Ocean that lies to the west of Europe, where these attributions were devised, and to the west is given the elementals known as the Undines, and also the archangel Gabriel. The lifeless ground in winter is black. Be aware that the color of the north itself is black, because winter brings desolation and darkness and barren soil is dark, but it is sometimes useful to associate the element Earth with the color green, since growing things spring up from the soil. The north is associated with the elementals known as the Gnomes and with the archangel Uriel.

	East	South	West	North
Element	Air	Fire	Water	Earth
Season	Spring	Summer	Autumn	Winter
Color	Yellow	Red	Blue	Black
Elementals	Sylphs	Salamanders	Undines	Gnomes
Archangel	Raphael	Michael	Gabriel	Uriel

Elemental Associations of the Quarters

These four categories allow the magician to more easily manipulate occult energies and spiritual beings of the lower elements. We do this by facing the quarter from which we desire to call the blind force or spirit that will serve our purpose. For example, when using these correspondences to attract the occult forces of elemental Fire or the fiery elementals known as Salamanders, we face the south. To attract the forces of elemental

Air or the airy elemental spirits known as Sylphs, we face the east. To attract the forces of elemental Water or the watery elementals known as Undines, we face the west. To attract the forces of elemental Earth or the earthy elementals known as Gnomes, we face the north. Similarly, the spirits of the spring are summoned from the east, the spirits of winter from the north, and so on. We may, if we wish, command the elementals of a quarter by the name of the archangel that rules in their quarter.

The Quintessence, which does not have its own direction, may be assigned to the point of the center, where the lines of east-west and north-south intersect.

Workings: The Five Elements

These workings are designed to give you an intuitive awareness of the nature of the elements and the classes of elemental spirits associated with them. Manipulating the forces of the elements forms a large part of the work you will do on a daily basis in your magic, so it is necessary that you fully understand what the elements are and the differences between them.

You may object, thinking that all you are doing in these workings is imagining things and that none of it is real. This is certainly true at the beginning of practice, but as you become better at concentrating your mind and focusing your willpower, you will find that the presence of the concentrated elemental forces becomes impossible to dismiss as mere wishful thinking. You will actually begin to feel the elements.

Fire is hot and prickly, the sensation you get on your face when you open a hot oven. Water is cool and damp, like cold sea mist on the face. Air tickles the little hairs on your arms and the back of your neck by its motion and is humid and thick, the way you feel in the summer when there is going to be a thunderstorm. Concentrated Earth feels dry and cool, and presses on your skin from all sides.

Working 1: Earth Element

Begin in the standing posture, facing north, with your arms at your sides and your feet four inches apart. Take a few slow, silent breaths to calm your mind and focus on what you are about to do.

Widen your stance to about twelve inches and extend your arms in the opening posture. Continue to gaze straight ahead. As you make this opening motion with your hands, visualize the transparent aura around your body expanding in all directions.

When your aura is a perfect transparent sphere that surrounds you like a giant soap bubble, raise your arms in the invoking posture and invoke the green energy of elemental Earth.

As this energy descends through the top of your aura and fills it, visualize the aura turning a transparent forest green. You are attracting the health-giving qualities of fertile soil and growing things, not the icy, sterile qualities of frozen ground in winter, so your aura is tinted rich, dark green instead of black. Hold this green color in your aura for a minute or so, with your arms upraised and face upturned. Be aware of the weight of elemental Earth all around you, pressing against you on all sides. It is cool and dry against your skin. Smell the freshly turned soil.

Lower your arms slowly and smoothly into the banishing posture, with your palms turned down, and turn your gaze downward. Use your will to push the green color and the heavy Earth energy out through the bottom of your expanded aura and into the ground below you.

When your aura is once again transparent and colorless, shift into the opening posture, with arms outstretched and eyes straight ahead. Connect with your expanded aura and transition smoothly into the closing posture by bringing your feet together and crossing your wrists in front of your chest, with your hands clenched into fists. As you draw your hands together, visualize the sphere of your aura deflating to its normal state close to your body. Close your eyes and hold the posture for a minute while you visualize your contracted aura.

Assume the standing posture and take a few silent breaths to relax and end the working.

Working 2: Gnomes

Assume the standing posture facing north, and draw a few slow, silent breaths to calm your mind and relax your body.

Become aware of your aura. Perform the opening posture to expand your aura into a sphere.

Shift to the invoking posture, with both arms raised, and draw Earth energy into your aura, turning it a deep transparent green. When your expanded aura is fully charged with the energy of elemental Earth, contemplate it for a minute. Be aware of the weight and coolness of this energy all around you.

Move from the invoking posture into the scrying posture by bringing your hands together, palms turned outward, so that a perfect upright triangle is formed between your thumbs and forefingers. Hold this triangle about twelve inches in front of your face and gaze through it as though looking through a window while at the same time remaining conscious of the green tint of your expanded aura.

Visualize through the triangle the image of a short, stocky figure dressed in old-fashioned leather work clothes. It can be a man or a woman, whichever you prefer. The Gnome is about four feet tall (120 cm), very broad in the shoulders and powerfully muscled, with dark brown or dark reddish hair braided in the back. Its skin is swarthy, its face broad, its eyes dark brown. Visualize it standing in a green field of tall grass and wildflowers beside a large gray standing stone that towers above its head.

See this figure as clearly as possible in your imagination, as though you are seeing it in a dream. If details of the Gnome's appearance or clothing suggest themselves to you, accept them and add them to your visualization. The image should not be static, but alive. See the Gnome breathing and moving as it regards you, aware of your attention. Hold the visualization for a minute or so.

Allow this image to vanish as you separate your hands and step back with your right foot into the warding posture, with elbows bent and close to your body, hands held up in front of your shoulders, with the palms turned forward.

Bring your right foot forward again into the medium stance, and make the banishing posture with your arms lowered in a V-shape, palms downward. With the force of your will, cause the green Earth energy that still fills your expanded aura to flow out through the bottom or your auric sphere and into the ground below you.

Transition smoothly into the opening posture. Connect with your expanded aura, then draw it inward as you slowly and smoothly shift into the closing posture. Shut your eyes and visualize your aura deflated to its normal position close to your body. Hold this posture for a minute or so.

Move into the standing posture and take a few deep, silent breaths to end the working.

Working 3: Water Element

This is similar to Working 1: Earth, but you are invoking the energy of elemental Water into your aura instead of elemental Earth.

Adopt the standing posture facing west. Take a few deep, silent breaths.

Make the opening posture and use your will to expand your aura. Hold it open and contemplate it as a colorless sphere.

Slowly and smoothly transition into the invoking posture and draw down the energy of elemental Water until it fills your expanded aura. Visualize it as a deep transparent blue. Feel this energy cool and damp against your skin, like morning mist.

Hold your aura filled with this blue energy for a minute or so, then move smoothly into the banishing posture and force the energy of elemental Water down and out of your aura, so that it pours into the ground below you.

Shift into the opening posture, connect with your expanded aura, and immediately transition into the closing posture. As you draw your arms slowly together to cross them over your chest, visualize your aura deflating to its normal shape around your body. Hold this posture with your eyes closed for a minute or so.

Move into the standing posture and take a few silent breaths to calm your thoughts and end the working.

Working 4: Undines

This working follows the pattern of Working 2: Gnomes. Begin in the standing posture facing west. Take a few silent breaths to prepare yourself.

Visualize your aura. Make the opening posture to expand it into a colorless, transparent sphere.

Shift smoothly into the invoking posture and draw down the energy of elemental Water so that it fills your expanded aura with transparent blue. Hold for a minute as you contemplate your aura filled with this cooling, moist energy.

Move into the scrying posture and visualize through the scrying triangle between your hands the figure of an Undine sitting on a rock with its feet in the water of a deep pool. The Undine has a slender body, blue or green eyes, pale white skin with a slight bluish cast, and long, wavy black hair. It wears flowing, translucent, silky garments. You may visualize the spirit as male or female, whichever you choose.

After holding this image in your imagination for a minute, separate your hands to dissolve it and step back into the warding posture.

Move into the banishing posture. Send the blue energy that fills your expanded aura into the ground below your feet.

Transition smoothly into the opening posture to connect with your aura, and then immediately cross your wrists in the closing posture. As you do so, visualize your aura contracting back to its normal position. Contemplate your aura for a minute with your eyes closed.

Shift back into the standing posture and take a few silent breaths to relax and end the working.

Working 5: Air Element

This working follows the same general pattern as workings 1 and 3. As you transition between the postures, remember to keep your movements smooth and slow.

Begin in the standing posture facing east. Visualize your aura as colorless around you, close to your body.

Make the opening posture to expand your aura into a colorless, transparent sphere. Move into the invoking posture and draw the energy of elemental Air down into your expanded aura. As it fills your aura, it turns it a bright transparent yellow. Contemplate the yellow tint and feel the energy of this element tickle the hairs on your skin. You may feel a slight breeze.

Transition into the banishing posture and use your will to force the energy of elemental Air down and out of your expanded aura. Send it into the ground below you.

Form the opening posture once again to connect with your aura, and immediately move into the closing posture, drawing your aura back to its normal shape around your body. Contemplate it for a minute or so with your eyes closed.

Assume the standing posture and take a few silent breaths to end.

Working 6: Sylphs

This visualization follows the pattern of workings 2 and 4.

Begin with the standing posture facing east.

Expand your aura with the opening posture.

Form the invoking posture and fill your expanded aura with the bright yellow energy of elemental Air. Feel this energy all around you.

Move into the scrying posture, and through the scrying triangle between your hands, visualize a Sylph. It is a slightly built spirit wearing loose, brightly colored garments, with blond hair, lightly tanned skin, pale blue or golden eyes, a pointed chin, and slightly pointed ears. It can be either male or female, as you choose. Regard it for a minute or two through your triangle, and make eye contract with the spirit. If details of the figure suggest themselves to you, mentally add them to the image.

Separate your hands to dispel the image and step back into the warding posture. Shift to the banishing posture. Send the yellow energy of Air into the ground beneath you. Contemplate your transparent, colorless expanded aura.

Move into the opening posture and then, without pausing, transition into the closing posture. As you cross your fists in front of your chest, draw your expanded aura back to its normal resting position close to your body. Hold for a minute with eyes closed.

Assume the standing posture and take a few silent breaths to end.

Working 7: Fire Element

This working follows the pattern of workings 1, 3, and 5.

Adopt the standing posture facing south.

Shift into the opening posture to expand your aura.

Form the invoking posture and draw down the energy of elemental Fire. See it in your mind as it fills your expanded aura with bright transparent red. Intensify the red tint in your imagination, and feel the heat and dryness against your skin. It is never an unpleasant sensation because you control it. The heat cannot burn you. By visualizing the warmth and the redness of elemental Fire, you attune your mind to its vibrational frequency, so to speak, and in this way attract and concentrate it in your expanded aura. You may begin to perspire from the warmth. This is natural and a sign of success. The heat you will feel is not quite the same as normal warmth but is a kind of frantic energy beating against your skin, similar to the heat that radiates from glowing metal.

Shift into the banishing posture and expel the Fire energy into the ground beneath you. As you do so, watch in your mind as your aura goes from red to colorless.

Move into the opening posture, then immediately transition into the closing posture, drawing your aura closer to your body as you bring your hands together to cross them over your chest. Close your eyes and contemplate your aura for a minute or so.

Resume the standing posture and take a few silent breaths to end.

Working 8: Salamanders

This working follows the pattern of workings 2, 4, and 6.

Begin in the standing posture facing south.

Move into the opening posture to expand your aura into a sphere.

Go to the invoking posture to fill your expanded aura with the transparent red energy of elemental Fire.

Form the scrying posture, and through the triangular scrying window between your hands, visualize the figure of a Salamander standing beside a bonfire. You may visualize the spirit as male or female. It is an athletic figure five feet or so in height, with wild fiery red hair that almost appears to be burning, skin that is flushed with inner heat, and penetrating charcoal-gray eyes. It wears tight-fitted garments that are predominantly red, orange, yellow, or black. Meet the gaze of this spirit with your eyes. Watch it leap repeatedly over the bonfire.

After contemplating the figure for a minute or two, open your hands and step back into the warding posture.

Lower your hands as you move into the banishing posture to empty the red energy of elemental Fire out of your expanded aura.

Make the opening posture to define your expanded aura, then at once move smoothly into the closing posture to contract your aura back to its normal shape near your body. Close your eyes and hold for a minute or so.

End the working by shifting into the standing posture and relaxing your mind with a few slow, silent breaths.

Working 9: Spirit Element

This working follows the pattern of workings 1, 3, 5, and 7.

Start in the standing posture facing east. Spirit has no direction, but the east is the nominal direction to face for most work.

Expand your aura with the opening posture, then attract the energy of elemental Spirit with the invoking posture.

As the energy of Spirit fills your expanded aura, visualize your transparent aura turning from clear to a transparent milky whiteness, the color of milky quartz. Feel this purifying energy around you, vitalizing and cleansing your body.

Use the banishing posture to expel the energy downward, and transition from the opening posture into the closing posture to collapse your aura back to its normal shape. Close your eyes and contemplate your aura for a minute or so.

Assume the standing posture and take several slow, silent breaths to end.

Working 10: Guardian Angel

This exercise follows the pattern of workings 2, 4, 6, and 8.

Start in the standing posture facing east.

Expand your aura with the opening posture.

Move to the invoking posture to draw down the energy of elemental Spirit, or Light. This is a pure white light that fills your expanded aura. It feels cool and clean against your skin.

Form the scrying posture and visualize through the triangle between your hands the figure of your own guardian angel. It will be a tall, graceful figure modestly clothed in white, black, or gray. Its complexion and hair color will be similar to your own. Usually the guardian angel appears as the opposite sex—if you are a man, it will be a woman; if you are a woman, it will be a man. Meet the tranquil gaze of this spirit for a minute or so.

Separate your hands to dispel the image, and step back into the warding posture. Hold briefly.

Move into the banishing posture to empty your expanded aura of the energy of elemental Spirit.

Move into the opening posture and then, without pausing, transition into the closing posture. Visualize your aura contracting to its normal position close to your body as you slowly draw your hands together and cross them at the wrists. Hold for a minute or so with eyes closed.

End the working by assuming the standing posture and taking a few silent, deep breaths.

CHAPTER 3
ELEMENTAL HAND GESTURES

WHEN USING THIS SYSTEM OF KINESIC magic, it is not necessary to make instruments to channel the energies of the elements or to use material substances to represent them. You don't even need to draw the traditional alchemical symbols of the elements, which are the barred and unbarred triangles described in the last chapter. The powers of the elements can be invoked, banished, received, projected, channeled, balanced, manifested, and more using only five simple hand gestures in combination with the twenty-four postures.

Always remember that the energies of the elements surround you at all times. We live within the elemental spheres of the four lower elements. The Earth upon which we stand is itself composed of all four lower elements, as are our physical bodies. Concentrated within us is the fifth element, that of Spirit, the essence of our life force that pervades everything in the universe. When we manipulate these energies using magic, we merely make them more or less manifest in particular locations.

It is never possible, nor would it be desirable, to send any of these elemental energies away completely. They are parts of us. Nor is it wise to allow one of them to predominate within us for a prolonged period, as this would create an imbalance. The ancient Greeks understood that the enlightened human being is one who is prudent in speech, moderate in action, and balanced in humours.

The four lower elements are the workhorses of Western magic. We use their energies often because they are easy to access and relatively easy to channel and concentrate.

Elementals, the spiritual beings of these elements, are the classes of spirits most interested in human affairs and most likely to interact with us. They are tied to the sub-lunar spheres by their natures, just as we are. Elementals can understand our motives, and we can understand theirs.

There are several basic principles that govern the manipulation of elemental energies, which I will state here. These occult potencies may be projected in straight rays, like the rays of the Sun or the rays that ancient astrologers conceived to descend from the planets and stars to influence our fates. Such rays twist as they propagate through space, like the twisting in the threads of a length of rope. Occult energies are concentrated by means of a contracting spiral and released by means of an expanding spiral. Spirals form the portals through which energies may be moved across barriers, either from inside to outside or from outside to inside.

The left side of the body is occultly female, or receptive, while the right side of the body is occultly male, or projective. We take in on the left hand and put out on the right hand. Of course we can receive or project through either side of the body if we force it. In kinesic magic, energy is sometimes invoked or banished with both hands when we use the general invoking posture or the general banishing posture. Even so, the naturally receptive side is the left, and the naturally projective side is the right.

Elemental gestures can be formed using either hand, or both hands together. In the illustrations in this book, the right hand is shown.

Earth

Hand Gesture of Earth

The gesture of elemental Earth is made by closing the hand into a fist, with the thumb inserted between the middle and ring fingers so that just the tip of the thumb projects between their knuckles. Do not clench your hand too tightly or it will become tired.

Figure 3.1: Hand Gesture of Earth

Meditation on Earth

Face the north in the standing posture, with hands relaxed at your sides and feet about four inches apart. Take a few silent breaths to focus your mind.

Think of soil and stone. Fill your mind with images of rocky ground, deserts, mountains, and tilled farmland with young green plants budding forth from it. Be conscious of the weight of the dirt, the hardness of the stones, the smell of the tilled soil.

Form the Earth gesture with both hands, and move into the spiral invoking posture, with your left hand high above your head and your right hand pressed to the center of your chest over your heart-center. Using the force of your will, draw Earth energy from the space around you into your left hand and send it in a contracting spiral down your left arm, across your back at the shoulders, and down your right arm into your heart-center.

As you do this, visualize the baseball-size sphere of your heart-center gradually turning from soft white to a dark green color, and its rate of counterclockwise rotation increasing as it gathers energy. Fill your heart-center with Earth energy to a level that is not uncomfortable.

Assume the ankh posture, with your feet together, your arms spread wide, and the palms turned forward, but hold the Earth gesture with each hand. Visualize the green Earth energy you have accumulated in your heart-center pouring down the left side of your body to your feet, crossing from your left foot to your right foot, then flowing up the right side of your body to the top of your head, and again down the left side of your body in a continuous cycle.

You should circulate this cool, heavy energy around the perimeter of your body for a dozen cycles or so in time with your breaths, visualizing its green color as it flows. Use audible breaths to pump the energy around your body. As you slowly exhale with an audible hissing between pursed lips, will the energy to flow down your left side from your head, and as you inhale audibly over your teeth with a hissing sound, will it to flow up your right side from your feet.

This energy is a source of solidity and strength, of resistance to change, of determination and steadfastness. It can be a useful energy if you're feeling doubt in your mind or weakness in your body. A minor benefit is that it can be used to stop trembling and twitching, such as may come from a facial tic or muscle fatigue.

From the ankh posture, separate your feet in the narrow stance and bring your hands together in front of you in the prayer posture. Continue to hold the Earth gesture with both hands. Draw the Earth energy circulating throughout your body into the center of your chest and compress it back into your heart-center, which turns green and spins more rapidly. Contemplate your heart-center for a minute.

Shift your arms into the spiral banishing posture, with your hands still in the Earth gesture. Your left hand is pressed over your chest and your right hand directed downward at your right side.

Mentally will the Earth energy that fills your heart-center to flow in an expanding spiral into your left hand, up your left arm, across your back at the shoulders, down your right arm, and out your right hand in a green stream of energy that twists down into the ground below where you stand. As your heart-center empties of Earth energy, it once more becomes a soft white color and its rate of spin slows to normal.

Shift to the closing posture, with feet together, hands made into fists, right wrist crossed in front of left wrist, and eyes shut. Contemplate your balanced inner state for a minute or so while breathing normally.

Relax your hands and assume the standing posture. Take a few silent breaths to end the meditation.

Water

Hand Gesture of Water

The hand gesture of Water is made by extending the thumb, index finger, and middle finger together and touching while folding down the ring and small fingers to the palm.

Figure 3.2: Hand Gesture of Water

Meditation on Water

Begin in the standing posture facing west and take a few silent breaths to focus on your purpose.

Fill your mind with the most watery images you can imagine—rushing rivers cascading over rocks, thundering waterfalls, a deep blue lake with ripples on its surface, the blue waves of the ocean turning white with foam and breaking on a beach. Hear the sound of the water. Feel its mist cooling and dampening your face.

Make the gesture of Water with both hands and shift into the spiral invoking posture. Use the power of your will to draw the energy of elemental Water into your upraised left hand, down your left arm, across your body at the shoulders and down your right arm. This energy flows into your right hand, where it jumps from your hand through your chest and into your heart-center, turning its sphere an ever-deepening blue and causing it to rotate faster around its vertical axis in a counterclockwise direction.

You must feel the coolness of this blue energy stream as it flows down your left arm, across your shoulders, and down your right arm. At first you will only be able to imagine this feeling, but the more you practice, the more real the feeling will become.

Shift to the ankh posture while holding the gesture of Water with both hands, and circulate around your body the blue energy of elemental Water that fills your heart-center. Send it down your left side, across your feet, up your right side to the crown of your head, and down the left side again.

Audibly exhale to push the blue energy down your left side, pause briefly when it is at your feet, then audibly inhale to pull it up your right side, and pause when it fills your head. Do this cycle a dozen times or so.

The energy of Water is useful for receiving impressions and visions. It can help restart your creative process when it has dried up and stopped working. It is a cooling, soothing, relaxing energy that is sensually quite pleasant. It has a calming effect when you are angry, frustrated, or troubled by worrying thoughts.

Shift to the prayer posture while continuing to hold the Water gesture with both hands. Compress the blue energy that fills your body back into the sphere of your heart-center, causing it to glow blue and rotate more rapidly. Contemplate this for a minute or so.

Change to the spiral banishing posture and send the energy of elemental Water that fills your heart-center flowing from your right hand in a blue stream into the ground below where you stand. As the energy flows out of your body, the sphere of your heart-center returns to its usual soft white color and spins more slowly.

Make the closing posture with your hands clenched into fists, and contemplate the inner balance of your four humours for a minute or so with eyes shut.

Return to the standing posture and take a few silent breaths to end the meditation.

Air

Hand Gesture of Air

The hand gesture of elemental Air is made by extending and spreading the thumb, index finger, and small finger while keeping the middle finger and ring finger curved down toward the palm. It is not necessary to actually touch the palm with the middle and ring fingers, as this puts excessive stress on the hand.

Figure 3.3: Hand Gesture of Air

Meditation on Air

You should meditate on the nature of elemental Air on a regular basis. This meditation will improve your ability to visualize and understand the Air energy, and will help link in your unconscious mind the hand gesture with the element.

Stand facing the east in the standing posture and draw several silent breaths to focus your mind.

Fill your mind with images and sensations associated with elemental Air. Imagine the sound of a rustling pine tree on a mountainside that has been bent by the prevailing wind. Feel a breeze brush against your cheeks and move your hair. Breathe deeply and be refreshed by it. Picture white clouds rolling across the open blue sky and birds flying high above you.

When you have filled your mind with airy imagery, make the Air gesture with both hands and adopt the spiral invoking posture. Using your will, draw yellow Air energy out of the atmosphere above you into your left hand, and send it down your left arm, across your back at the shoulders, down your right arm, and into your heart-center. This causes your heart-center to gradually change from soft white to bright yellow, and its rate of counterclockwise spin to increase.

When you have filled your heart-center, shift into the ankh posture, but continue to hold the Air gesture with both hands. Use the force of your will to cause the Air energy in your spinning heart-center to flow out and down the left side of your body to your feet, then up the right side of your body to the crown of your head.

Circulate the energy a dozen times or so. Use audible exhalations to force it down your left side and audible inhalations to pull it up your right side.

The Air energy fills you and makes you light and open. Feel it expanding your consciousness. It refreshes and cleanses your organs, tissues, and bones, blowing away the psychic dust that has settled there.

Part your legs slightly and bring your hands together in front of you in the prayer posture, but continue to hold the Air gesture with both hands. You should touch together the tips of your thumbs, index fingers, and small fingers when you do this. Concentrate the Air energy back into your heart-center until it spins with great speed and glows bright yellow. Contemplate your heart-center for a minute or so in this posture.

To restore the elemental balance inside your body, shift into the spiral banishing posture while holding the Air gesture with both hands. Visualize the Air energy flowing from your heart-center into your receptive left hand, and use the power of your will to carry it up your left arm, across your back at the shoulders, and down your right arm. Send the energy out your right hand in a twisting yellow stream into the ground, where it is earthed.

Change to the closing posture, with your forearms crossed and hands clenched lightly into fists. Contemplate your inner energy balance for a minute with your eyes shut. You should feel refreshed, with your thoughts clearer and more sharply focused.

Adopt the standing posture with your arms at your sides and your hands relaxed. Take a few silent breaths to end the meditation.

Fire

Hand Gesture of Fire

The gesture of Fire is made by spreading wide the middle finger, index finger, and thumb while keeping the ring finger and small finger folded down near the palm.

Figure 3.4: Hand Gesture of Fire

Meditation on Fire

Face the south, the quarter ruled by Fire, in the standing posture. Calm and focus your mind with a few silent breaths.

Visualize the most fiery things you can imagine—a roaring furnace, a forest fire, a house engulfed in flames, an erupting volcano, glowing molten lava flowing down a slope, or iron heated bright red and radiating heat.

Form the gesture of Fire with both hands, and shift into the spiral invoking posture to draw down the energy of Fire into your left hand. Using visualization and the force of your will, cause this fiery energy to descend in a contracting spiral through your upper body and down your right arm into your heart-center, which slowly changes from soft white to bright red as it rotates more rapidly counterclockwise.

You should feel the heat of this energy in your arms and across your shoulders as it descends and accumulates in the center of your chest. This is not a painful sensation, but a radiant warmth. The energy cannot burn you because you control it.

Once your heart-center is filled with the energy of Fire, assume the ankh posture while continuing to hold the gesture of Fire with both hands. Use the force of your will to send the Fire out of your heart-center and down your left side, across to your right foot, up your right side to the crown of your head, then back down your left side.

Circulate the fiery energy in this way a dozen times or so, using audible exhalations to drive it down the left side of your body and audible inhalations to pull it up the right side.

This Fire energy has an invigorating and purifying effect, especially in burning away sickness or infection. It can help to cut through confusion and focus the mind on a single purpose. It is also useful for banishing fatigue or weakness from the body.

Transition from the ankh posture to the prayer posture, but instead of pressing your palms flat together, as in the ideal form of the prayer posture, join your hands while maintaining the Fire gesture with both hands. The tips of your extended thumbs, index fingers, and middle fingers should touch. Use the power of your will to compress the energy of Fire that circulates through your body back into the sphere of your heart-center, turning it bright red. Contemplate your heart-center for a minute.

Shift slowly and smoothly into the spiral banishing posture, but continue to make the Fire gesture with both hands. Draw the fiery energy out of your heart-center, up your left arm, and across your back at the shoulders, and with the force of your will, push it down your right arm and out your right hand so that it flows in a twisting red stream downward into the ground, where it is earthed.

Make the closing posture with hands lightly closed into fists and forearms crossed at the wrists in front of your chest. Hold this pose for a minute or so with your eyes shut, and be aware of the balance and harmony of elements within your body.

Open your eyes and move into the standing posture. Take several silent breaths to conclude this meditation on elemental Fire.

Spirit

Hand Gesture of Spirit

The gesture of Spirit is formed by extending the index finger with the thumb spread away from it, so that an approximate right angle is formed between the index finger and thumb. The middle, ring, and small fingers are folded down to the palm.

Figure 3.5: Hand Gesture of Spirit

Meditation on Spirit

This meditation will improve your ability to visualize and understand Spirit energy, and will help link in your unconscious mind the hand gesture with the element.

Adopt the standing posture facing the east, since there is no quarter associated with Spirit, and take several slow, silent breaths to calm your emotions and focus your thoughts.

Take a minute to fill your mind with thoughts and feelings associated with elemental Spirit. These will be spiritual associations, but their exact nature will depend on your personal spiritual beliefs. For example, you might visualize a church, the statue of a saint, or a crucifix if you are Christian, but if you are pagan, you might picture a pagan deity or a circle of standing stones. Call up images in your mind that you associate with spiritual feelings that are pure and true.

When you have filled your mind with Spirit imagery, make the Spirit gesture with both hands and assume the spiral invoking posture. Draw cool white Spirit energy down from the heavens into your left hand and send it down your left arm, across your back at the shoulders, down your right arm, and into your heart-center. This causes your heart-center to gradually change from soft white, which is slightly yellowish, to a neutral white, and its spin to increase.

When you have filled your heart-center, shift into the ankh posture, with your hands in the Spirit gesture. Use the force of your will to cause the Spirit energy in your spinning heart-center to flow out and down the left side of your body to your feet as you exhale audibly, then up the right side of your body to the crown of your head as you inhale audibly. Do about a dozen of these cycles, feeling the energy of Spirit circulate through your body.

Spirit energy purifies your mind and banishes trivial, materialistic thoughts. It liberates and elevates you above the earthly plane, and gives you a sense of union with limitless space. Use it to banish brooding or obsessive thoughts and to cleanse yourself of bad memories or dark feelings.

Make the prayer posture while holding the Spirit gesture with both hands so that your thumbs and index fingers touch. Concentrate the Spirit energy back into your heart-center until it spins with great speed and glows a pure white. Contemplate your energized heart-center for a minute or so in this posture.

Shift into the spiral banishing posture while continuing to hold the gesture of Spirit with both hands. Visualize Spirit energy drawn from your heart-center into your receptive left hand, and use the power of your will to carry it up your left arm, across your back at the shoulders, and down your right arm. Send the energy out your right hand in a white stream that twists into the ground, where it is earthed.

Move into the closing posture and contemplate your inner state for a minute or so with your eyes shut, forearms crossed, and hands closed into fists. You will feel renewed, and your mind will be tranquil.

Adopt the standing posture, with your arms at your sides and your hands relaxed. Take a few silent breaths to end the meditation.

Workings: Elemental Hand Gestures

Use the following exercises to practice moving elemental energy through your hands by means of the five elemental gestures. By keying each gesture to its element repeatedly while visualizing its elemental energy, the link between the element and the gesture becomes automatic, to the point where simply making the gesture will be enough to call forth the corresponding elemental force. The gestures evoke the energies, and the postures direct them and apply them.

Working 1: To Invoke an Element

Gaze at the horizon. Adopt the standing posture facing the quarter that is associated with the element with which you are working, or facing east if you are working with Spirit. Take a few silent breaths to calm and focus your mind.

Form the gesture of the element with both hands and shift into the spiral invoking posture, with your left hand raised above your head as you press your right hand to your chest over your heart-center.

Use the force of your will to draw the occult energy of the element into your receptive left hand from the elemental sphere that surrounds you. The four lower elements are like Russian dolls that nest one inside another, but they also overlap and interpenetrate. You are standing on the sphere of Earth. The sphere of Water flows over it and falls upon it as rain. The sphere of Air supports the clouds and fills your lungs. The sphere of Fire is the source of the lightning. Spirit does not have a sphere, but pervades everything in the universe.

Be aware of the nature of the elemental energy you have attracted on the skin of your left hand. Fire is hot and prickly, Water is cool and damp, Air is warm and dry, and Earth is heavy and cool. Spirit feels light and penetrating but has no specific sensation of its own.

Cause this accumulated energy to descend down your left arm, across your back at the shoulders, and down your right arm in a contracting spiral that has as its focus your right hand. Will the elemental energy to flow from your right hand through your chest and into your heart-center.

The heart-center is to be visualized as a soft white sphere about the size of a baseball. As it fills with elemental energy, it turns the color of the element. Fire is red, Water is blue, Air is yellow, and Earth is dark green (if you are dealing with the life-giving quality of Earth) or black (if you are dealing with its sterile, dead quality). Usually you will invoke the green energy of Earth. Spirit turns the sphere of your heart-center from a warm soft white to a neutral white.

As you accumulate elemental energy in the sphere of your heart-center, it spins more rapidly on its vertical axis in a counterclockwise direction. Your heart-center is always spinning, but the more energy it receives, the faster it spins.

When your heart-center is spinning rapidly like a dynamo, make the closing posture by drawing your feet together, clenching your fists, and crossing your forearms at the wrists in front of your heart-center. Close your eyes and hold this posture for a minute while you contemplate your energized heart-center.

Shift into the standing posture to end this exercise, with hands open and relaxed at your sides, your gaze directed forward at the unseen horizon. Hold it for several silent breaths.

This working to invoke an element should be done immediately prior to the working that follows, if you are merely practicing the method.

Working 2: To Banish an Element

This working is best done as a practice immediately following the previous working, while your heart-center is still filled with the energy of the element you invoked.

Facing the quarter of the element, or facing east if you have invoked Spirit, assume the standing posture. Take several slow, silent breaths.

Form the gesture of the element with both hands. Adopt the spiral banishing posture—press your left hand over your heart-center and point with your right hand downward at the floor near your right foot. As you do this, continue to hold the gesture of the element with both hands.

Use the force of your will to draw the elemental energy out of your heart-center and into your left hand. Cause it to flow in an expanding spiral up your left arm and across your back at the shoulders, and send it down your right arm.

As the energy of the element leaves the sphere of your heart-center, your heart-center changes from the color of the element back to a soft, warm white that has a slight yellowish tinge, like the light of an incandescent light bulb. Let the energy stream downward in a twisting ray from your right hand into the ground beneath the floor on which you stand, where it is harmlessly dissipated.

When your heart-center has returned to its natural color and slowed to its normal rate of spin, draw your feet together and shift into the closing posture, with your wrists crossed and hands clenched. Hold it for a minute or so with eyes shut as you contemplate the elemental balance within your body.

Separate your feet slightly. Open and relax your hands, then lower them to your sides as you return to the standing posture. Take a few slow, silent breaths to end.

Working 3: To Receive an Element

The purpose of this working is to receive into your heart-center elemental energy that is already concentrated in a place, person, or object. You transfer the energy from the thing into yourself.

Begin in the standing posture facing the quarter of the element with the thing you wish to drain of excess elemental energy on your left side. For purposes of practice, you could use a large piece of rock for elemental Earth, a glass bowl of water for Water, the rising column of smoke from a rose incense stick for Air, a candle flame for Fire, or a living flower or plant for Spirit.

Take a few silent breaths to calm yourself and focus your mind. Form the gesture of the element with both hands.

Shift into the receiving posture by stepping to the left with your left foot and pointing your left hand at the thing from which you intend to draw the Earth energy, palm up, with your right hand pressed to your chest over your heart-center. Continue to hold the gesture of the element with both hands as you do this.

Use the force of your will to draw the energy of the element from the object into your receptive left hand, and send it up your left arm, across your back at the shoulders, and down your right arm into your right hand, where it flows through your chest into your heart-center. As the spinning soft-white sphere of your heart-center fills with the energy of the element, it spins faster and turns the elemental color.

It is possible to draw elemental energy from a person, place, or thing over a considerable distance by pointing your receptive left hand at it, but the closer you are to the thing, the stronger the flow of energy will be.

When your heart-center is spinning rapidly, bring your feet together and make the closing posture, with crossed wrists and clenched fists, to cut off the flow of elemental energy. Shut your eyes and spend a minute in this pose contemplating your energized heart-center.

Move into the standing posture, with hands open at your sides, and take a few deep, silent breaths to end the working, which should be done together with the working that follows if you are merely practicing the technique.

Working 4: To Project an Element

For purposes of practice, you should perform this working shortly after you have charged your heart-center with elemental energy drawn from a place, person, or object during the previous working.

Face the quarter of the element with the thing you intend to charge with energy on your right side. If you wish, you may use the same objects you used in the previous working, by moving them from your left side to your right side.

Begin in the standing posture, and take a few silent breaths to focus your mind on what you are about to do as you gaze at the unseen horizon.

Form the gesture of the element with both hands and adopt the projecting posture—step to the right with your right foot and point your right hand at the object you intend to charge with energy, your palm turned downward, as you press your left hand to the center of your chest. Continue to hold the gesture of the element with both hands.

Use the force of your will to send elemental energy flowing from the sphere of your heart-center into your left hand, up your left arm, across your back at the shoulders, and down your right arm in an expanding spiral. Visualize it as it exits out your right hand in a stream that is tinted with the color of the element. The stream of Spirit is a clear white. The energy stream enters the object you point at with your right hand and fills it. As you draw this energy from the sphere of your heart-center, it spins more slowly and turns from the color of the element to its natural soft white.

Step back to bring your feet together and make the closing posture, with wrists crossed over your chest and hands clenched into fists. This will cut off the flow of elemental energy out from your body. Shut your eyes and contemplate the balance of elements within yourself for a minute.

Shift into the standing posture, with your hands relaxed and open at your sides, and take a few long, silent breaths to end.

Working 5: To Charge with Elemental Energy

At times you may need to charge something with energy you gather from its elemental sphere without drawing this energy out of your own energized heart-center. For this purpose, you will employ the magician posture.

Begin the working facing the quarter associated with the element, or in the case of Spirit, face the east. The person or thing you wish to charge with energy should be on your right side.

Adopt the standing posture and draw a few silent breaths to focus on what you are about to do.

Form the gesture of the element with both hands and shift into the magician posture, with your left hand high in the air and your right hand directed at the thing you seek to charge with elemental energy. Continue to look forward at the horizon. It is best to actually touch the object or person with your right hand if you can do so.

Will the energy of the element to flow from its sphere into your left hand. Visualize your hand as a kind of occult magnet for this energy that attracts and concentrates it. When your left hand is filled with energy, send it flowing through your upper body and out your right hand in a stream that enters the thing you are charging.

The energy stream is visualized in the elemental color. Be aware of it as it flows down your left arm and into your chest, and cause this energy to circle once around your heart-center counterclockwise without entering your heart-center, so that the stream forms a contracting spiral. Then direct it across the right side of your chest and down your right arm in an expanding spiral.

When the thing you are charging is filled with elemental energy, make the closing posture to end the flow of energy through your body. Stand with your forearms crossed, your hands closed into fists, and your eyes shut for a minute or so as you contemplate the normalized state of your heart-center.

Shift to the standing posture and draw a few silent breaths to end.

Working 6: To Drain of Elemental Energy

To channel elemental energy out of something in order to drain it of this energy, begin in the standing posture facing the direction of the element you are working with, and draw a few silent breaths to focus your intention.

Form the gesture of the element you wish to draw out with both hands, and shift into the Baphomet posture. Point at the thing you wish to drain with your left hand, or actually bring your left hand into contact with it. At the same time, raise your right hand high into the air. Continue to gaze forward at the unseen horizon.

Use the force of your will to draw the element out of the thing you seek to drain and send it through your body in a double spiral. The first half of its transit through your body is a contracting spiral, while the second half is an expanding spiral. It flows up your left arm and through the left side of your chest to circle your heart-center once in a counterclockwise direction, then it flows from around your heart-center through the right side of your chest and up your raised right arm. Visualize the elemental energy stream expanding from your right hand in a clockwise spiral (from your perspective) above your head. The energy spins outward from your right hand and disperses harmlessly in all directions.

Make the closing posture to end this flow of energy through your body, and hold it for a minute or so with your eyes shut.

Adopt the standing posture and take a few slow, silent breaths to relax and conclude the working.

Working 7: To Channel an Element

At times you may wish to channel the energy of an element through your body from one thing to another thing without accumulating that energy inside your heart-center.

Begin as usual with the standing posture. The thing from which you intend to draw energy should be on your left side, and the thing you intend to infuse with that energy on your right. Take a few silent breaths to focus your mind.

Make the gesture of the element you intend to channel with both hands as you widen your stance and shift into the channeling posture. The transfer will be strongest if you can actually touch both objects with your hands, but if you cannot touch these things, point at them with your hands while holding the elemental gesture.

Use your will to channel the energy through your body. Draw it out of the source with your left hand and pass it in a double spiral through your upper body and out your right hand into the target. The energy stream flows up your left arm and to the center of your chest in a contracting spiral, and around your heart-center once in a counterclockwise direction, then across to your right shoulder and down your right arm in an expanding spiral. Visualize it in the color of the element.

When you have transferred the energy, close your stance and make the closing posture, with your hands clenched lightly into fists and crossed at the wrists in front of your chest. Shut your eyes and contemplate your inner balance for a minute or so.

End the working by shifting to the standing posture and taking a few silent breaths to relax.

Working 8: To Balance the Humours

The nominal position for the balancing posture can be used for a general balancing of the four humours within the body.

Begin with the standing posture, facing east. Take a few silent breaths to focus your purpose.

Widen your stance and shift into the balancing posture, with your palms pressed together in front of your solar plexus, the right hand held palm up and the left hand above it held palm downward.

Visualize your heart-center inside the center of your chest as a sphere about the size of a baseball that is spinning counterclockwise when viewed from above. It is a soft white color.

Become aware of your dominant elemental state. One of the four lower elements will very likely predominate over the others at a given time, and it will be coloring your emotions, impulses, and urges, as well as the sensations in your body.

Fire will produce anger, irritability, impatience, impulsiveness, carelessness, haste, and rashness. Water will cause dreaminess, listlessness, languor, laziness, fantasies, erotic desire, sleepiness, and lack of ambition. Air will cause the mind to race, obsessive thoughts, swiftly changing emotions, talkativeness, arguing, contrariness, restlessness, an inability to concentrate, wittiness, and spontaneous laughter. Earth will generate feelings of inertia, heaviness, depression, brooding, stubbornness, resistance to change, callousness, insensitivity, coldness, and hardness of heart.

Allow this dominant element to color your heart-center. Fire will redden it. Water will tint it a transparent blue. Air will yellow it. Earth will darken it to a deep forest green or even to a dark gray or black. Do not try to force the color—allow your inner state to define it within your heart-center.

Separate your palms by about four inches and make the gesture of the element that tints your heart-center with your left hand. With your right hand, make the elemental gesture of the opposite color. Fire is opposite Water, and Air is opposite Earth.

Will the sphere of your heart-center to pass out through your chest so that it floats between your hands. Feel the sphere touching your hands just as if it were solid and you were holding it between them.

The elemental discoloration in the projected sphere of your heart-center is caused by the elemental imbalance within you. Cleanse the sphere by rebalancing it. Do this by rhythmically rotating your hands at the wrists while continuing to visualize the spinning sphere of your heart-center held between them. Slowly rotate your hands as if an actual ball was held between them, so that your left hand, which was on the top, is now on the bottom, and your right hand, which was on the bottom, is now on the top. Your forearms move very little when you do this—most of the motion is in your wrists and hands. This can be practiced with an actual ball until the motion becomes second nature.

As you rotate your hands, visualize the spinning sphere turning over so that its north pole becomes its south pole, and its south pole becomes its north pole. It now appears to spin in the opposite direction, from your point of view above it. The rotation that was counterclockwise when viewed from above is now seen as clockwise.

Hold this position for a silent breath, then rotate your hands at the wrists back to their original position and hold it for a breath. Continue in this way for a dozen rotations or so, until the elemental discoloration in the sphere has been washed to a pure soft white.

Will the ball to pass back into your chest, and visualize it cleansed and rotating at a moderate speed in its normal counterclockwise direction. Flatten your hands and close your palms together, with the left hand above and the right below, to resume the starting position of the balancing posture.

Shift to the standing posture and take a few silent breaths to end the working.

Working 9: To Manifest an Element

Adopt the standing posture facing the quarter associated with the element you intend to manifest. If you seek to manifest Spirit, face the east. Take a few silent breaths to focus your intention on what you are about to do.

Widen your stance and shift into the general invoking posture. Make the gesture of the element with both hands. Draw the energy of the element around you with the force of your will so that it swirls around you counterclockwise like a whirlwind that is tinted with the transparent color of the element.

When the elemental energy is thick around you, flatten your hands and bring them together to form a horizontal triangle that points away from you as you step forward on your right foot into the manifesting posture. Visualize the swirling elemental energy around you concentrating itself into a ball about the size of a basketball that floats in the air just in front of the point of the triangle formed by your joined thumbs and forefingers. It is the color of the element and rotates rapidly in a counterclockwise direction.

You may notice that the air of the room in which you are working is affected by the presence of so much elemental energy. If you have manifested Fire, it will be warmer; if Water, the air will become damp and cool; if Air, there will be a draft; if Earth, the air around you will feel heavy, stifling, and motionless.

To disperse the energy ball harmlessly, shift into the general banishing posture and make the gesture of the element with both hands. Will the ball to descend into the ground below the floor on which you are standing. Visualize it floating downward and vanishing into the floor.

Bring your feet together in the closing posture, with your hands closed into fists and your forearms crossed at the wrists in front of your chest. Shut your eyes and contemplate the silence within you for a minute or so.

Make the standing posture and take a few silent breaths to relax and end.

Working 10: The Elemental Microcosm

Face east in the standing posture and take a few silent breaths to focus your mind.

Move into the invoking posture, with both hands raised in the gesture of Spirit, and draw around you a swirling column of Spirit energy. It is clear and cool and fresh, tinted a neutral white. Feel it brushing your skin like a whirlwind.

Step forward into the manifesting posture and focus this energy into a spinning ball just beyond the point of the triangle formed by your joined thumbs and forefingers. It should be visualized around the size of a basketball, spinning counterclockwise and shining with neutral white light.

Make the gesture of Spirit with both hands. Reach forward to gently press the spinning ball between your hands. Bring your feet together to touch and raise the ball above your head as you shift into a modified version of the macrocosm posture. Hold the ball of Spirit energy over your head while maintaining the gesture of Spirit with both hands. Take a slow, silent breath while holding this posture.

Spread wide your stance and open your arms into the microcosm posture, flattening your hands as you do so and turning the palms forward. Use the power of your will to extract balls of the four lower elements from the ball of Spirit energy that floats just above your head, while leaving a ball of Spirit still spinning above your head. Direct the ball of Fire around your right foot, the ball of Air around your left hand, the ball of Water around your right hand, and the ball of Earth around your left foot.

Hold the microcosm posture for a minute or so, and be aware of these five balls of elemental energy at the extremities of your body, which is spread wide in the shape of a star with five points. Feel the differences in the energy balls radiating against your hands, feet, and the top of your head. Fire is hot and dry, Air is hot and moist, Water is cool and moist, Earth is cool and dry, and Spirit is a kind of penetrating effervescence.

Resume the macrocosm posture. As you bring your feet back together and raise your hands, draw the four balls of lower elemental energy upward into the ball of Spirit above your head. Make the gesture of Spirit with both hands, and will the four lower energies to merge into the ball of Spirit between your hands and become Spirit.

Widen your stance to medium and shift into the loosing posture, with your hands still in the gesture of Spirit. Release the ball of Spirit energy upward through the ceiling of your room, to expand and dissipate into the air above you.

Make the closing posture and hold it for a minute or so with eyes shut while contemplating your inner silence.

Move into the standing posture and take several silent breaths to relax and end.

CHAPTER 4
THE SEVEN PLANETS

ANCIENT ASTROLOGERS IN PERSIA LOOKED UP at the night sky and saw that there were seven lights that moved in regular ways that were independent of the seemingly fixed background of the stars. All the stars appeared to sweep across the night sky from east to west, due to the rotation of the Earth, but these seven lights moved in other ways that were predictable, unlike the movements of comets and meteors, which came and went.

These seven visible lights are the planets of traditional astrology, and they are still shining down on us today, just as they shone down on the magi of Persia five thousand years ago.

Why, you may wonder, does a worker of ritual magic need to know about the ancient planets? You need to know about them because all of Western magic is based, to a greater or lesser degree, on astrology, which we may call the mother of all magic.

The planets are quite useful in practical magic operations. Each planet has its own unique nature, and the natures of the planets are linked, in an occult way, with sets of symbols, classes of objects, kinds of environments, human personality types, and hierarchies of spirits. By manipulating the energy of a planet, you can control the things, events, and beings that lie under the authority of that planet.

In our modern age, we understand that the planets revolve around the Sun, and that there are more of them than are visible to the naked eye. However, the cosmology of magic is based on the ancient geocentric model that was accepted by most of the ancient world, where the Earth is the fixed center of the universe, surrounded by concentric, rotating, transparent spheres in which are set the planets and the stars, like jewels set in the surface of hollow glass balls.

The seven spheres of the planets nest one inside the other, and they turn on an invisible cosmic axis running through all of them. This turning makes the planets move across the sky. Surrounding them all is the sphere of the fixed stars. All of the visible stars are set in the surface of this crystalline outer sphere, and their locations relative to each other always remain the same, fixed into place. This is the ancient view of the cosmos—the stars were believed not to wander like the planets.

You may scoff and say that's not an accurate model of the solar system. From a scientific perspective, it is not accurate, but it is a very natural way to regard the cosmos. When you stand looking up at the sky, does the ground appear to move beneath your feet or does it feel stationary? Unless there's an earthquake, the ground never moves. The lights in the sky are points, with the exception of the Sun and Moon. It was natural to call those that did not appear to change position the "fixed stars," and those points of light that moved the "wandering stars." It was natural to assume that the Sun moved around the Earth, just like all the other planets. After all, doesn't the entire universe revolve around you, when you look out at it from the perspective of your mind? Aren't you at the center of everything, from your own point of view? Of course you are. That's the natural way of looking at the world.

Science has taught humanity to adopt an artificial viewpoint, where our awareness must hover somewhere in space high above the plane of the solar system, and of course from that elevated and detached perspective, we see that the planets do indeed revolve around the Sun. In view of the contempt science holds for magic, it is ironic that this projection of the viewpoint is a magical act.

To work magic, we much retain our natural viewpoint at the center of the universe. When we adopt this view, we see that everything—planets, the Sun, the stars and galaxies—revolves around us. A skilled magician can also shift his point of view at will outside his body to any place he chooses, and then the universe revolves around that projected point of view.

Gods of the Planets

The seven planets of traditional astrology share the names of seven of the most prominent gods and goddesses in the pantheon of the ancient Greeks, and represent the seven days of the week, which in Latin are named after the Roman versions of these gods and goddesses. In other cultures, different gods were identified with the planets.

The Germanic names for the gods of the week have mostly prevailed in the English language, with the exception of Saturday, named after the Roman Saturn. In the following table, I've given the Greek, Roman, and Germanic names for the gods of the week, bracketed on either side by the English and Latin names for the days of the week.

English Name of Day of Week	Greek God	Roman God	Germanic God	Latin Name of Day of Week
Monday	Selene	Luna	Moon	*Lunae dies*
Tuesday	Ares	Mars	Tew	*Martis dies*
Wednesday	Hermes	Mercury	Woden	*Mercurii dies*
Thursday	Zeus	Jupiter	Thor	*Iovis dies*
Friday	Aphrodite	Venus	Frija	*Veneris dies*
Saturday	Kronos	Saturn	Saturn	*Saturni dies*
Sunday	Helios	Sol	Sun	*Solis dies*

The Seven Days and Their Gods

Although the ancient Romans largely adopted the mythology of the Greeks, and came to consider the Greek gods associated with the days of the week to be the same as their own Roman equivalents, they are not exactly the same gods, because they had different origins. There are differences between the Greek god Kronos and the Roman god Saturn, between the Greek Hermes and the Roman Mercury (although these two are very close), between the Greek Aphrodite and the Roman Venus, and so on. What I have given in this chapter is the general understanding of these gods used by modern Western magicians. If you wish to learn about the subtle differences between the Greek and Roman gods, you must study the mythologies of these two cultures.

Observing Times

For the most part, the names of the gods of the planets used by the Romans are employed in modern magic. Each day is devoted to the particular deity who bears its name. Monday, for example, is the day of the goddess Luna. Those who prefer to observe times in magic will work rituals that fall under the influence of this goddess on her own day.

Is it necessary to observe times in magic? No, it is not absolutely necessary, but it does help the concentration of the mind, and anything that helps to intensify the focus of the imagination and the will is not to be discarded lightly. The seven days of the week are ancient. Working a planetary ritual on the day of the ruling deity can strengthen the effects of the ritual and make a successful outcome more likely.

Not only are the days of the week assigned to these deities, but also the twenty-four hours of each day. This is done by assigning the planets to the hours of the seven days of the week in the Ptolemaic order of the planets. The planets are arranged from the outermost and slowest-moving to the innermost and quickest-moving, from the perspective of the fixed Earth at the center of everything: Saturn ($\hbar$), Jupiter ($\mathrm{2\!\!\!\!4}$), Mars ($\mathrm{\sigma'}$), Sun ($\odot$), Venus (Q), Mercury ($\mathrm{\varphi}$), Moon (D). The first hour of each day is assigned to the planet of that day, and the successive twenty-three hours receive the planets in the descending Ptolemaic order repeated over and over. When the end of the day is reached, the planets begin on the first hour of the next day.

It is fascinating to see how elegant this system of planetary hours is in its arrangement. The loop of the planets assigned to the hours moves seamlessly from one day to the next, and yet each day always begins with its own planet. This can scarcely be a coincidence. We must assume that the order of the days of the week was arranged to achieve this result, which means that the planetary hours must be very ancient indeed.

Originally, the hours of the day and night were not all of equal length. The day was divided into twelve hours from sunrise to sunset, and the night was similarly divided into twelve hours from sunset to sunrise. Since the days and nights are only of equal length on the two days of the equinox, unless you lived on the equator, an hour of the day was seldom of the same duration as an hour of the night. Days are longer than nights in the months of summer, and shorter than nights during the months of winter.

Hour	Sun.	Mon.	Tues.	Wed.	Thurs.	Fri.	Sat.
1	☉	☽	♂	☿	♃	♀	♄
2	♀	♄	☉	☽	♂	☿	♃
3	☿	♃	♀	♄	☉	☽	♂
4	☽	♂	☿	♃	♀	♄	☉
5	♄	☉	☽	♂	☿	♃	♀
6	♃	♀	♄	☉	☽	♂	☿
7	♂	☿	♃	♀	♄	☉	☽
8	☉	☽	♂	☿	♃	♀	♄
9	♀	♄	☉	☽	♂	☿	♃
10	☿	♃	♀	♄	☉	☽	♂
11	☽	♂	☿	♃	♀	♄	☉
12	♄	☉	☽	♂	☿	♃	♀

Planetary Hours of the Day

Hour	Sun.	Mon.	Tues.	Wed.	Thurs.	Fri.	Sat.
13	♃	♀	♄	☉	☽	♂	☿
14	♂	☿	♃	♀	♄	☉	☽
15	☉	☽	♂	☿	♃	♀	♄
16	♀	♄	☉	☽	♂	☿	♃
17	☿	♃	♀	♄	☉	☽	♂
18	☽	♂	☿	♃	♀	♄	☉
19	♄	☉	☽	♂	☿	♃	♀
20	♃	♀	♄	☉	☽	♂	☿
21	♂	☿	♃	♀	♄	☉	☽
22	☉	☽	♂	☿	♃	♀	♄
23	♀	♄	☉	☽	♂	☿	♃
24	☿	♃	♀	♄	☉	☽	♂

Planetary Hours of the Night

Consequently, if you wish to use the planetary associations for the hours of the days in the ancient manner, you must discover the time of sunrise and the time of sunset on the day of your ritual working, then calculate the length of time between sunrise and sunset in minutes and divide those minutes by twelve. Similarly, if you are working at night, you must convert the hours between sunset and sunrise into minutes, and divide those minutes by twelve, which will give you the length of an hour of night on that date. Having determined the length of the hour, you then plot out how many of those hours elapse from sunrise until the time of your ritual, or, if you are working at night, how many hours elapse from sunset until the time of your ritual.

This is not higher mathematics, but it does require some time with a pencil and paper. In my own magic, I seldom work with the planetary hours. I regard them as an unnecessary complication. They are given here for those who may wish to work with them. But I do observe the planetary associations for the days of the week. For example, if I have a work of magic that involves gambling or luck, I will do it on Wednesday, the day of Mercury, the planetary god who is most strongly associated with games of chance. Works involving love I would do on Friday, the day of Venus, and works involving conflict I would do on Tuesday, the day of Mars, and so on.

The division of the week into planetary days is a way for the magician to focus his mind strongly on the particular planetary energy he is working with, and it also serves to bind the planetary energies to the day of working, so that those energies are stronger on that day. When you set aside a day of the week for working with a particular planet, you dedicate that day to the deity of the planet. It is a kind of offering to the deity.

The ancients seldom made a clear distinction between the planets in the heavens and the deities after which they were named. When they spoke of Mars, they might refer to the god or the planet. They regarded the planets as the chariots of the gods. The planets carried the gods across the heavens, and at times the gods might leave their chariots and descend to the surface of the Earth to interact with humanity.

Meanings of the Planetary Glyphs

The planets are composed of combinations of elemental energies. This is clearly indicated by their ancient glyphs.

The Sun is a pure form of celestial Fire, and its opposite, the Moon, is a pure form of celestial Water. Earth is represented by a cross surrounded by a circle, or more simply by a cross with equal arms, which expresses the four directions.

The glyph of Venus, which contains the Sun symbol (circle above cross), represents Fire dominant over Earth, and the glyph of its opposite, Mars (cross above circle), stands for Earth dominant over Fire.

The glyph of Jupiter, which contains the Moon symbol (crescent above cross), shows Water dominant over Earth, and the glyph of its opposite, Saturn (cross above crescent), shows Earth dominant over Water.

Mercury stands alone and apart with its threefold glyph (crescent above circle above cross), which indicates Water dominant over Fire dominant over Earth.

You may object that the glyph of Mars has an arrow, not a cross, but there is an older variant form of the glyph for Mars that shows a cross above a circle, and even an intermediate form that has an arrow with a very widely splayed point that resembles a cross.

You will find a fascinating discussion about the composition of the planetary glyphs in Alfred H. Barley's book *The Rationale of Astrology* (London, 1905).

⊙ Sun—Fire (circle = spirit)
☽ Moon—Water (crescent = soul)
⊕ Earth—Earth (cross = body)

♀ Venus—Fire (circle) over Earth (cross)
♂ Mars—Earth (cross) over Fire (circle)

♃ Jupiter—Water (crescent) over Earth (cross)
♄ Saturn—Earth (cross) over Water (crescent)

☿ Mercury—Water (crescent) over Fire (circle) over Earth (cross)

You will remember that the four elemental spheres below the sphere of the Moon have a set order. Earth is at the center, or bottom; around and above the Earth flows the sphere of Water; around and above the watery sphere is the sphere of Air; and around and above Air is the sphere of Fire. This natural order of the elemental spheres is important in understanding the composition of the planets. Also, notice that Fire and

Earth are compatible elements, and Water and Earth are also compatible, but Fire and Water are antagonistic.

Venus is composed of Fire above Earth. This is the natural order of these compatible elements. This makes Venus a healthy and stable expression of their energies. It is the Sun beaming down upon the warm, fertile ground below. The Earth is the base element and plays the dominant role in the expression of the energy of Venus, which may be said to be earthy but crowned with celestial flame. Notice that Fire and Earth are at opposite extremes in the sequence of the four elemental spheres. This separation creates a dynamic tension in the makeup of Venus that gives the planet an energetic expression.

Mars is composed of Earth above Fire. This is an unnatural order for these compatible elements. This makes Mars an unhealthy and unstable expression of their energies. It is a volcano about to erupt. Fire, the base element, is ceaselessly striving to ascend above the crowning element of Earth. This gives the planet great force but also makes the action of this force unpredictable and explosive. The extreme separation of these elements in the sequence of the elemental spheres gives this planet a dynamic tension similar to that of Venus.

Jupiter is composed of Water above Earth. This is the natural order for these compatible elements, which are the least energetic of the elements, making this planet very stable and healthy in its influence. It is rain quenching the thirst of the dry earth and making it fertile. Water and Earth are adjacent in the sequence of the elemental spheres, minimizing the dynamic tension in this planet. Its force is mild, regular, predictable, and beneficent.

Saturn is composed of Earth above Water. This is an unnatural order for these two compatible elements, but because they are adjacent in the sequence of elemental spheres, and because they are low-energy elements, Saturn is seldom unpredictable. It is, however, never completely content with its condition, as the Water ceaselessly tries to flow above the Earth. Water concealed in the depths of Earth gives this planet a brooding darkness and a secretive nature.

Mercury is composed of Water above Fire above Earth. Fire and Earth are compatible elements, as are Water and Earth, but Water and Fire are antagonistic. When brought together, the result is steam, a form of Air that is warm and moist. So even though Air is not explicitly expressed in the symbols of the glyph for Mercury, it is implied. It is the expanding cloud of steam that rises when you throw water on a bonfire. The separations between the elements is great—Fire is the highest elemental sphere and Earth the lowest; Water and Fire also have a large separation. This gives the planet a very energetic expression. Fire above Earth is the natural order, but Water above Fire is unnatural, and this makes the planet unpredictable, capricious, and mercurial, sometimes beneficial and sometimes malicious.

Colors of the Planets

One of the main ways to conceptualize and differentiate the planets is by color. There are traditional colors associated with the seven planets of classical astrology that have been recognized for centuries. Several of these traditional colors I use in my own work, but I find the others to be irrational, and for this reason I have changed them.

On the traditional pigment color wheel used by painters to mix their colors there are three primary colors (yellow, red, blue) and three secondary colors (purple, green, orange). Since the six planets apart from Mercury are arranged in three pairs of opposites, it seems to me to make sense to assign these planets to the six colors on the color wheel, placing each pair of planets on opposite sides of the wheel. In so far as possible, I retain the traditional colors for the planets (figure 4.1).

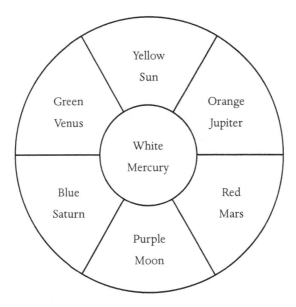

Figure 4.1: The Seven Planets on the Color Wheel

At the top of the wheel I place the Sun on its traditional color, yellow. At the bottom I put the Moon on the opposite color, purple. On red I put Mars, which has red as its traditional color. The opposite of Mars is Venus, which is placed on the opposite color, green, and this happens to be the traditional color of Venus. The traditional color of Jupiter is blue, but here we encounter a problem—if we place Jupiter on blue in the color wheel, we must put its opposite, Saturn, on orange, which is the color opposite blue on the color wheel. Orange seems grossly inappropriate for Saturn, a cold, distant planet. On the other hand, the actual color of the planet Jupiter itself, as seen through a telescope, is orange. For this reason I place Jupiter on orange and put its opposite, Saturn, on blue. Blue is a cool color and seems to me to suit the nature of Saturn.

This takes care of the six paired planets, but what of Mercury, the planet that stands apart and alone? When the spectrum of colors in light is combined, the result is pure white light. White light contains all colors and is itself colorless. Mercury, as I have shown, combines the essential natures of all the other planets in itself, being made up of circle, crescent, and cross. This has led me to place Mercury in the center of the color wheel and to assign it the color (or rather, non-color) white.

Although these color assignments, which I use in my personal system of magic, make good sense to me, they may not make sense to you. If you wish to use the traditional colors for all the planets in your magic, there is no reason why you should not do so. They are provided in the individual descriptions of the planets in the next section. There are no right or wrong color assignments for the planets—there are only color assignments that feel right to you intuitively and make sense to you rationally.

Natures of the Seven Planets

The kind of ritual work that is undertaken on the day of a planet should be in accord with the basic nature of the god or goddess of that planet. I will list here the nature of each planet, and also the general kinds of operations that are best suited to do under each influence.

Moon (Monday): Purple (Traditional Colors: Silver, White, Black)

The energy of this day is female. The Moon is both earthy and watery by nature; hence, she has a natural association with wet earth, or mud. She presides over secret things and what is hidden beneath the surface of the water or what lies buried in mud. The Moon concerns sleep, dreams, fantasies, illusions, appearances, and self-deception. She rules over psychic phenomena and psychic abilities of a passive, receptive kind, such as clairvoyance and premonitions.

Figure 4.2: Symbol of the Moon

The Moon represents the eternal female in all her guises, from innocent youth to wise old age. This is usually divided into three stages: the maiden, the mother, and the crone. She is not primarily the female as seductress but the female as mother, although she is filled with mystery and holds many secrets. Of course, the psychic, impressionable qualities of this planet can occur in both sexes.

The Moon also presides over germination, the beginnings of life in the darkness and in hidden places. This includes the germination of seeds buried in the moist ground and the germination of the embryo in the womb. Until recent centuries, the crawling things that live in the mud were believed to arise from the mud itself. This was known as "spontaneous generation." It is a superstition, but it does indicate the kind of generation that is thought to be caused by the rays of the Moon upon the Earth.

One of the key aspects of the Moon is changeability. The face of the Moon never remains the same, but is constantly expanding or contracting. At times it disappears completely. This expansion of the Moon, followed by contraction, naturally lends itself to the association with pregnancy and birth. The Moon grows round just as a woman's belly enlarges during pregnancy, and then the Moon deflates, just as a pregnant woman's abdomen shrinks after giving birth.

There are often said to be three phases of the Moon: the waxing crescent, the full orb, and the waning crescent. A fourth, secret phase is the dark of the Moon, when her face is hidden. Evil magic, which needs to be concealed from view, is often worked in the dark lunar phase. Magic that seeks an increase or expansion of some kind is done in the waxing phase. Magic that seeks a decrease, a reduction, or a wasting away is done in the waning phase. Magic seeking some type of fulfillment or achievement or attainment is best done during the full Moon.

Lunar foods are those that tend to be insipid in taste, like the white of eggs, rice, cauliflower, and bean sprouts, as well as foods that are pale or white in color, such as milk, mushrooms, animal fat, and the flesh of fishes.

Crawling and creeping things are strongly lunar, especially those that move under the cover of darkness, such as mice, worms, and beetles. So are those things that dwell in the mud or under the surface of water, especially those that live on the bottom of lakes or oceans, such as eels, crayfish, and lobsters. So are the creatures of the night, such as spiders, moths, cats, owls, and bats. So are beasts renowned for their fertility, such as rabbits.

Silver is the metal of the Moon, imitating by its luster the shining face of this wandering body of the heavens. Indeed, silver is the most highly reflective of all metals. Like the lunar orb itself, it is by turns bright when polished and black when tarnished. Mirrors are strongly lunar in nature, especially when backed by the lunar metal. (They are sometimes backed by aluminum, which is somewhat less lunar than silver.) Mirrors are lunar not only because of their silver backing but also because they resemble the surface of water, a lunar substance. Glass and rock crystal resemble water, and they are both highly lunar in nature. Crystal balls are lunar.

The traditional colors of the Moon are white and black, but the traditional color of Saturn is also black, which can lead to confusion. In my own work, I prefer to use the color purple for the Moon. Purple has no traditional association with any other planet, and it is a color that suggests putrefaction, a transformative lunar process. Purple is opposite yellow on the color wheel used by painters, just as the Moon is the natural opposite of the Sun.

The energy of the Moon is a pure celestial Water, which is more rarefied and lighter than earthly elemental Water. It may be represented symbolically by the dew that falls from the sky during the night. Dew is sometimes said to be the sweat of the Moon. This energy is variable, cyclical, inconstant, bright or shadowed, and by turns stronger or weaker, depending on the circumstances in which it expresses itself.

The goddess of the Moon has many names, but here we are using Luna, a name for both the planet and the lunar goddess. She is a mysterious deity with hidden purposes, many secrets, and changing moods, and a goddess of contradictions, both dark and light. At times she is nurturing and protective, but at other times barren and cold. She presides over the germination of seeds in the moist, dark soil and over the creeping things that live there or that swim beneath the surface of water.

Elemental Water is associated with feelings in the body generated by the emotions, but the celestial Water of the Moon functions in the higher realm of the emotions on a mental level. The energy of the Moon is linked with emotional currents in the mind—with conceptual sadness, joy, dread, contentment, desire, disgust, attraction, and revulsion.

The Moon's energy is the Water of dreams, visions, regrets, hopes, longings, phobias, wonders, fantasies, self-doubt, night terrors, and the shadows of the mind. In a practical sense, it may be applied to matters of mental health, dreamwork, psychic activity, scrying, visions, and spirit communications.

Some of the works that fall naturally under the Moon's nature are fertility, pregnancy, childbirth, the health of young children, motherhood, menstruation, the breasts and ovaries, mental health, insomnia, dreams, appearances, masks, glamour, illusions, fantasies, and anything dealing with travel over water. Scrying, especially when done in water, a mirror, or a crystal, is a lunar activity.

Efforts to make a woman conceive a child should be done on the lunar day of the week during the nighttime, and if possible under the direct rays of the Moon when it is in its earliest waxing crescent.

Therapeutically, the occult energy of the Moon may be used to alleviate headaches, to banish nightmares or obsessive thoughts, to cure childhood complaints, to increase fertility, and to strengthen and heal the sexual parts of women, such as the womb, ovaries, and breasts.

Mars (Tuesday): Red (Traditional Color: Blood Red)

The modern glyph for Mars is a circle with an arrow that points toward the upper right, but here I have used an earlier version of the glyph in which the arrow points straight up. I find this to be a better symbolic expression of the energies of this planet. Elsewhere in this book I have used the conventional glyph for Mars for convenience, but this is the form I prefer.

Figure 4.3: Symbol of Mars

The energy of the day of Mars is strongly masculine. This planet is fiery by nature, and also airy—an explosive combination. The redness of the planet Mars is clearly visible in the night sky. This coloring of the planet reinforces two of the primary associations of Mars—fire and blood, both of which are red. Both are prominent during warfare. Mars is concerned with military battles, fights, conflicts, and strife of all kinds, but also with victory, dominance, command, and incisive actions.

The god Mars is represented by a virile man who is mature but not yet middle-aged, and bearded, but with a beard that is not yet full. This planet is typified by the soldier, the commander, the leader, the fighter, the explorer, and the athlete. The personality of Mars is sharp, direct, and domineering. It can be found in both men and women. This kind of person does not like to be contradicted and has to get in the last word or the final blow.

Mars is most potent in governing the affairs of military personnel, the police, prison guards, security guards, boxers, and those who study the martial arts, as well as those who use weapons, knives, and sharp instruments in their work or who cause blood to flow, such as butchers, those who work in slaughterhouses, barbers, surgeons, and hunters; also those who work with fire, such as blacksmiths, welders, bakers, foundry workers, glass blowers, pottery makers, and firefighters.

All things that are naturally hot to the taste are associated with Mars, such as black pepper and peppermint; also plants and spices that burn the tongue, among them red peppers, radishes, cloves, garlic, and onions; also ointments that generate heat when rubbed on the skin.

Strong alcoholic drinks, particularly hard liquors such as whiskey and rum that burn the throat, are associated with Mars. Intoxication often inclines people to fight. Smoking, by its very nature, is a martial activity—it involves fire, heat,and smoke and is a stimulant.

Iron is the metal of Mars, as is steel, which is chiefly composed of iron. When iron and steel rust, they turn a red color, the traditional color of this planet. Iron is the hardest and strongest of the planetary metals. Red brass is also associated with Mars due to its reddish color.

The main stone of Mars is the diamond for its hardness, because it is the hardest of stones and scratches lesser stones but is not scratched by them. Also given to Mars are the bloodstone and the lodestone, the first due to its blood color and the second because of its power of domination. Sulphur is linked with Mars because it burns.

All weapons of war, combat, or slaying of any kind are martial by nature. Knives, swords, axes, spearheads, and arrowheads—all of which are made from the martial metal, iron, in the form of steel—fall under this planet, along with guns, artillery, bombs, and missiles of all types. Also under this planet are helmets and armor of all kinds, as well as military equipment, vehicles, ships, and planes, and military installations, strongholds, and bases. Battlefields are martial.

The hunting falcon is martial, as is the hunting hound, and the horse because of its historical use in warfare. The leopard is martial for its fierceness, and the dragon for its fiery breath and greatness in combat. The wolf is martial. It was used as one of the symbols of the Roman legions before all the legions adopted the symbol of the golden eagle. The twin brothers Romulus and Remus, the mythical founders of Rome, were said to have been suckled and reared by a she-wolf.

Works that fall naturally under the action of Mars include warfare, all forms of combat, strategies, tactics, confrontation, domination, and competitive sports, plus all tasks that involve courage and daring, leadership, boldness, and physical risk-taking. You would use the energy of Mars to win a scholarship, to get a promotion, to take a position from someone else, to prevail over a rival, to win a prize that involves risk or effort, to win a competition or battle, or to dominate others.

The energy of Mars can be invoked to cause a climax or catastrophe, in the sense of bringing events to a head so that a resolution can be achieved. It can provoke the decisive battle that decides the outcome of the conflict.

The occult energy of Mars may be used therapeutically to increase male potency and virility and to strengthen or heal the sexual parts in men. It is also useful in bodybuilding and in acquiring skill in sports or other physical activities, particularly those involving effort and risk.

Mercury (Wednesday): White (Traditional Color: Orange)

Mercury is unique among the planets in that it is composed of three essences—those of the Sun, the Moon, and the Earth. All of the other planets are made up of either a single essence or two essences.

Figure 4.4: Symbol of Mercury

The day of Mercury is the day of communications and travel. The expression of this planet's threefold composition is airy by nature, involving thoughts and mental images, along with words both spoken and written. Mercury has to do with messages and messengers; with games of fortune, such as gambling with cards and dice; and with intellectual games, such as chess; also with the manipulation of money and with the process of buying and selling—as opposed to the amassing of wealth for security, which falls under Jupiter, or the hoarding of wealth, which is under Saturn.

The symbolic human type for this planet is a youth or a young man, unbearded, who is slender of body and light of step, quick yet precise in his movements, with a witty mind and talkative nature, learned in academic subjects and shrewd in debate. He is not virile in a masculine sense, but is somewhat feminine in appearance. The male ballet dancer represents the Mercurial physique, as does the jockey or the gymnast.

Things associated with Mercury include communication devices such as the pen, the typewriter, and the word processor; also the calculator, mathematics in general, cards, dice, and money, especially coins.

The metal of Mercury is quicksilver. It is unlike all other planetary metals in that it is liquid at room temperature. The liquid nature of metallic Mercury makes it highly mobile. It rolls around in the form of globules. It is a toxic metal, so it is wise to avoid handling it or breathing in its vapor.

Mercury the metal is shiny and highly reflective, like silver. The traditional color associated with Mercury is orange. This may be due to the color of this metal when it oxidizes—mercuric oxide powder is orange or dark orange in color. In modern magic, the color given to this planet is often either a pure transparency, like air, or a rainbow of changing iridescent colors, like those on the wing of a dragonfly.

The ability of Mercury to assume any color of the rainbow is useful. It allows us to temporarily assign different colors to the heart-center, which in kinesic magic is associated with Mercury. The specific color I have linked with Mercury in this system of magic is soft white. I chose this color because the combination of all color wavelengths of light produces white, and the glyph of Mercury is a combination of all three symbols used to form the various glyphs of the other planets—the circle, crescent, and cross.

The foods linked with this planet are sweet and light, such as melons, fruits, grapes.

Animals given to Mercury are those with keen senses that are quick and light in their movements, among them the fox, weasel, monkey, and dog. The butterfly, which is light, airy, quick, and colorful, is of the nature of this planet. So are songbirds such as the lark and nightingale. The parrot is Mercurial for its tendency to speak. The dolphin, which is intelligent and quick and which breathes air, is also a beast of Mercury.

The primary creature falling under the nature of this planet is the serpent, which represents both quickness and subtlety. It was also said to be deathless, due to the shedding of its skin several times a year. The shedding was looked upon as a renewal of youth.

The serpent is the symbol of Hermes, the Greek version of Mercury. Hermes and Mercury are both associated with medicine. The staff of Hermes, which has two serpents coiled around it, is often confused with the staff of the physician god Asclepius, which has only a single serpent coiled around it and is used as a symbol by the medical profession.

Lawyers best exemplify the energy of this planet, because they engage in extended and complex legal arguments in which they are mainly concerned with having their argument prevail over the arguments of others, rather than with reaching a true understanding. Mercury loves reasoning and eloquence for their own sake.

The occult energy of this planet naturally lends itself to healing and renewal. Other works falling under this planet are communications of all kinds, the transmission of messages, school and college studies, reading and writing, calculation, mathematics, gambling, stock market speculation, financial risk-taking, intellectual games and challenges, formal debates, and travel by land, sea, or air. The influence of this planet increases eloquence and skill in debates.

Jupiter (Thursday): Orange (Traditional Color: Blue)

This day concerns home and family. Jupiter is by nature expansive. Its energy is jovial, generous, and beneficent. This planet stands for the patriarch, for the maintenance and support of the family, hearth, and home, and by extension for all father figures. Jupiter energy is enlarging and nourishing. It causes growth or increase, particularly growth in the body such as weight gain, and robustness of health.

Figure 4.5: Symbol of Jupiter

The symbolic human type that represents this energy is a mature man with a full beard, in good health and possessed of both strength and endurance, with a body that is tending to fullness and flushed in complexion. His virility has not yet failed him, but it is the virility to rule in a just and prudent manner, with sound judgment and generosity of spirit. There is nothing mean or small in this type of person. This is the king in his castle, whether that be his family home or his place of business.

Wine, mead, and ale are associated with Jupiter, along with rich foods having a pleasant flavor, such as puddings, cakes, dates, figs, pineapples, melons, fatty meat such as pork and lamb, tender meat such as chicken, shortbreads, the yolk of eggs, nuts, cream, chocolate, caramel, ice cream, grapes, cherries, raisins, liquorice, sugar, honey, and so on.

Jupiter is associated with lavish tastes in possessions and expensive and showy clothing, and also with medals, awards, and signs of office. The energy can be fruitfully invoked in matters involving displays of wealth and social status.

The golden eagle is the primary symbol of Jupiter. In general, this planet is linked to beasts with intelligence and an even disposition, having some nobility or loftiness in their nature, such as the elephant, the hart, and the mountain sheep.

Jupiter is associated primarily with the oak tree, but in a more general way with all trees that are considered fortunate, such as the beech and poplar, and with trees that bear fruit, such as the pear, the apple, the fig, and the olive.

The metal of Jupiter is tin, a bright and shiny metal that does not rust or readily tarnish. Centuries ago it was sometimes used as the backing of mirrors because of this property.

The color traditionally associated with Jupiter is the blue of the sky at its zenith. One form of tin oxide, the form known as stannous oxide, is a very dark blue, and it may be this that caused tin to be associated with the color blue; but it seems more likely that the god Jupiter, as father of the gods, was linked to the heavens, which are blue in color, and the planet Jupiter received blue in this way. In kinesic magic, orange is assigned to Jupiter, and this is, in fact, the actual color of the planet as seen through a telescope.

Works that fall under this planet by their nature are honors earned or conferred, the spending of money, expensive possessions of all kinds, status symbols, property or land holdings, construction work, business or empire building, politics, and the amassing of wealth and security.

Venus (Friday): Green (Traditional Color: Green)

This is the day of the week devoted to the goddess of love, both romantic love and sexual love. Its energy is passionate and erotic, but also ardent, devoted, and joyful, a blending of Air (romance) and Water (sexuality). Whereas Luna is the goddess of fertility and childbirth, Venus is the goddess of love and love-making.

Figure 4.6: Symbol of Venus

The energy of this day is symbolized by a naked or scantily clad, beautiful young woman who is neither mother nor virgin. She is tender of heart, loving, kind, and generous but uninterested in intellectual matters. She is all feeling.

Ripe sweet fruits such as melons, pears, and figs are associated with Venus, as are sweet peas. The pomegranate in particular is the fruit of Venus, as is the apple.

Among her birds are the turtle dove, the pigeon, the swan, the sparrow, and the swallow. Her animals are those of an amorous and passionate nature, given to frequent and energetic sexual coupling, such as the rabbit, the goat, and the bull, and also animals with a loving nature, such as the dog.

Brightly colored, sweet-scented flowers are given over to Venus, as are sweet perfumes and sweet incense of all kinds, such as rose incense, musk, and sandalwood.

Cosmetics and unguents used to beautify the face and the skin are of Venus. All forms of makeup and adornment fall under the rule of this planet, as does fashion in clothing and hairstyles.

The metal of Venus is copper, which is soft and easily shaped. The traditional color associated with this planet is green. This is usually understood to be a reference to green growing plants and trees, which are given over to Venus. It is possible that this color association comes from the color of verdigris, a bright green substance created when copper corrodes.

The stone of this planet is emerald, but also jade, green jasper, lapis lazuli, and coral—in general, stones that are green or white, white being a reference to the fairness of the skin of this goddess.

All forms of prostitution are ruled by Venus, and so are sex therapy and marriage guidance counseling. Dance and song of an emotional, lyrical kind and romantic poetry are of Venus. Escort services, dating services, and matchmakers reside here as well.

Magic works that naturally fall under this planet are love charms, relationships, sexual relations and activities, a glamorous appearance, attraction of a lover, skill in lovemaking, exciting desire in others, bonding couples together, engagements, and weddings.

Saturn (Saturday): Blue (Traditional Color: Black)

Saturn is the slowest and most remote of the seven ancient planets. This god is very earthy and cold by nature. The day of Saturn is the best day for magic that concerns declining health, physical infirmities, and old age, but it's also good for deep and obscure studies, the acquisition of wisdom, and shrewdness in the accumulation of wealth.

Figure 4.7: Symbol of Saturn

In Greek mythology, Saturn is one of the Titans, a race of ancient giants who ruled over the world prior to the coming of the Olympians. This god, called Kronos or Cronos by the Greeks, ascended to the throne of heaven by castrating his father, Uranus, with a stone sickle. Kronos learned of a prophecy that he would be deposed by one of his own sons, and to prevent this he swallowed his children one after another as they were born, so that none could grow to adulthood. When Zeus, the Roman Jupiter, was born, the wife and sister of Kronos hid her baby son and replaced him with a black stone, which she handed to Kronos, who promptly swallowed it. Zeus grew up and eventually overthrew his cannibalistic father, taking the throne for himself.

The usual modern representation of Saturn is that of a very thin, old man with a bald head and a long white beard. There is no fat on his body and no joviality in his nature. He is stern, sour, and humorless. The hermit who hoards his money in the ground is of a saturnine nature. Nonetheless, this saturnine person is shrewd and calculating and often possesses arcane or occult wisdom.

The influence of Saturn is said to be most potent over those who are solitary and withdrawn by nature, deep thinkers, those who brood and keep their own counsel, and those who are not lovers of social gatherings or casual conversation.

In the human body, this planet governs the health of the bones and joints.

Lead is the metal of Saturn. It is the densest of the planetary metals and very heavy. It is also dead in the sense that it does not ring when struck, but gives back a dull thud. When lead is polished, it has a shiny silvery surface, but this quickly tarnishes to a dark gray when exposed to air.

Saturn is linked with the element Earth and with both weight and coldness.

The traditional color associated with Saturn in Western magic is black. This may have been suggested by the remoteness of this planet in the midnight darkness of the heavens, or perhaps by the dark gray of tarnished lead.

In my own work, I use the color blue for this planet, but a deeper blue than the blue traditionally assigned to Jupiter. Feel free to use the traditional black for this planet if you wish. You should be comfortable with whatever colors you choose for the planets.

The traditional stones of Saturn include the onyx for its blackness and the lodestone for its heaviness. To these I would add jet and obsidian, both black stones, and to a lesser degree brown jasper for its earthy coloring.

Foods linked to Saturn are sour, bitter, or rotten and include lemons, limes, walnuts, and cranberries, and also black fruits and black berries, but not those with a sweet taste; also meat and fish that has begun to rot and stink, and black bread and moldy bread.

Trees of this planet are the cypress and yew, both of which traditionally grew in graveyards. Plants include the opium poppy, mandrake, hellebore, hemlock, and in general plants and herbs associated with poison, death, and sleep.

Beasts of Saturn are the mule, the camel, the bear, the hog, the toad, the scorpion, and the mythical basilisk; among birds, the owl for its solitude and dwelling in darkness, crows and ravens for their black feathers and ravenous appetite, the ostrich because it swallows small stones, and the peacock for its harsh voice—in general, creeping things, things of darkness, solitary and sad creatures, and those that tend to eat their own young.

The scents of this planet are earthy and heavy, tending to provoke dullness or stupefaction, such as hashish and opium; also the odor of grave mold and decay. Burned pitch provides an appropriate incense, and also frankincense.

Professions falling under the rule of Saturn include scholars, teachers, monks and nuns, priests, magicians, astronomers, scientists generally, and philosophers.

Afflictions of the body under this planet are all illnesses and infirmities associated with age, especially those associated with the bones and joints, such as arthritis, and all wasting diseases, such as cancer.

Works that fall under the rule of Saturn are those that deal with endings, conclusions, death, wrapping up a business, dissolving a partnership, calculating earnings, or maintenance of essential systems; also hidden knowledge, ancient wisdom, and occult studies and books, especially those of a mathematical nature, such as numerology and the Kabbalah.

Sun (Sunday): Yellow (Traditional Colors: Yellow, Gold)

This day of the Sun is best devoted to works of wholeness and integration of the personality and identity. The Sun is fiery and warm, but constant and dependable rather than fitful and explosive, as is the fiery Mars. It is the sustainer of all life upon Earth, for without the golden warmth of the Sun, there would be no heat in living things.

Figure 4.8: Symbol of the Sun

The human figure that usually represents the Sun is a great, smiling, masculine face. The Romans conceived Sol as a god in a golden chariot who rode across the heavens each day from east to west. Sol is similar to Jupiter in many ways, but whereas Jupiter concerns most particularly the family and the home, Sol presides over the well-being of all the world and everything in it that requires warmth and light.

The precious stones of the Sun are those that are yellow or golden in color and those that are transparent and seem to radiate rays of light when illuminated. Amber, which is petrified tree resin, was regarded as a precious stone in ancient times. It is highly solar in nature. Tiger-eye is a solar gemstone. Topaz and chrysoprase are also solar when yellow in color.

Solar trees are those that have purifying or cleansing properties, such as the cedar and the bay tree, and those that enjoy the heat of the Sun, such as the palm tree, and also the ginger tree, which has heat in its roots. The pine is solar for its blond wood.

Mistletoe, which grows green in the midst of winter, is a solar plant, as was understood by the druids, who harvested it with a golden sickle. The sunflower is the most solar of all flowers, because it is shaped like the full face of the Sun and because it turns its face toward the Sun and follows it across the heavens throughout the day. In general, any round, golden flower is solar.

Solar spices include saffron, cinnamon, cloves, and balsam, and in general those that are yellow or golden in color and warm on the tongue. Rosemary makes a solar incense, as does sweet calamus, which is a kind of sweet-smelling grass, and mastic, which is the golden resin of a tree.

The lion, called the king of beasts, is the most solar of animals for its nobility, its steadfastness, its golden coat, its radiating mane of hair (which is like the rays surrounding the face of the Sun), and its love for the warm regions of the world. The horse is solar for its speed, endurance, nobility, and beauty. The bull is solar for its strength.

The mythical phoenix is the most solar of all birds because it is deathless, because it is solitary and alone, and because it rises renewed from its own ashes. The cock that crows at the rising of the Sun is solar, as are hawks, which fly higher than almost any other bird and have extraordinarily keen eyesight.

Among foods, butter is solar for its color and nourishing qualities, as is the yolk of eggs. Honey and the honey wine known as mead are both highly solar because they are sweet and preserve freshness, and also because they are the product of the bee, one of the most solar of all creatures. Beeswax is solar. All sweet syrups and anything that is golden, sweet, and nourishing is of the Sun.

Gold is the metal of the Sun for a number of reasons. It shines like the Sun when it reflects light. It has the unusual property of never tarnishing. A golden object lost under the ground and dug up a thousand years later will still be as bright and shiny as when it was buried. It is a mild and easily worked metal that can be hammered to an almost transparent thinness in the form of gold leaf.

The traditional color that represents the Sun is bright yellow. This color may derive from the color of gold or from the color of the Sun itself.

The Sun's energy is the celestial Fire of the planetary spheres, which is a more rarefied, light, expansive form of elemental Fire. We see this expressed in the nature of sunlight, which is warm, constant, radiant, penetrating, and life-giving rather than life-destroying. It is Fire in the form of radiation.

The god of the Sun, who has various names but whom we may call Sol (a name for both the planet and the solar god), is a benevolent deity who brings both light and warmth to the Earth—without Sol there would be no life. Even so, when angered, Sol can send down blazing beams of heat that wither and kill crops in the field, dry up lakes and rivers, and cause heatstroke.

Elemental Fire functions in the human body in the form of sensations, emotions, and urges, and also in the material world with which the body interacts. Solar Fire, because it shines from the heavenly seat of a god, functions in the higher human realm of intentions, decisions, and willed actions.

The Sun's energy is the Fire of human purpose, the strength of will, the determination to finish a task, decisiveness, taking control of a situation, and steady intention. In a practical sense, this energy may be applied in matters that concern the identity and self-fulfillment in life, the use of talents, the accomplishment of life goals, and the realization of one's destiny. It is the expression of True Will in the world, which is the inner motivation to achieve perfect attainment of life's purpose.

Professions in harmony with the Sun are clock and watch makers and all those who measure the hours, optometrists who use lenses to correct the vision, trades that deal with lighting and illumination, window makers and installers, investigators, police detectives, and in general any profession that makes clear, that illuminates, that opens the way, or that regulates or reveals what is hidden.

Works ruled by Sol include those that pertain to prosperity, charity, and generosity; works of inclusion such as invitations to join clubs or attend parties or to join a partnership or business; harmony and teamwork; politics; volunteer work; psychiatry and psychological counseling; and lifestyle and career planning.

The Seven Chakras

The heart-center of your body, which has already been described with regard to the manipulation of elemental energies, is not the only center. There are many other occult centers, but in modern Western magic the main ones are usually understood to be seven in number, arranged on a vertical line that runs down the head and torso directly in front of the spine (figure 4.9). These seven centers are called *chakras* (Sanskrit: wheels, circles). They are usually described in modern magic as spheres.

By associating the chakras with the seven planets, it becomes possible to concentrate and manipulate the forces of the planets, or even to summon and control planetary spirits, by awakening their corresponding chakras.

This does require some preparatory work. To use the chakras in this way, you must understand clearly the natures of the seven planets. You must be able to visualize in a tactile way the seven chakras inside your body. And you must create a link between each chakra and its corresponding planet.

Once you do this, the benefits in kinesic magic are enormous. It becomes possible to awaken the forces of each planet in moments, without the use of any tools, materials, or symbols. The planets become linked to your energy centers in the same way we linked the elements to hand gestures.

The concept of the chakras is Eastern in origin. It probably originated in India as part of the system of Kundalini yoga, and from there was carried to other lands when Buddhism spread around the world. The number of chakras and their exact locations vary from one Eastern authority to another, but the major ones are usually said to number seven in Hindu and Buddhist texts, which is convenient for our purposes.

In Western magic, these occult centers are located at the perineum, just in front of the anus; in the lower belly below the navel; in the stomach region above the navel; in the center of the chest at the level of the heart; in the pit of the throat; between the eyebrows behind the forehead; and over the entire surface of the crown of the head. The Sanskrit names given to them are unimportant—we will call them the root, bowel, stomach, heart, throat, brow, and crown chakras.

It is usual to place these centers either along the spine itself or within the body just in front of the spine. Bear in mind that they are occult centers, not physical parts of the body. Some authorities claim that they have correspondences with various nerve ganglia, and others deny it. I find it useful not to try to link these centers with any body organs or nerve junctions, but to think of them as wholly occult. I imagine them to lie in front of the spine, along a line that runs down through the center of the torso.

How are we to arrange the planets on the chakras? One common arrangement is to use the Ptolemaic order of the planets, beginning with the quickest planet, the Moon, at the root-center, and moving upward through the planetary spheres to Mercury (bowel), Venus (stomach), Sun (heart), Mars (throat), Jupiter (brow) and Saturn (crown). Another arrangement puts the Sun in the crown-center, the Moon at the brow, Mars at the throat, Mercury at the heart, Jupiter at the stomach, Venus at the bowel, and Saturn at the root. Yet another arrangement places Sun on the crown and Moon on the brow, but puts Mercury at the throat, Venus at the heart, Mars at the stomach, Jupiter at the bowel, and Saturn at the root. And there are still other arrangements.

What do all these different systems of placing the planets on the chakras tell us? That it does not matter where the planets are located, so long as the location makes sense to the person who places them. If the placement seems rational and feels natural, then a link can be formed between each planet and its corresponding chakra. There is no single right way, although in my opinion some arrangements make better sense than others.

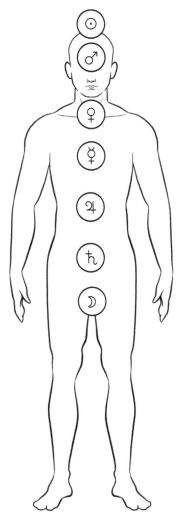

Figure 4.9: The Seven Chakras on the Human Body in Kinesic Magic

There are two plausible candidates among the planets for the central heart chakra: the Sun and Mercury. Good reasons can be advanced for placing either one in the center of the column of chakras. I have chosen to place Mercury in the center and the Sun on the crown of the head, as shown in figure 4.9. I will explain my reasoning briefly.

All the traditional planets of astrology are arranged in pairs of opposites except Mercury, which stands alone. Mercury is fundamentally different and apart from the other planets. The Sun has its opposite, the Moon. Mars has its opposite, Venus. Jupiter has its opposite, Saturn. This is very clearly expressed by the astrological glyphs of the planets, which are quite ancient.

The chakras can be divided into pairs of opposites along the vertical axis of the body, except for the central chakra, which has no opposite. For this reason, among others which I will not delve into here, I place Mercury on the heart-center, in the middle of the body chakras.

The Sun I place on the crown chakra, just above but touching and penetrating the crown of the head, since that center is usually depicted in occult texts as radiant and golden. I put the opposite of the Sun, the Moon, on the opposite, lowermost chakra, the root, which is located at the perineum, where the legs meet.

Mars I put on the brow chakra due to the piercing, penetrating nature of this planet, which accords well with the psychic third eye. On the throat chakra I place the natural mate of Mars and its opposite, the emotional, expressive Venus. Both the glyph of Mars and that of Venus contain the circle of the Sun, so it seems to make good sense to put them both close to the Sun, in the upper, illuminated part of the body.

Saturn, the cold, dark, hard planet, I place in the lower bowel, the region where solid waste is generated, and next to Saturn I place its natural mate and opposite, Jupiter, in the region of the stomach, where food is received and transformed into warmth and nourishment. The glyphs of both Saturn and Jupiter contain the crescent of the Moon, so it makes sense to place them both close to the Moon, in the lower, shadowed portion of the body.

I have given this explanation of my placement of the planets on the chakras not to persuade you that it is necessarily better than other arrangements but to show you that it has been seriously considered and tested. I've been using it for decades with good results. If you wish to change the order of the planets on the chakras in your own work—for example, moving the Sun to the heart chakra—feel free to do so, but only if you have a clear reason in your own mind for making the change.

Be aware that the colors applied to the chakras come from the colors assigned to the planets by me on the color wheel. They are not the same colors that are given to the chakras in traditional Hinduism or Buddhism, where they have elaborate symbolic forms and associations. It is not necessary to know Kundalini yoga to use the concept of the seven energy centers of the body in Western magic.

Moon (Root)

The root chakra at the perineum is associated with the voiding of wastes from the body, both solid and liquid wastes. It is also associated with the organs of reproduction. This gives it a natural link with the Moon and the goddess Luna, who is goddess of Water and of Earth in the form of mud and its creatures, of the night and its creatures, of secret and hidden things, and of pregnancies.

Saturn (Bowel)

The bowel chakra is located at the level of the intestines, where food is held and processed, nourishment is extracted, and wastes are generated. These holding and containing qualities suggest Saturn, the old miser and hermit who presides over arcane works; the grinding and breaking down of things the way bones are ground to powder in a mortar and pestle; and the unfolding of complex processes.

Jupiter (Stomach)

The stomach chakra at the level above the navel, where food is deposited, can be most easily linked to fat and jovial Jupiter, who enjoys indulging himself in rich foods and good wines. This center is considered in Eastern nations to be the source of strength in the body. Sumo wrestlers of Japan hold that their great strength flows from their bellies. The images of the Buddha in China and India are usually obese, their bellies prominently displayed.

Mercury (Heart)

The heart chakra is located just above the base of the sternum. It is the central chakra, with three others above it and three below. Here is where I have placed Mercury, the most balanced yet solitary of the planets, as I explained earlier. This is the center that regulates and coordinates the other centers as they work together. It is the intermediary, the gateway between the upper and the lower body, just as the god Mercury conveys messages of the gods between the supernal and infernal regions.

Venus (Throat)

The throat chakra relates to vocal expression through cries, words, poetry, and song. Here is placed Venus, the goddess of romantic and sensual love. Lovers are seduced with flattering words and promises, making this a natural place for this goddess. The emotions are articulated in the form of sounds. Song and poetry combine emotion with reason. What the heart feels, the voice expresses.

Mars (Brow)

The brow chakra is the center of willpower and the concentration of purpose, of clarity, of foresight—all necessary qualities in a warrior. Mars is located in this center, which is in harmony with the resolve and fearlessness of this god. It is the center of the psychic ability of clairvoyance. This center should not be thought of as located just behind the forehead, as is usually the case, but deeper inside the brain at this level.

Sun (Crown)

The crown chakra has to do with inspiration and enlightenment. This center receives the Sun, giver of light, dispeller of darkness, whose constant heat enables generation of all kinds. In Eastern occultism, it is represented by a great golden lotus flower with a thousand petals that spread themselves over the entire top of the head. The Sun radiates downward on what lies beneath, warming and illuminating it. As all is revealed by the light of the Sun, so is the crown chakra associated with spiritual enlightenment.

Workings: The Seven Planets

The seven planets represent the most potent set of forces that can be invoked in Western magic, but to harness that power effectively you must clearly understand their natures, their relationships with one another, and their assigned correspondences. This cannot be done in a purely intellectual way, by memorizing sets of associations or meanings. It is necessary to actually feel the different natures of the planets in the chakra centers of your body, and this can only be accomplished by repeated visualizations and meditations upon them. These exercises are designed to help you understand the planetary energies not only symbolically but also on a sensual level, as living forces that move through you.

Working 1: The Planetary Wheel

This is a visualization that will link the planetary colors with the astrological symbols of the planets on the subconscious level.

Adopt the sitting posture facing the east. Take two or three silent breaths to focus your intention. Close your eyes.

THE SEVEN PLANETS | 137

Visualize a featureless gray mist in front of you. In your imagination, create a small white disk. Draw the glyph of Mercury in black upon the disk. Hold this clearly in your mind while you take a deep, slow breath and release it.

Extend a yellow spoke upward from the top of the white disk and imagine on the end of it a yellow disk that is the same size as the white disk. Draw in black the glyph of the Sun upon the yellow disk. Breathe slowly and deeply as you hold the image in your mind.

Extend a purple spoke downward from the white disk and form a purple disk on the end of it. Draw the glyph of the Moon upon the purple disk in black. Breathe.

Extend a red spoke diagonally down from the right side of the white disk and make a red disk on the end of it. Draw the glyph of Mars upon the red disk with black lines. Breathe.

Extend a green spoke diagonally up from the left side of the white disk and put a green disk on the end of it. Draw the glyph of Venus upon the green disk in black. Breathe.

Extend a blue spoke diagonally down from the left side of the white disk and put a blue disk on the end of it. Upon the blue disk draw with black lines the glyph of Saturn. Breathe.

Extend an orange spoke diagonally up from the right side of the white disk and make an orange disk on its end. Mark the glyph of Jupiter on this orange disk with black lines. Breathe.

While still holding this figure of six spokes radiating from a central hub in your mind, shift your attention to the yellow disk. Draw a yellow arc from the yellow disk to the orange disk on the upper right. Draw an orange arc from the orange disk to the red disk on the lower right. Carry a red arc from the red disk to the purple disk at the bottom. Carry a purple arc from the purple disk to the blue disk on the lower left. Make a blue arc from the blue disk to the green disk on the upper left. Finally, connect the rim of this wheel by making a green arc from the green disk to the yellow disk at the top. Hold the fully completed color wheel of the planets in your imagination for several slow, deep breaths.

Allow the image of the wheel to dissolve into nothingness and open your eyes.

Working 2: Root Chakra

Begin in the standing posture facing east. Take a few silent breaths to focus your mind.

Shift into the scrying posture and visualize in the upright triangle formed between your thumbs and forefingers the astrological symbol of the Moon, a crescent. This should be visualized standing on its end and open to the left, as it appears in the glyph of the planet Jupiter. This is a waxing crescent—one that is increasing—and is a healthy and positive expression of lunar energies (which are twofold and have a dark side). It should be visualized in the color assigned to the Moon, a rich purple.

Press the symbol of the Moon between your palms as you shift into the balancing posture, with your left palm turned downward on top of the right palm, which is turned upward. Mentally hold this symbol of the Moon pressed between your palms in front of your chest.

Slowly separate your palms by raising your left hand and lowering your right hand until a gap of about three inches is between them. As you draw your hands apart, visualize the formation of a counterclockwise-spinning purple sphere between them, with the glyph of the Moon inside it.

Scoop this sphere into the cupped palm of your left hand and press it into your chest. The energy of the purple sphere enters and fills the white sphere of your heart-center, turning it purple. Feel it inside your heart-center.

As you do this, at the same time reach down and press your right palm against your groin, where your root-center is located. Cup your hand to your groin.

Use the force of your will to draw the purple energy rotating in your heart-center into your left hand and send it in an expanding spiral along your left arm, across your shoulders, down your right arm to your right hand, where it enters your root-center. As the purple energy of the Moon leaves your heart-center, your heart-center becomes a soft white sphere once again.

Build up the sphere of the Moon in your root-center—it should be pictured as a purple sphere about the size of a tennis ball that spins in a counterclockwise direction just in front of your anus in the flesh between your legs. Visualize the symbol of the Moon inside this spinning sphere. The lunar symbol is stationary and the sphere spins around it.

Shift to the closing posture and contemplate with your eyes shut your energized root-center. Feel there the coolness, the moistness, the earthiness of the Moon.

Change to the standing posture and take a few silent breaths to end.

Working 3: Bowel Chakra
Begin in the standing posture facing east, and draw a few silent breaths to focus on what you are about to do.

Adopt the scrying posture. Visualize the astrological symbol of Saturn in the scrying triangle between your hands. It is a deep blue color.

Transfer this symbol between your palms to a position in front of your chest as you shift to the balancing posture.

Open a space between your palms and visualize a spinning blue sphere between them, with the symbol of Saturn inside it.

Press this sphere into your heart-center with your left palm and visualize its blue energy filling your heart-center. At the same time, press your right palm to your belly just below your navel.

Send the blue energy of Saturn up your left arm, across your shoulders, and down your right arm in an expanding spiral from your heart-center into your bowel-center, and visualize it there as a spinning blue sphere about the size of a tennis ball with the symbol of Saturn inside it. Your heart-center returns to a soft white color as the Saturn energy leaves it.

Shift to the closing posture and contemplate your energized bowel-center with your eyes shut for a minute or so. Feel the nature of Saturn, which is heavy, dark, silent, and cold.

Relax your mind as you change to the standing posture and draw a few silent breaths to end this exercise.

Working 4: Stomach Chakra

Adopt the standing posture facing the east, and take a few silent breaths to prepare.

Shift to the scrying posture and visualize the astrological symbol of the planet Jupiter in the triangle between your hands. It is a deep orange color.

Press this glyph between your palms as you bring them in front of your chest in the balancing posture.

Slowly separate your palms to about three inches. Use the power of your will to create a counterclockwise-spinning orange sphere between them, with the glyph inside it.

Press this sphere through your chest into your heart-center with your left palm so that the orange energy of Jupiter fills the sphere of your heart-center and causes it to spin more rapidly counterclockwise. Be aware of the Jupiter energy in your heart-center, which is vitalizing, invigorating, and expansive.

As you fill your heart-center with this orange energy, press your right palm to your stomach above your navel.

Use the power of your will to draw the Jupiter energy out of your heart-center into your left hand and send it in an expanding spiral up your left arm, across your shoulders, down your right arm, and into your right hand. From there it enters your stomach-center, where it becomes a spinning orange sphere about the size of a tennis ball.

When all the energy of Jupiter has been drawn from your heart-center, shift to the closing posture and contemplate the energy spinning in your stomach-center for a minute or so with your eyes shut. Feel its warm, energizing nature.

Change to the standing posture and take a few silent breaths to end.

Working 5: Heart Chakra

Begin facing east in the standing posture. Take several slow, silent breaths to prepare.

Move into the scrying posture and formulate the glyph of Mercury inside the scrying triangle between your hands. It is a soft white in color.

Change to the balancing posture as you carry this glyph between your hands to just in front of your chest.

Slowly separate your hands to create a spinning soft-white sphere with the glyph of Mercury inside it. This sphere is larger than the others—about the size of a baseball.

Press this sphere into your heart-center so that the energy of Mercury fills your heart-center. This energy lacks a strong emotional tendency, but is light, airy, and refreshing. Visualize the glowing white glyph of Mercury inside this spinning sphere.

As you press this Mercury energy into your chest with your left palm, press your right palm over the back of your left palm and hold it there for several slow breaths.

Change to the closing posture and contemplate your energized heart-center for a minute or so with your eyes closed. Feel the energy of Mercury inside you, light and quick of motion.

Assume the standing posture and draw a few slow, silent breaths to end.

Working 6: Throat Chakra

Assume the standing posture facing east and focus your mind with several silent breaths.

Shift to the scrying posture. Form the green glyph of Venus between your hands in the scrying triangle.

Transfer this glyph to just in front of your chest between your palms as you change to the balancing posture.

Separate your palms and create a spinning green sphere between them that is about the size of a tennis ball, with the glyph of Venus inside it.

Press this green sphere into your heart-center with your left hand while touching your throat center with your right hand. Feel the vital, sensual, emotional energy of Venus spinning inside your heart-center.

Transfer the green energy of Venus into your throat-center with an expanding spiral through your upper body. As you draw this energy out of the sphere of your heart-center, your heart-center becomes soft white in color once again.

Change to the closing posture and visualize for a minute or so with eyes closed the green sphere of Venus spinning in your throat-center with the glyph of Venus inside it.

Go back to the standing posture and take a few silent breaths to end.

Working 7: Brow Chakra

Begin with the standing posture facing east, and draw a few silent breaths to focus your purpose.

Shift to the scrying posture and create the glyph of Mars in red within the scrying triangle between your hands.

Change to the balancing posture and hold the Mars glyph pressed between your palms in front of your chest.

Slowly separate your palms as you use the power of your will to create a spinning red sphere between them that is about the size of a tennis ball. It surrounds the glyph of Mars.

With your left palm, press this red sphere into your heart-center so that the red energy of Mars fills the soft white sphere of your heart center and makes it spin more rapidly. Feel the hot, harsh, sharp energy of Mars.

At the same time that you press this Mars energy into your chest, put the fingers of your right hand to your forehead, where your brow-center is located.

Use the force of your will to send the Mars energy through your upper body in an expanding spiral and into your brow-center. Create a red, spinning sphere between and behind your eyebrows, with the glyph of Mars inside it.

Change to the closing posture and contemplate the Mars energy in your brow-center for a minute or so with eyes shut.

Resume the standing posture and draw a few silent breaths to end.

Working 8: Crown Chakra

Assume the standing posture facing east, and draw a few silent breaths to focus your mind.

Move into the scrying posture and create the yellow glyph of the Sun within the scrying triangle.

Transfer the glyph of the Sun to just in front of your chest as you change to the balancing posture.

Slowly separate your palms and create a spinning yellow sphere between them that is about the size of a tennis ball, with the Sun glyph inside it.

Press this yellow sphere into your heart-center with your left hand so that the energy of the Sun fills it and turns it from soft white to a bright yellow. Feel the warming, gentle, nourishing energy of the Sun.

At the same time, press your right palm down against the top of your head.

Use your will to send the Sun energy in an expanding spiral through your upper body, so that it creates a spinning yellow sphere at your crown-center on the top of your head. This yellow sphere is about the size of a tennis ball and is halfway inside and halfway above your skull. Let its energy stream over the surface of your skull in golden rays.

Shift to the closing posture and contemplate your energized crown-center for a minute or so.

Change back to the standing posture and draw several silent breaths to end.

Working 9: The Planetary Pillar

Start in the standing posture facing the east, and take a few silent breaths to focus your mind on the work ahead.

Widen your stance and raise your arms in the invoking posture to draw down from the lunar sphere the purple energy of the Moon. Let it flow into you through your upturned face so that it fills your entire body.

Narrow your stance and change to the prayer posture. Visualize the astrological symbol of the Moon inside your root-center at your groin. Use your will to focus and concentrate the transparent purple energy that circulates throughout your body into your root-center.

Resume the invoking posture and draw down into your body the blue energy of Saturn from the sphere of this planet so that it fills you.

Shift to the prayer posture and compress this blue energy into your bowel-center with the power of your will. Visualize the symbol of Saturn inside the sphere of your bowel-center.

Go back to the invoking posture and draw down orange energy from the sphere of Jupiter so that it fills your body.

Change to the prayer posture and concentrate this orange energy in your stomach-center. Visualize the symbol of Jupiter in this spinning orange sphere.

Move back into the invoking posture and draw down the energy of Mercury from its sphere to fill your body.

Resume the prayer posture and focus this soft white energy into your heart-center, where you visualize the symbol of Mercury.

Once again assume the invoking posture. Draw down the green energy of Venus from its sphere to fill your body.

Move into the prayer posture and concentrate this green energy in your throat-center while visualizing the symbol of Venus there.

Change to the invoking posture and draw down the red energy of Mars from its sphere to fill your body.

Change to the prayer posture and concentrate the Mars energy in your brow-center while visualizing the glyph of Mars behind your forehead.

Assume the invoking posture to draw down into your body the yellow energy of the Sun from the solar sphere.

Change to the prayer posture to concentrate this energy at the crown of your head in your crown-center. Visualize as you do this the glyph of the Sun in the sphere of your crown-center, which is half inside and half above your skull.

Shift into the ankh posture. Visualize the Moon glyph inside the purple sphere of your root-center. Use the power of your will to draw a portion of this lunar energy out of this sphere and send it upward in a rising column to touch your bowel-center.

Change the focus of your mind to your bowel-center, and visualize its blue sphere with the Saturn glyph inside it. Use your will to draw some of this blue Saturn energy upward in a rising column until it touches your stomach-center.

Focus your mind on your stomach-center and visualize its orange sphere with the Jupiter glyph inside it. Use your will to draw part of this orange energy upward in a column until it touches your heart-center.

Focus on your heart-center and visualize the glyph of Mercury inside its white sphere. Use your will to draw soft white Mercury energy upward in a rising column until it touches your throat-center.

Change your attention to your throat-center and visualize the Venus glyph inside its green sphere. Cause the green energy to rise upward in a column until it touches your brow-center in the middle of your skull at the level of your eyebrows.

Focus on your brow-center and visualize the glyph of Mars inside its red sphere. Send part of this red energy upward in a column to touch your crown-center.

Change your attention to your crown-center and visualize the Sun glyph inside its yellow sphere. Allow the solar energy to fountain upward and spill out in all directions over your skull. Cause it to flow down the entire length of your body to the soles of your feet in a shimmering, golden cascade of light.

Move into the closing posture to stop this cascade of solar energy. Stand for a minute or so with your eyes shut, contemplating the seven colored planetary spheres arranged one above the other, and the six colored segments that connect them.

Shift into the standing posture and draw a few silent breaths to end.

Working 10: The Planetary Spiral

The planetary energies in your seven body centers have two primary modes of motion. The first is linear, as demonstrated in the preceding working. The second mode is spiral, which we will examine here. The connecting arcs of energy described in this working form a continuous expanding spiral that begins in your heart-center and passes through each of your body centers in turn until it terminates at your crown center. Be aware that the larger arcs of the spiral extend beyond the boundary of your body.

Start in the standing posture facing the east, and take a few silent breaths to prepare your mind.

Widen your stance and change to the balancing posture, with palms pressed together horizontally in front of your chest. Visualize the glyph of Mercury inside the white sphere of your heart-center. Speak the following words:

Mercury the center makes,
From all others he partakes;

Press your left palm to your heart-center and your right palm to your stomach-center, just above your navel. With the power of your will, draw a stream of soft white Mercury energy from your heart-center and send it in a semicircular arc down the left side of your body so that it connects with your stomach-center. This arc of energy does not follow your arms, but flows in a crescent through the left side of your abdomen directly from heart-center to stomach-center.

Visualize the orange sphere of your stomach-center with the glyph of Jupiter inside it. Feel it beneath your right hand. Speak these words:

Jupiter rules the vault of heaven,
Most fortunate of all the seven;

Move your left hand up to press against your throat-center while leaving your right hand on your stomach-center. Use the power of your will to send an orange stream of Jupiter energy curving in a semicircular arc from your stomach-center up the right side of your torso to connect with your throat-center. Hold the two arcs of the spiral in your imagination.

Visualize the green sphere of your throat-center with the glyph of Venus inside it. Speak these words:

Venus draws sap up from roots,
Makes flowers bloom upon the shoots;

Move your right hand to your bowel-center, below your navel, while leaving your left hand on your throat-center. Use your will to send the green Venus energy in your throat-center arcing down the left side of your body to touch your bowel-center. Sustain all three arcs of the spiral in your mind, and with your inner eye see their different colors.

Visualize the blue sphere of your bowel-center with the glyph of Saturn inside it. Speak these words:

Saturn, lonely, dark, and cold,
Holds all secrets great and old;

Move your left hand to your brow-center, but leave your right-hand on your bowel-center. Send the blue energy of your bowel-center arcing up the right side of your body to touch your brow-center. Hold all four arcs of the spiral in your mind.

Visualize the red sphere of your brow-center with the glyph of Mars inside it. Speak these words:

> Mars is master of the foe,
> His flaming sword, the widow's woe;

Move your right hand down to your root-center while leaving your left hand pressed to your brow-center. With the power of your will, cause the red energy of your brow-center to arc down the left side of your body to touch your root-center. Continue to sustain in your mind the other loops of the spiral.

Visualize the purple sphere of your root-center with the glyph of the Moon inside it. Speak these words:

> Moon shows a bright or darkened face,
> Above the clouds her hounds give chase;

Move your left hand upward to press down against your crown-center on the top of your head, but leave your right hand on your root-center. Will the purple lunar energy of your root-center to arc up the right side of your body to touch your crown-center.

Visualize the yellow sphere of your crown-center with the glyph of the Sun inside it. Speak these words:

> Sun is source of warmth and light,
> A shining shield against the night.

Be aware of the continuous spiral of energy expanding from your heart-center to your crown-center through and beyond your body in six semicircular, colored arcs. Change into the macrocosm posture by bringing your feet together and pressing your hands palm to palm above your head, fingers pointing upward. Visualize a ray of golden light ascending straight up from the crown of your head into the heavens like the beam of a searchlight. It continues upward into infinity. Hold this golden ray intensely in your imagination for several deep breaths as you allow the spiral to fade away.

Assume the closing posture to cut off the ray streaming upward from the crown of your head. Contemplate the seven spheres of your body centers in balance within you for a minute or so with eyes closed.

Resume the standing posture and take a few silent breaths to relax and end.

CHAPTER 5
PLANETARY HAND GESTURES

IN KINESIC MAGIC, THE SEVEN PLANETS of traditional astrology are represented by hand gestures. This eliminates the need for instruments, substances, charms, and inscribed sigils associated with the planets. These things can still be used, but once a link has been formed between a hand gesture and the planet it represents, simply by making the hand gesture of a planet alone, the mind is aligned with the occult potential of that planet.

In combination with the twenty-four postures, these hand gestures invoke, manipulate, and banish the energies of the seven planets. With them you can more easily infuse your body with these energies, concentrate planetary energies into objects and places, or project these energies into other people.

Those who are afflicted with an excess of one planetary energy can be brought to a state of internal harmony by withdrawing a portion of that energy from their body or by infusing them with the planetary energy of the opposite planet. For example, if a person is afflicted with an excess of Mars to the extent that he has fits of violent rage and commits reckless actions, he may be harmonized by withdrawing a portion of the Mars energy from his brow-center using the Mars hand gesture, or by infusing into his throat-center the energy of the opposite of Mars, gentle and loving Venus.

Conversely, if a person is suffering from a deficiency of a planetary energy, that energy can be projected into the body center of that planet in order to restore a more healthy overall balance to the body. For example, if someone is timid and fearful, it may be useful to load their brow-center with the energy of Mars.

It might be argued that this treats only the symptoms of the disorder and does not address the root of the problem that created the energy imbalance. This is true, but through regular therapy sessions to balance the body centers, the body and mind of an individual can be trained to accept a balanced planetary state as normal, and to seek to recreate it when it is absent.

All of the planets have their natural opposites, with the exception of Mercury, which is balanced within itself. The Moon is opposite to the Sun, Venus is opposite to Mars, and Saturn is opposite to Jupiter. When necessary, an excess of the energy of Mercury can be countered by the concentrated energy of elemental Earth. The energies of Mercury and Earth are not perfect opposites, but they have contrary tendencies.

By using the balancing posture, it is possible to equalize the energies between pairs of opposite planets in your own body or in the body of another person. You can also use this posture to add the energy of any planetary center to any other planetary center. For example, by forming your receptive left hand in the gesture of Mars and pressing it to your forehead, over your brow-center, and by forming your projective right hand in the gesture of Saturn and pressing it to your lower belly over your bowel-center, you can draw out the energy of Mars and transform it (by passing it around your heart-center) into the energy of Saturn to fortify your Saturn energy.

It may be useful here to reiterate a few general principles of magic before describing the planetary hand gestures. Always remember that the right side of the body is projective and the left side is receptive. The right side sends out and the left side absorbs. Occult energies are transmitted along straight rays of force that twist as they propagate in the same way that the strands of a rope are twisted. They pass into and out of magic circles, such as the aura that surrounds your body, by means of spirals, which open esoteric gateways through expanded center points. Any point in a circle may be regarded as its center, since all mathematical points are identical. The center of anything is determined by point of view. Occult energy is shaped and directed by visualization, but it is moved using the force of the will.

When you hold your left hand pressed to a planetary chakra and extend your right hand, you are forming a channel that is shaped like an expanding spiral. Energy runs from the chakra into your left hand (which is receptive), along your left arm, across your shoulders, down your right arm to your right hand (which is projective), and outward into the macrocosm.

When you hold your right hand to a body center and extend your left hand, you form a contracting spiral that focuses on that chakra. Energy from the macrocosm flows into your left hand, along your left arm, across your shoulders, down your right arm, and into the planetary chakra under your right hand.

You should practice the accompanying meditations and exercises with all seven of the planetary energies until you become familiar with their natures and how they differ. You must be able to clearly visualize the energy streams, and feel them flowing through your body.

Hand Gesture of the Sun

The Sun is represented by the clenched fist, which forms a roughly spherical shape. The thumb should be outside the fingers, held tight across the second joints of the index and middle fingers. If you cannot form this fist perfectly, get as close to it as you are able without straining your hand.

Figure 5.1: Hand Gesture of the Sun

Meditation on the Sun

This meditation is designed to familiarize you with the energy of the Sun. If possible, face the direction of the Sun. Otherwise, face east. Adopt the standing posture, with hands relaxed at your sides. Take a few slow, silent breaths to focus on what you are about to do.

Form the Sun gesture with both hands and move into a modified form of the spiral invoking posture, with your left fist high above your head and your right fist pressed to the crown of your head, where your Sun center is located. Visualize your Sun center as a yellow sphere about the size of a tennis ball that projects halfway above the center of your skull. It is an astral form that penetrates through your right hand without being obstructed.

Using the force of your will, draw solar energy down from the celestial sphere of the Sun into your left hand and send it in a contracting spiral down your left arm, across your back at the shoulders, and along your bent right arm into your crown-center.

You can use audible breaths to help pump this solar energy through your body and into your crown-center. Breathe in slowly and audibly as you use your will to draw energy into your left hand and send it in a spiral to your right hand, then breathe out slowly and audibly as you concentrate the energy in your crown-center.

As you do this, the sphere of your crown-center gradually turns a brighter yellow color, and its rate of counterclockwise rotation increases. Continue to fill your crown-center with Sun energy for several minutes or until it feels full.

Assume the prayer posture, with palms pressed flat together in front of your chest, fingers pointed upward, your head inclined downward slightly, and your gaze lowered. Contemplate for a minute the Sun energy accumulated in your crown-center.

This energy is wholesome and purifying. Feel its pleasant warmth on the top of your skull and inside your head. It is constant, reliable, and changeless. Warmth is life. The warmth of the Sun causes seeds to germinate in the ground, and the rays of the Sun allow plants to grow upward and stand tall. Solar energy is the energy of self-awareness and self-reliance. The Sun's rays dispel all shadows. Use this energy to examine who you are and where you're going in your life. Use it to burn away infection and disease, both physical and spiritual. This energy engenders a healthy body and an open, honest mind.

Widen your stance and shift slowly and smoothly into the opening posture, pushing outward with your palms until your arms are fully extended to the sides. As you do so, mentally cause the yellow energy that fills your crown-center to expand outward in a flaming yellow ring that floats on the air at the level of your crown-center. Spend a minute or so contemplating this flaming yellow ring, which floats just beyond your extended, outward-turned palms. You can, if you desire, expand the ring further by the force of your will.

Smoothly narrow your stance and transition back into the prayer posture. As you do so, shrink the flaming yellow ring back into the sphere of your crown-center, which once again becomes bright yellow and spins more quickly. Maintain this posture for a minute as you contemplate your charged crown-center.

Form your hands in the Sun gesture and transition into a modified spiral banishing posture, with your left fist pressed down on the crown of your head and your right fist directed downward at your right side. Mentally will the excess Sun energy that fills your crown-center to flow in an expanding spiral into your left hand, through your bent left arm, across your back at the shoulders, and down your right arm. The energy exits your right fist in a twisting yellow stream that flows into the ground below where you stand.

You can, if you wish, use audible breaths to pump the solar energy out of your crown-center. Use audible inhalations to draw the energy into your left fist and through your arms, and audible exhalations to push it from your right hand into the ground. As your crown-center empties its excess solar energy, it becomes a paler yellow color and its rate of spin slows to normal.

Shift to the closing posture, with your feet together, forearms crossed at the wrists in front of your chest, and eyes shut. Contemplate the balanced energies within your body and mind for a minute or so.

Relax your hands at your sides and assume the standing posture. Take a few silent breaths to end the Sun meditation.

Hand Gesture of the Moon

The Moon is represented by the flat of the hand with the thumb and fingers extended together but very slightly curved to form a crescent when the hand is viewed from the edge. The open, flat hand is the natural opposite of the clenched fist, just as the lunar crescent is the opposite of the solar circle.

Figure 5.2: Hand Gesture of the Moon

Meditation on the Moon

All of the planetary meditations follow the same general outline already described in the meditation on the Sun. Face the direction of the Moon, if you can. Otherwise, face east. Adopt the standing posture and take a few silent breaths.

Form the Moon gesture with both hands and widen your stance into a modified form of the spiral invoking posture, with your left hand extended above your head and your right hand cupped to your groin, where your root-center is located. Draw purple lunar energy down into your left hand from the celestial sphere of the Moon and send it in a contracting spiral through your body into your root-center.

It may help you to use audible breaths to pump this energy through your body, as described in the previous meditation. As you do this, the sphere of your root-center gradually turns a deeper purple color and rotates more rapidly. Fill your root-center with lunar energy.

Shift smoothly into the prayer posture and contemplate for a minute or so the Moon energy you have gathered in your root-center.

This energy is secret and mysterious, filled with deep emotions and giving rise to fantastic thoughts and images. It feels pleasantly cool, like moonlight on a summer's night. It stirs sexual energy within you. Feel it tingle inside your sexual organs, constantly shifting and changing, never remaining the same. It is the power of dreams and visions, the power to scry into the mysteries of the universe. It engenders all manner of thoughts and possibilities. You can use this energy to heal or invigorate your reproductive organs or those in other individuals. It can also be used to encourage fertility and conception.

Shift slowly and smoothly into the opening posture. As you do so, mentally expand the purple energy that fills the sphere of your root-center outward in a flaming purple ring that floats on the air at the level of your groin. Spend a minute contemplating this ring of power.

Smoothly transition back into the prayer posture. As you do so, shrink the flaming purple ring back into your root-center. Hold the prayer posture for a minute as you contemplate your charged root-center once again.

Form both hands into the Moon gesture and transition into a modified spiral banishing posture, with your left palm cupped to your groin and your right hand directed downward at your right side. Mentally will the Moon energy that fills your root-center to flow in an expanding spiral into your left hand, up your left arm, across your back at the shoulders, and down your right arm, where the energy exits from your right hand into the ground in a purple stream. If you wish, you can use audible breaths to better pump this energy out of your body.

Shift to the closing posture and contemplate your balanced energy for a minute in inner stillness.

Relax into the standing posture and draw a few silent breaths to end the Moon meditation.

Hand Gesture of Mars

Mars is represented by a clenched fist with the thumb extended straight out, away from the fist. This is similar to the hand gesture hitchhikers use. The thumb is a phallic symbol. In this gesture, it signifies male potency.

Figure 5.3: Hand Gesture of Mars

Meditation on Mars

Face Mars, if you can. Otherwise, face east. Adopt the standing posture and take a few deep breaths.

Form the Mars gesture with both hands and shift into a modified form of the spiral invoking posture, with your left hand extended high above your head and your right hand pressed to your forehead, where your brow-center is located. Draw martial energy down into your left hand from the sphere of Mars and send it in a contracting spiral through your arm and shoulders into your brow-center. If you wish, use audible breaths to more strongly pump this energy through your upper body.

The sphere of your brow-center, which lies within your head at the level of your eyebrows, gradually turns a deeper red and rotates more rapidly. Fill your brow-center with Mars energy.

Shift smoothly into the prayer posture, with palms pressed together in front of your chest, and contemplate the Mars energy you have gathered in your brow-center for a minute or so.

This energy is hot and penetrating. It focuses your thoughts and intensifies your concentration. It hardens your resolve and dispels doubts and fears. It can be used to heighten your courage or, when it is projected, the courage of another individual. It is useful when you need to come to a decision on an uncertain issue. Held under control, it increases the likelihood of victory in any dispute or conflict, but if allowed to run out of control, it can make you hot-headed and reckless. For this reason, it can be used to provoke recklessness and bad decisions in others. It can also be used to project thoughts into the minds of others, or to cause others to act in the way you will them to act. The brow-center is the site of the third eye, from which psychic force is projected.

Shift into the opening posture, and as you do so, mentally expand the red energy that fills the sphere of your brow-center outward in a flaming scarlet ring that floats on the air at the level of your forehead. Spend a minute contemplating this scarlet ring.

Smoothly transition back into the prayer posture. As you do so, shrink the flaming red ring back into your brow-center. Hold the prayer posture for a minute as you contemplate the charged sphere of your brow-center.

Form your hands into the Mars gesture once again and transition into a modified spiral banishing posture, with your left hand pressed to your forehead and your right hand directed downward at your right side. Mentally will the Mars energy that fills your brow-center to flow in an expanding spiral through your left arm, across your shoulders, and down your right arm, where it exits from your right hand into the ground in a twisting red stream. If you wish, use audible breaths to help pump this excess Mars energy out of your body, until your brow-center has returned to its normal energy state.

Move to the closing posture and contemplate for a minute the balance of energies within you.

Relax into the standing posture with a few silent breaths to end the Mars meditation.

Hand Gesture of Venus

Venus is represented by a clenched fist with the thumb held inside the fist. It is the opposite of the Mars hand gesture. The fingers curled around the thumb symbolize the vagina. Hold your fingers loosely around your thumb so there is no strain.

Figure 5.4: Hand Gesture of Venus

Meditation on Venus

Face Venus, if you can. This will be just before sunrise or shortly after sundown, depending on whether Venus is rising in the east or setting in the west. Otherwise, face east. Adopt the standing posture and take a few deep breaths.

Form the Venus gesture with both hands and shift into a modified spiral invoking posture, with your left hand extended above your head and your right hand pressed to the pit of your throat, where your throat-center is located. Draw green Venusian energy down into your left hand from the celestial sphere of Venus and send it through your arms and shoulders into your throat-center, using audible breaths to pump the energy if you find it helpful.

The sphere of your throat-center, which lies within your neck at the level of the pit of your throat, gradually turns a deeper emerald green and rotates more rapidly. Fill it with Venus energy for several minutes.

Shift smoothly into the prayer posture and contemplate the Venus energy you have gathered in your throat-center for a minute or so.

This energy is gentle and soothing. It awakens and intensifies all tender emotions, but particularly the emotion of love, both physical and sexual. You may feel a lump in your throat and find yourself remembering emotional moments in your life. This energy can be useful for breaking down emotional barriers and softening those who have hardened their heart. It increases the appreciation of poetry and song, because both depend on the voice, but more generally awakens an understanding and appreciation of artistic forms of expression. Artists will find that the invocation of this energy will make them more creative and expressive. It can be used to help heal the throat and larynx and soothe a sore throat, and by projection can hasten the healing of throat problems in others.

Shift into the opening posture, and as you do so, mentally expand the green energy that fills the sphere of your throat-center outward in a flaming emerald ring that floats on the air at the level of your collarbones. Spend a minute contemplating this green ring.

Smoothly transition back into the prayer posture. As you do so, shrink the flaming green ring back into your throat-center. Hold the prayer posture for a minute as you contemplate the charged sphere of your throat-center.

Form your hands into the Venus gesture and transition into a modified spiral banishing posture, with your left hand pressed to the pit of your throat and your right hand directed downward at your right side. Mentally will the Venus energy that fills your throat-center to flow in an expanding spiral through your left arm, across your shoulders, and down your right arm, where it exits from your right hand into the ground in a twisting green stream. It may help to use audible breaths to pump this excess Venus energy from your body.

Change to the closing posture and contemplate the energy balance within you for a minute or so in silence with your eyes shut.

Relax into the standing posture, with your hands open at your sides. Take a few silent breaths to end the Venus meditation.

Hand Gesture of Jupiter

Jupiter is represented by the flat of the hand, fingers together, with the thumb extended away from it at a right angle, or as close to a right angle as your hand will naturally form without strain. The extended thumb represents masculine phallic energy, but it is lunar in its expression rather than solar, as in the case of Mars.

Figure 5.5: Hand Gesture of Jupiter

Meditation on Jupiter

Face Jupiter in the night sky, if you can conveniently do so—it is not visible at all times of the year. Otherwise, face east. Adopt the standing posture and take a few silent breaths.

Form the Jupiter gesture with both hands and shift into a modified spiral invoking posture, with your left hand high above your head and your right hand pressed to your abdomen above your navel, where your stomach-center is located. Draw orange Jovian energy down into your left hand from the sphere of Jupiter, which is always above you regardless of whether Jupiter is visible in the sky, and send it through your arms and shoulders into your stomach-center.

You can use audible breaths to help pump this energy through your body and into the sphere of your stomach-center. Fill your stomach-center with Jupiter energy. As the sphere fills, it gradually turns a deeper orange and rotates more rapidly

Shift smoothly into the prayer posture and contemplate the Jupiter energy you have gathered in your stomach-center for a minute or so.

This energy is nourishing and sustaining. It is a source of strength that you may draw upon in times of need, especially physical strength and endurance. It has a calming and focusing effect on the mind, and dispels worries with quiet self-confidence. Jupiter conveys the authority of the father and the patriarch. It can be used to give others confidence in your leadership and decision-making abilities. It can also be called upon to protect the family and the home. This energy is characterized by confidence, generosity, good humor, and the enjoyment of life. It can be used to help heal complaints of the stomach such as indigestion or heartburn, and to clear the mind after too much alcohol.

Shift into the opening posture, and as you do so, mentally expand the orange energy that fills the sphere of your stomach-center outward in a flaming orange ring that floats around you on the air at the level of your stomach. Spend a minute contemplating this orange ring.

Smoothly transition back into the prayer posture. As you do so, shrink the flaming orange ring back into your stomach-center. Hold the prayer posture for a minute as you contemplate the charged sphere of your stomach-center.

Form both your hands once again into the Jupiter gesture and transition into a modified spiral banishing posture, with your left hand pressed to your abdomen and your right hand directed downward at your right side. Mentally will the Jovian energy that fills the sphere of your stomach-center to flow in an expanding spiral up your left arm, across your shoulders, and down your right arm, where it exits from your right hand into the ground in a twisting orange stream.

Change to the closing posture to terminate this stream, and hold it for a minute while you contemplate the balanced energies within you.

Relax into the standing posture, with your hands open at your sides, and take a few silent breaths to end the Jupiter meditation.

Hand Gesture of Saturn

Saturn is represented by the flat of the hand, fingers together, with the thumb folded across the palm to the base of the little finger, or as far across as can be held comfortably. It is the opposite of the gesture of Jupiter. The folded thumb symbolizes the penis in its flaccid state and indicates a masculine energy that is latent or subdued, with lunar feminine energy dominant. Fold the thumb as far down as you can comfortably hold it, but don't strain your hand.

Figure 5.6: Hand Gesture of Saturn

Meditation on Saturn

Face Saturn, if you can easily do so. It is not visible in the night sky in all seasons. Otherwise, face east. Adopt the standing posture and take a few silent breaths.

Form the Saturn gesture with both hands and shift into a modified spiral invoking posture, with your left hand raised high above your head and your right hand pressed to your lower belly, below your navel, where your bowel-center is located. Draw blue Saturnian energy down into your left hand from the sphere of Saturn that is always above you, and send it through your arms and shoulders into your bowel-center.

The sphere of your bowel-center gradually turns a deeper blue and rotates more rapidly counterclockwise. Fill your bowel-center with Saturn energy. It can be pumped through your upper body with the aid of audible breaths—you should experiment doing the exercise both with and without audible breaths to see which method suits you best.

Shift smoothly into the prayer posture and contemplate the Saturn energy you have gathered in your bowel-center.

This energy is cold, heavy, and hard. It focuses your thoughts on serious subjects and dispels distracting emotions while deepening your ability to concentrate and study. For this reason, it is excellent for students studying for examinations or anyone who studies intensely any difficult or obscure matter, especially occult subjects. Too much of this energy will cause moroseness and depression. It tends to engender cynical and selfish thoughts, but can be excellent for solving problems that threaten your personal security or financial status. On a physical level, this energy can be used to cure constipation and problems associated with the bowels and anus. It is also good for joint aches.

Shift into the opening posture, and as you do so, mentally expand the deep-blue energy that fills the sphere of your bowel-center outward in a flaming ring that floats on the air at the level of your lower belly. Spend a minute contemplating this blue ring of astral fire.

Smoothly transition into the prayer posture once again. As you do so, shrink the flaming blue ring back into your bowel-center. Hold the prayer posture for a minute as you contemplate the rapidly rotating, charged sphere of your bowel-center.

Form both hands into the Saturn gesture and transition into a modified spiral banishing posture, with your left hand pressed to your belly below your navel and your right hand directed downward at your right side. Mentally will the Saturn energy that fills the spinning blue sphere of your bowel-center to flow in an expanding spiral up your left arm, across your shoulders, and down your right arm, where it exits from your right hand into the ground in a twisting blue stream. You can, if you wish, facilitate this flow with audible breaths.

Change to the closing posture and contemplate the balanced state of your body centers for a minute.

Relax into the standing posture. Take a few silent breaths to end the Saturn meditation.

Hand Gesture of Mercury

Mercury, which has no opposite among the seven planets, is represented by the flat hand with the fingers and thumb widely separated so that they do not touch each other. Mercury embodies the qualities of the enlightened magus, and the hand with the fingers spread into five points suggests, by the symbolism of the pentagram, the intellectual abilities and moral virtues of our human species. Five is the number of humankind.

Figure 5.7: Hand Gesture of Mercury

Meditation on Mercury

Face Mercury, if you can. It is only visible at certain times either very low in the east before sunrise or low in the west just after sunset, but it is much more difficult to see than Venus, which similarly appears in either the east or the west. If it is not convenient for you to face the planet Mercury, then face east. Adopt the standing posture and take a few silent breaths.

Form the Mercury gesture with both hands and shift into the spiral invoking posture, elevating your left hand high above your head and pressing your right hand to the center of your chest, where your heart-center is located. Draw white Mercurial energy down into your left hand from the celestial sphere of Mercury, which is always above you even when the planet itself is not visible in the sky, and send it through your arm and shoulders into the rotating sphere of your heart-center. You will recall that this is a larger sphere than the other planetary centers of the body—it is visualized as being around the size of a baseball, whereas the other centers are visualized as being about the size of a tennis ball.

The sphere of your heart-center—which lies toward the back of your chest, just in front of your spine, at the level of your heart—gradually turns a brighter white and rotates more rapidly. The white of Mercury is a warm soft white, as opposed to the white of the stars, which is a cool blue-white, and the white of Spirit, which is a neutral white. Fill your heart-center with Mercury energy. If you wish, use audible breaths to move this energy with greater force.

Shift smoothly into the prayer posture and contemplate the Mercury energy you have gathered in your heart-center for a minute or so.

This energy is very quick and light, in constant darting motion. It quickens the working of your mind and makes your thoughts race. It can be used to heighten your ability to speak in public and debate issues, particularly issues dealing with politics and business. It also tends to make you more witty in conversation. It is useful when composing speeches or reports and when entertaining others with words or stories, and also when it is necessary to mediate between parties in a debate or dispute. It can facilitate the outcome of legal matters. Too much of the Mercurial energy tends to induce a love of gambling and puzzle solving, as the restless mind seeks intellectual diversions with which to occupy itself. There is no emotional intensity here. It is mental energy that computes, analyzes, and reaches conclusions. On a physical level, it can be used to regulate the functions of the body such as pulse rate, hormonal balance, and blood pressure. Invoke it particularly in matters dealing with communication or travel.

Shift into the opening posture, and as you do so, mentally expand the soft white energy that fills the sphere of your heart-center outward in a flaming white ring that floats on the air at the level of your heart. Spend a minute contemplating this ring of astral fire.

Smoothly transition back into the prayer posture. As you do so, shrink the flaming white ring back into your heart-center. Hold the prayer posture for a minute as you contemplate the recharged white sphere of your heart-center.

Form both hands into the Mercury gesture and transition into the spiral banishing posture, with your left hand pressed to the center of your chest and your right hand directed downward at your right side toward the ground below where you stand. Mentally will the Mercury energy that fills your heart-center to flow in an expanding spiral up your left arm, across your shoulders, and down your right arm, where it exits from your right hand into the ground in a twisting white stream. You can facilitate the expulsion of this excess Mercury energy with audible breaths if you wish.

Change to the closing posture to cut off the flow of energy, and stand for a minute with your eyes shut and forearms crossed, contemplating your balanced planetary centers.

Relax into the standing posture, with your arms at your sides, and take a few silent breaths to end the Mercury meditation.

Workings: Planetary Hand Gestures

The following practices involving the use of the planetary hand gestures should be done while facing the direction of the planet you are working with, if this is possible. This will create a stronger link between the hand gesture and the planet it represents. However, if you don't know the direction of the planet, or for some reason it is not convenient to face in that direction, the exercises may also be done while facing east. It is the usual custom in modern Western magic to begin rituals facing the east when no other direction is indicated.

It is best to do the working of a planet on the day of that planet. For example, the workings involving Sun energy are best done on Sunday, if possible while facing the Sun. You may even wish to observe planetary hours and do the workings associated with a planet not only on its day of the week but also during one of its own hours.

Of course, it is not absolutely necessary to perform planetary magic on the day of the planet, or in the hour of the planet, or facing the planet, but these associations can be helpful in achieving the best results. Those who want to simplify their practice can perform these exercises at any time while facing in any direction. There are no specific points of the compass associated with the seven planets in Western magic, because the compass has reference to the surface of the Earth, and the spheres of the planets are above the earthly spheres of the four lower elements. Whether you wish to link directions and times with the planets is up to you.

I suggest that you do one or more of the workings for a planet immediately after performing the meditation on that planet. The purpose of the workings is to associate the occult energies of the planets with the planetary hand gestures and planetary body centers.

Each working below is described in general terms but should be practiced with all seven planets and all seven centers of the body, ideally on the different days of the week, with the workings of the Sun on Sunday, those of the Moon on Monday, and so on. In this sense, each working is really seven workings. If you have the time and stamina, you can do all of the workings for a particular planet together on its own day, but you may find it easier to break them down into selected sets. Workings 1–2 go together, as do 3–4, 5–6–7, and 8–9. Working 10 stands alone.

The associations in the following table should be adhered to when performing these workings, unless you have reasons for departing from them. For example, you may wish to use the traditional colors of the planets rather than the color-wheel colors I have assigned to them.

Day of Week	Ruling Planet	Chakra	Color
Sunday	Sun	Crown	Yellow
Monday	Moon	Root	Purple
Tuesday	Mars	Brow	Red
Wednesday	Mercury	Heart	White
Thursday	Jupiter	Stomach	Orange
Friday	Venus	Throat	Green
Saturday	Saturn	Bowel	Blue

Associations of the Seven Days

Working 1: Invoking Planetary Energy

It is best to face in the direction of the planet you are invoking. If this is not possible, face east. Begin in the standing posture, with arms at your sides and eyes directed straight ahead. Take a few silent breaths to calm and focus your mind.

To invoke into a chakra of your body the energy of the planet linked with that center, form both hands in the gesture of the planet. Shift into the spiral invoking posture by pressing your right hand over the center associated with the planet while raising your left hand high in the air. Energy is drawn from the celestial sphere of the planet high above into your left hand, and passes through the contracting spiral of your arms and shoulders to exit from your right hand into the planet's body center. The center should be visualized as a sphere that is the color associated with its planet.

As you cause planetary energy to flow into the sphere in a contracting spiral through your upper body, visualize the sphere rotating more rapidly in a counterclockwise direction and glowing more brightly with the planet's color.

Continue to charge the center with planetary energy until it feels fully energized. To cut off the flow of energy, shift into the closing posture, with your forearms crossed over your chest at the wrists and your hands closed into fists. Close your eyes. Hold this posture for a minute or so as you contemplate your charged center.

Shift into the standing posture, with your arms at your sides and hands relaxed and open as you gaze forward. Take a few silent breaths to end. Unless you have some purpose for sustaining a charge of energy in your planetary center, the working that follows should be done shortly after you finish in order to restore the balance of energies in your body.

Working 2: Banishing Planetary Energy

This working will usually be done soon after Working 1: Invoking Planetary Energy, while your charged body center is still filled with planetary energy.

Begin in the standing posture facing the planet, or facing east. Take a few silent breaths to calm and focus your mind.

Form the gesture of the planet with both hands and adopt the spiral banishing posture. Press your left hand over the charged planetary center, and at the same time point your right hand down at the floor beside your right foot.

The energy is drawn out of your charged center and into your left hand, then pushed by the force of your will in an expanding spiral up your left arm, across your back at the shoulders, and down your right arm, where it exits downward from your right hand in the form of a twisting stream that is the color associated with the planet. This stream flows downward through the floor into the ground, where it is earthed.

As the excess planetary energy flows out of the sphere of your body center, that sphere spins more slowly counterclockwise and the brightness of its color dims. When you have returned the center to its normal state, cut off the flow of energy by adopting the closing posture, with hands closed into fists and forearms crossed at the wrists over your chest. Hold it with your eyes closed for a minute while you contemplate the condition of your body centers.

Change into the standing posture and take a few silent breaths to end.

Working 3: Receiving Planetary Energy

Begin in the standing posture facing the planet, or the east, with the object or person from which you wish to drain planetary energy on your left side. If it is not possible to face the planet or the east, at least position yourself so that the thing or person from which you will draw energy is on your left. Take a few deep breaths.

Form both your hands into the gesture of the planet as you prepare to shift into the receiving posture. Step to the left with your left foot. Extend your left hand toward the thing from which you intend to receive the energy, with your palm turned upward, while at the same time turning your head to look over the top of your left hand, and press your right hand to the body center of that planet. The flow of energy will be stronger if you are able to actually touch the person or object with your left hand.

Use your willpower to draw the energy of the person or object into your receptive left hand. Send it along your left arm, across your back at the shoulders, and along your right arm into your right hand, where it passes into the body center of the planet. As the spinning sphere of the planet's center fills with the energy of that planet, it spins faster and its planetary color becomes more intense.

Bring your feet together and face forward as you make the closing posture, with wrists crossed over your chest and fists clenched, your eyes shut, to cut off the flow of planetary energy. Spend a minute in this pose contemplating your energized planetary center.

Move into the standing posture, with hands open at your sides, head level, and gaze directed forward, and take a few silent breaths to end the working. This working will usually be done shortly before the working that follows, unless you have some reason for sustaining the energy charge in your planetary center.

Working 4: Projecting Planetary Energy

You will usually perform this working directly after Working 3: Receiving Planetary Energy.

Face the planet, or the east, in the standing posture, with the thing you intend to charge with energy on your right side. If this is not possible, at least position the thing you will charge on your right. Take a few silent breaths to focus your mind.

Form the gesture of the planet with both hands as you step to the right with your right foot and shift into the projecting posture, with your right hand directed toward the person or object you intend to charge with planetary energy and your left hand pressed over the charged body center of that planet. The palm of your right hand should be turned downward and your gaze directed above it at the thing to be charged.

Use the force of your will to send energy out from the charged sphere of the body center associated with the planet and into your left hand. Send it up your left arm, across your back at the shoulders, and down your right arm in an expanding spiral. It exits out your right hand in a stream that flows into the thing at which you point. If you can actually touch the thing you are charging, the flow of energy will be stronger. As you draw this energy from the body center of the planet, its sphere spins more slowly and its color becomes paler.

Make the closing posture, with wrists crossed over your chest, hands clenched into fists, and eyes shut, to cut off the flow of planetary energy out from your body. Contemplate the body center you have just drained of excess planetary energy for a minute or so.

Shift into the standing posture, with your hands relaxed and open at your sides and eyes directed forward, and take a few silent breaths to end.

Working 5: Concentrating Planetary Energy

To draw planetary energy directly from the celestial sphere of the planet and accumulate it in a place, person, or object without absorbing that energy into your planetary center, begin in the standing posture and take a few silent breaths.

Form the gesture of the planet with both hands as you shift into the magician posture. Raise your left hand high in the air, and at the same time point your right hand at the thing you will charge with energy. Keep your gaze directed forward. If you can actually touch your right hand to the thing you are charging, the flow of energy will be facilitated.

Use the power of your will to draw down planetary energy from the celestial sphere of the planet into your left hand. The energy is gathered from the heavens and streams down your left arm and into your chest, where it swirls once counterclockwise around the sphere of your heart-center without entering it. From there it moves across to the right side of your body and down your right arm, passing from your right hand into the thing you are charging. The energy stream flowing through your body should be visualized in the color associated with the planet.

To cut off the flow of energy, shift from the magician posture into the closing posture, and hold it for a minute or so with your eyes shut.

Assume the standing posture and take a few silent breaths to end.

Working 6: Dispersing Planetary Energy

To channel planetary energy out of a person, place, or object in order to drain it of this force but without absorbing the energy into your own planetary center, begin as usual in the standing posture. Take several silent breaths to clear and focus your mind.

Form the gesture of the planet with both hands, and shift from the standing posture into the Baphomet posture. Point at the thing you wish to drain of energy with your left hand, or actually bring your hand into contact with it. At the same time, raise your right hand high into the air. Keep your gaze directed forward at the horizon.

Use your will to draw planetary energy out of the thing you seek to drain and send it through your body and out your raised right hand. The energy stream should be visualized in the color associated with the planet. It flows into your left hand and arm, goes once counterclockwise around the sphere of your heart-center, and continues up your right arm. Visualize the energy spinning clockwise outward from your right hand like a pinwheel and dispersing into the heavens, where it rejoins its planetary sphere.

Make the closing posture to end this flow of energy through your body, and stand in this pose for a minute as you contemplate the balance of energies within you.

Adopt the standing posture and take a few silent breaths to conclude the exercise.

Working 7: Cross-Channeling Planetary Energy

To channel planetary energy from one thing to another thing without accumulating it in your body, begin the exercise in the standing posture and take a few silent breaths to calm your mind and focus your purpose.

Make the gesture of the planet with both hands and shift from the standing posture into the channeling posture. The thing you wish to draw the energy from should be on your left side and the thing into which you will infuse the energy on your right. If you can actually touch the two things involved with your hands, the transfer will be more potent.

Use your willpower to draw planetary energy out of the thing on your left side with your receptive left hand and send it in a stream through your upper body and out your right hand into the thing on your right side. Visualize this stream, which is colored with the color of the planet, flow along your left arm to the center of your chest in a contracting spiral, swirl once counterclockwise around the spinning white sphere of your heart-center without actually entering it, and then flow in an expanding spiral down your right arm and out your right hand. Visualize the counterclockwise spin of your heart-center propelling the stream onward like a whirling spindle as the stream of energy circles around it.

To cut off the flow of energy through your body, make the closing posture, with your hands clenched into fists, your forearms crossed, and your eyes shut, and hold it for a minute or so as you contemplate your inner balance of forces.

Shift into the standing posture and take a few silent breaths to end the exercise.

Working 8: Transforming Planetary Energy

It is a mysterious truth that there is only one root occult energy in the universe. All of the various types of different energies are merely expressions of this single source, which the mystics of China know as *chi*, and which in the Star Wars movies was aptly called *the Force*.

This occult truth is reflected in the material world. All of the various colors of the spectrum are caused by varying the wavelength of light—there is no essential difference between them. All sounds are vibrations on the air of different frequencies. Similarly, all of the elemental energies are expressions of the element Spirit, and all of the planetary energies are variations of that same root energy of Spirit that underlies both the entire universe (macrocosm) and the mind and body of human beings (microcosm).

A practical consequence of this truth is that we can transform one planetary energy into another through the use of visualization and the force of our will.

To transform the energy of one planet into the energy of another planet as it passes through your body, begin in the standing posture and take a few silent breaths to focus your mind. The thing you will draw energy from should be on your left side and the thing you will project energy into on your right side.

Form your left hand into the planetary gesture of the energy you will draw out from the source, and form your right hand into the planetary gesture of the energy you will project into your target. The energy will be transformed by spiritual alchemy as it passes through you. This is the true meaning of the fable of transforming lead into gold.

Shift into the channeling posture, and direct your left hand at the source of energy and your right hand at the target while gazing straight ahead. If you can actually touch your hands to these two things, the energy transfer will be stronger.

Draw the energy of the planet that is indicated by the gesture of your left hand from the source into your left hand, and visualize it flowing along your left arm and across your torso to your spinning heart-center. This is the center of Mercury, the planet of alchemy. Allow the colored stream to wrap itself once counterclockwise around the white sphere of your heart-center.

Will the color of this energy stream to change from the color of the planet you indicate with your left hand into the color of the planet indicated by your right hand as the stream swirls once around your heart-center before continuing onward. Send the stream into the right side of your body, down your right arm, and out your right hand into the target you are charging with transformed planetary energy.

When you feel you have transformed a sufficient amount of energy, cut off the flow through your body by assuming the closing posture, with your hands closed into fists and your wrists crossed, and contemplate the soft white sphere of your Mercury center for a minute or so with your eyes shut.

Move into the standing posture and take a few silent breaths to end.

Working 9: Balancing Planetary Energy

Sometimes the centers of the body become unbalanced. They either accumulate an excess of planetary energy or become depleted of that energy. You can become aware of this imbalance by adopting the standing posture and inwardly visualizing the column of seven planetary centers in your body. If your faculty of psychic perception is open and sensitive, you will see that some of these spheres spin more rapidly and glow more brightly than others.

It is possible to restore them to balance by linking pairs of centers with the hands and channeling the energy from one center to another, transforming the energy by spiritual alchemy in the process.

This working will give you practice in moving planetary energies between the body centers and in transforming the energy of one center into the energy of another. Although you will be working with your own centers in this practice, be aware that this technique may also be used to balance the body centers of others by a laying on of hands.

Begin as usual in the standing posture and take a few silent breaths to focus your mind on what you will do.

With your left hand, form the gesture of the planet of the center you will draw energy from, and with your right hand form the gesture of the planet of the center you will charge with alchemically transformed energy.

Shift into a modified balancing posture, with your left hand pressed to the center from which you will draw excess energy and your right hand pressed to the center into which you will cause that transformed energy to flow.

Visualize the center you wish to draw energy from, and with the power of your will, cause that energy to flow into your left hand and along your left arm. Carry it through your chest to your heart-center and wrap it once around this spinning white sphere before sending it to your right shoulder, down your right arm, and from your right hand into the center you are charging.

As the energy flows into your receptive left hand and along your left arm, visualize the stream in the color of the planet indicated by the gesture of your left hand. The color changes as the stream of energy swirls around your heart-center, transforming into the color of the planet indicated by the gesture of your right hand.

For example, if your left hand is pressed to your brow-center, you will be making the Mars gesture with your left hand, and the energy stream that flows from your brow-center along your left arm will be red. It will transform into orange as it swirls around your heart-center if your right hand is formed in the Jupiter gesture and pressed against your stomach-center. But if your right hand is pressed to your throat-center and shaped in the Venus gesture, the energy stream will change from red to green as it flows around your heart-center.

Cut off the flow of energy when the two body centers feel balanced by shifting to the closing posture, and contemplate the state of your seven energy centers for a minute or so.

Move into the standing posture and take a few silent breaths to conclude.

Working 10: Spirit Scrying

Practice invoking and visualizing the pagan deities of the seven planets with the following working.

Begin as usual in the standing posture. Face the planet with which you are working on its day of the week, or if this is not convenient, face east. Take a few silent breaths to focus your mind.

Form the gesture of the planet with both hands and shift into the general invoking posture, with your hands raised high overhead, your arms spread in a V-shape, and your face tilted upward. Don't forget to widen your stance to medium. The palms of your hands should be turned upward. With the power of your will, draw down the energy of the planet into your body and into your aura through the crown of your head. Your aura will turn from a colorless transparency to a pale tint of the planet's color. Your aura is not expanded for this exercise. Feel the planetary energy swirling around you and throughout your entire body.

Narrow your stance as you shift smoothly into the prayer posture, with hands pressed flat together in front of your chest, head bowed slightly, and gaze directed downward at an angle. For a minute or so, visualize your tinted aura and feel the planetary energy saturating your body.

Bring your feet together and spread your arms wide in the ankh posture, with your flattened palms turned forward and your gaze at the level of the horizon. Speak the following incantation. Insert the name of the planet with which you are working in the space on the first line.

Ruler of _____ (name of planet), descend to me,
show your face that I may see;
Reveal yourself in fine array,
Here in this place, upon your day.

Widen your stance and adopt the scrying posture as you bring your hands together in front of you at the level of your face, with your thumbs and index fingers touching at the tips to form an upright equilateral triangle. Look through this triangle and scry the image of the deity who rules the planet whose energy you have invoked into your body. Visualize the god or goddess in classical garments, as represented in Greek and Roman statues. Meet the eyes of the deity and hold this visualization for at least a full minute with intense concentration. Strive to form a mental link with the deity you are visualizing through the triangle.

At first, you will only be using your imagination to visualize the deity, but as you work with this exercise, you will find that the deity becomes more aware of you, and more animated, and begins to interact with you using facial expressions and body gestures. The degree to which you can actually see the deity will depend on your level of psychic development.

If the deity gives you a sign of some kind, take a mental note of it—it may have application to circumstances in your life. It could be a smile, a frown, a nod, a hand gesture, or something else. It may come in response to your thoughts.

Dispel the image of the deity from your mind by stepping back with your right foot as you shift smoothly into the warding posture. Hold this posture for several silent breaths while clearing your mind. Your hands should be opened flat, palms facing forward, in this posture.

Move into the general banishing posture, with arms lowered in an A-shape, and as you do so, make the gesture of the planet with both hands. Using the force of your will, send the excess planetary energy out of your body and aura through the soles of your feet and into the ground beneath you.

Shift into the closing posture, with your feet touching, arms crossed over your chest at the wrists, hands closed into fists, and eyes shut. Contemplate the clarity of your aura and the balance of your body centers for a minute or so.

Move to the standing posture and take several silent breaths to end.

CHAPTER 6
THE TWELVE ZODIAC SIGNS

KINESIC MAGIC RELIES ON THREE SETS of occult energies that divide the wholeness of our reality into categories of meaning. The first set is the five elements, which divide the lower physical world and the elemental spheres around it into four essences called Fire, Water, Air, and Earth. These four are energized and sustained by a fifth essence, or quintessence, called Spirit, or Light. The second set of occult energies is represented and defined by the seven wandering lights of the heavens visible to the naked eye—the Moon, Mercury, Venus, the Sun, Mars, Jupiter, and Saturn—which occupy the zone between the elemental spheres around the Earth and the sphere of the fixed stars that lies beyond Saturn. The third set of occult energies is the twelve signs of the zodiac, located in the sphere of the fixed stars.

Understand that when I refer to the elemental spheres around the Earth, the spheres of the planets, and the sphere of the fixed stars, I am referring to symbolic or philosophical structures, not physical structures. Of course we know today that there is no actual crystalline sphere in which the stars are embedded. The stars nearest us that we can see in the night sky with the naked eye are scattered throughout space at varying distances, from a few light years to thousands of light years. But the concept of a celestial sphere of the fixed stars was employed by philosophers and magicians for many centuries because it was useful, and it is still a useful concept in modern magic.

The celestial equator is an imaginary circle that runs through space directly above the equator of the Earth. Think of it as a circle on the imaginary sphere of the fixed stars that lies above the equator (another imaginary circle) around our planet. The zodiac is a broader band of the heavens that follows the celestial equator like an invisible belt.

The astrologers of ancient Persia divided the belt of the zodiac into twelve segments, called *signs*, which they associated with twelve of the more prominent star patterns, or constellations. Each segment of the zodiac has its own distinct occult significance. The seven astrological planets move in front of the twelve signs, viewed from our perspective on the surface of the Earth, and astrologers derive information by combining the meanings of these planets with the meanings of the signs. For example, Mars in the sign Virgo means something different from Mars in the sign Aries.

Don't worry, I'm not going to get into the mechanics of astrology, which is a complex study. In kinesic magic, you don't need to know how to cast astrological charts in order to use the energies of the zodiac signs. But you do need to understand the natures of the signs in order to manipulate their energies.

Elements and Qualities in the Signs

The zodiac is divided into three groups of four signs each, known in astrology as the *quaternities*, because they can be graphically represented on the zodiac by squares. These three groups are called the Cardinal signs, the Mutable signs, and the Fixed signs. They express three different kinds of occult energy, which are known in astrology as the *qualities* (figure 6.1): Cardinal energy is linear and direct, Mutable energy vibrates or oscillates back and forth, and Fixed energy rotates around a fixed center point.

The zodiac is also divided into four groups of three signs each, known in astrology as the *trines*, because they can be graphically represented on the zodiac by triangles (figure 6.2). These groups are known as the Fire signs, the Water signs, the Air signs, and the Earth signs. The four groups echo the four lower elements in the zodiac. These celestial elements are a kind of heavenly, spiritual reflection of their earthly natures. The lower elements never ascend above the sphere of the Moon; rather, it is the influence of the stars that descends as rays to the sphere of the Earth to influence earthly events.

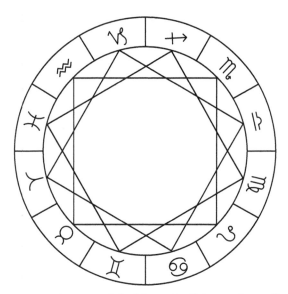

Figure 6.1: Squares of the Three Qualities on the Zodiac

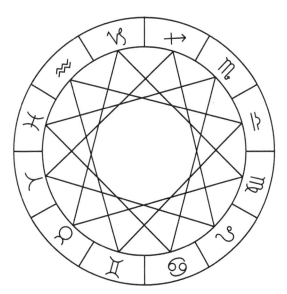

Figure 6.2: Triangles of the Four Elements on the Zodiac

The fifth element, Spirit, is present in all of the signs, just as it is present in all of the planets and all of the four lower elements. Spirit is the vitalizing principle of these twenty-four occult energies.

As you can see in the following table, each sign receives one of the three qualities and one of the four elements. The combination of its quality and its element determines a sign's essential significance. I have also indicated the ruling planet of each sign. Each planet passes through all the zodiac signs, but its power is exalted in a certain sign, or pair of signs, which for this reason it is said to rule.

Zodiac Sign	Element	Quality	Ruling Planet
Aries	Fire	Cardinal	Mars
Leo	Fire	Fixed	Sun
Sagittarius	Fire	Mutable	Jupiter
Cancer	Water	Cardinal	Moon
Scorpio	Water	Fixed	Mars
Pisces	Water	Mutable	Jupiter
Libra	Air	Cardinal	Venus
Aquarius	Air	Fixed	Saturn
Gemini	Air	Mutable	Mercury
Capricorn	Earth	Cardinal	Saturn
Taurus	Earth	Fixed	Venus
Virgo	Earth	Mutable	Mercury

Associations of the Zodiac Signs

The relationship between a zodiac sign and its ruling planet may seem random at first glance, but it is based on a division of the zodiac into a solar side defined by the Sun ruling in Leo, and a lunar side, defined by the Moon ruling in Cancer.

A line may be drawn down the middle of the zodiac wheel between Cancer and Leo that divides the wheel into these two sides (figure 6.3). The Moon casts a general lunar influence over the planets ruling the signs on the lunar side of the zodiac, and the Sun casts a general solar influence over the planets ruling the signs on the solar side.

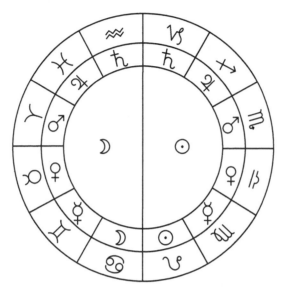

Figure 6.3: The Assignment of the Ruling Planets on the Zodiac

This effect is mild, but it should not be discounted. Venus ruling in Taurus, on the lunar side, will express itself slightly differently than Venus ruling in Libra, on the solar side. The solar influence may be described as masculine in nature—direct, straight, outgoing, forthcoming, revealing, upright, active, and projective. The lunar influence is feminine in nature—indirect, curved, introspective, withholding, concealing, supine, passive, and receptive.

The opposite masculine and feminine qualities assigned to the Sun and the Moon ultimately derive from the physical differences between the penis and the vagina, but by extension they are also based on the general behavioral differences between men and women observed and recognized since ancient times. The Sun epitomizes traditional male qualities, and the Moon epitomizes traditional female qualities. Both are equal in importance and both are necessary—neither could exist without the other. The Sun could not give without the Moon to receive; the shadows of the Moon could not exist without the light of the Sun to define them.

Color Assignment of the Signs

In kinesic magic, colors are assigned to the signs of the zodiac by using a color wheel (figure 6.4). There are other ways to assign colors to the signs. If you feel drawn to a different system of color assignment, by all means use it. In my own work, I have found assigning the colors by the color wheel to be a practical system.

Figure 6.4: The Color Wheel of the Twelve Signs

Beginning with the traditional first sign of the zodiac, Aries, the three primary colors are placed on the three Fire signs: Aries (red), Sagittarius (yellow), and Leo (blue). The three Air signs, which fall directly between the three Fire signs on the wheel of the zodiac, are given the secondary colors, which are derived by mixing the two primary colors on either side: Libra (yellow + blue = green), Gemini (red + blue = purple), and Aquarius (yellow + red = orange). The three Water signs and the three Earth signs receive the tertiary colors, which are created by mixing the primary color on one side with the secondary color on the other side. Cancer (blue + purple = blue-purple), Pisces (red + orange = red-orange), Scorpio (yellow + green = yellow-green), Capricorn (yellow + orange = yellow-orange), Virgo (blue + green = blue-green), and Taurus (red + purple = red-purple).

By the way, these are the colors used by painters when they mix pigments together. The three primary colors given here are the primaries that reflect from painted surfaces, and are not quite the same as the primary colors that are separated out of white light with a glass prism. I mention this merely to avoid confusion.

Birth Signs and Body Zones

In astrology, everyone has a birth sign determined by the position of the Sun in the band of the zodiac at the moment of birth. Our birth sign is considered to have a special influence on our personality, innate abilities, and behavior in life. We can discover our birth sign by knowing our date of birth, as shown in the following list. Please note that the cutoff dates for the signs can vary by a day or two depending on the year.

Aries: March 21–April 19

Taurus: April 20–May 20

Gemini: May 21–June 20

Cancer: June 21–July 22

Leo: July 23–August 22

Virgo: August 23–September 22

Libra: September 23–October 22

Scorpio: October 23–November 21

Sagittarius: November 22–December 21

Capricorn: December 22–January 19

Aquarius: January 20–February 18

Pisces: February 19–March 20

The energy of a sign can be invoked into your body to infuse your body and mind with its nature, and make you more adept and skillful in the area of life that falls under the sign, and the potency of a sign can be used to treat specific injuries and illnesses in various parts of the body. The association of the zodiac signs with zones of the human body is thousands of years old in astrology. This division can be quite useful when working magic for healing purposes. In kinesic magic, I have used the traditional locations of the signs on the human body (figure 6.5).

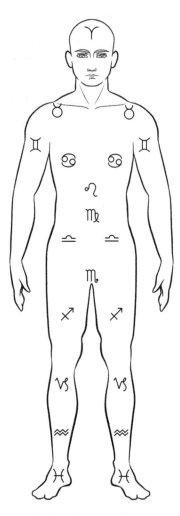

Figure 6.5: Zodiac Signs on the Human Body

General Meanings and Uses of the Signs

Each sign of the zodiac has its own unique nature that derives from its polarity, the combination of its element and its quality, and its mythological associations. The signs are linked to various parts of the human body and influence health, but they also can be used to influence different types of human emotions and behavior.

Aries: Cardinal Fire (Red)

Aries is generally regarded as the first sign of the zodiac. Of course, the zodiac is a wheel, and a wheel has no beginning and also no end. But the sign of Aries ascends the eastern horizon in the spring, the nominal start of the year. Again, the year of the seasons is a wheel, and a wheel has no start and no end. The wheel of the zodiac turns through the seasons of the year, so that each sign ascends in the east in its own time.

Figure 6.6: Aries, the Ram

The ancient symbol representing this sign is the ram (figure 6.6). Some of the understanding of this sign may be derived from the behavior of this animal, which is noted for its strong horns, which it butts against rivals during mating and uses to fight off predators. The ram is known for its virility. The ramming of its head mimics the action of the penis during sex. It is a thrusting, penetrating, forceful energy that knocks aside obstacles and knocks open doors.

This thrusting nature of the ram is supported by the quality and the element of this sign. The Fire element is energetic and expansive, and the Cardinal quality is linear and direct. This gives a thrusting, fiery force that seeks to pierce through veils and knock aside barriers.

Use the energy of this sign to achieve an ambition, to fight for a cause, or to overcome the opposition of others. This is the imposition of will by force, but it lends itself best to helping the underdog and righting injustices.

In the human body, Aries presides over the head and all its internal organs and parts, but in particular the eyes. The energy of Aries can be applied to cure headaches, earaches, and toothaches, as well as eye strain and sinus pressure. It can focus and sharpen the working of the mind. The heat of Aries can help dry up the sinuses during head colds.

The planet Mars rules this sign in astrology. This means that the force of Mars is less hindered and more free to act in Aries than in the signs that Mars does not rule. Scorpio is also ruled by Mars, but Scorpio is on the solar side of the zodiac, whereas Aries is on the lunar side. This means that the action of Mars in Aries is more lunar in nature and the action of Mars in Scorpio more solar.

Sagittarius: Mutable Fire (Yellow)

This is the ninth sign of the zodiac, moving around it counterclockwise from Aries, but it is useful to examine the signs in their elemental groups for purposes of comparison.

Figure 6.7: Sagittarius, the Bowman

Sagittarius is represented by the figure of an archer drawing back a bowstring to release an arrow. The symbol of the arrow is key to understanding this sign. It flies in a straight line with vigorous force and has a penetrating aspect, just like the energy of Aries, but whereas Aries batters down barriers, Sagittarius pierces them. An arrow may be shot in any direction. When released into the air, no one can be certain where it will fall. It lacks the persistence of the ram—when it strikes something hard and unyielding, it is blunted and broken.

The symbolism of the bow itself must also be considered. It relies on energy that is slowly accumulated by pulling back the bowstring, then suddenly released. Once released toward its objective, that energy is spent, and must be accumulated again by drawing back the bowstring.

The force of this sign is active, energetic, and questing but also unfocused and easily distracted. There is a tendency for it to fly off in all directions. It is more a mental energy than the fiery force of Aries. In Sagittarius, the fire is the fire of ideas, the fire of possibilities, the fire of intention.

The energetic expansion of elemental Fire is frustrated and held in check by the vacillating Mutable quality, which will not easily allow it to focus on only one goal until that goal has been achieved. The burning here is on the surface—deep emotional commitment is not present, nor is there sustained persistence. It is the energy of heated debate where successive points are made quickly, one after another, for a cumulative effect.

Use the energy of this sign in works requiring quickness, enthusiasm, and accuracy, and where there is a need to make a point or an example. It is suitable for sports that require an accurate aim and repeated, brief periods of focus, such as basketball, target shooting, hunting, archery, or darts. Use it where you wish to make your mark in society or in your profession. Use it when you wish to try something new in your life.

This sign presides over the region of the hips and the thighs, particularly the muscles of this part of the body, and also the liver. Call upon it to build up strength in the thighs and to help heal problems with hip joints and the liver.

In astrology, the planet Jupiter rules this sign, which lies on the solar side of the zodiac.

Leo: Fixed Fire (Blue)

The figure that represents the sign Leo in the zodiac is the male lion, who even in ancient times was regarded as noble and the natural ruler of the animal kingdom. The energy of this sign is that of this mythological lion, the king of beasts. For those who are familiar with C. S. Lewis's Narnia novels, this energy is exemplified in the character of Aslan, a wise lion king.

Figure 6.8: Leo, the Lion

The elemental Fire of Leo is moderated by the Fixed quality, which holds its explosive, expansive tendencies in check. This causes the Fire to burn steadily and constantly, like the fire in a furnace. It can be relied upon not to sputter out and fail.

You find this kind of Fixed Fire in good rulers and in those who have natural leadership ability. It is not something that can be learned or faked. It requires honesty and integrity of purpose, along with unwavering courage and steadfast determination. It can be abused by the person who possesses it, and when it is, the result is intimidation, a dominating of others, or even bullying.

This is not the Fire of Aries that batters down and overcomes or the Fire of Sagittarius that makes incisive hits that pierce to the bone; it is the slow, steady Fire that burns with a constant heat, the fire of determination to prevail, of being in control of situations, of leadership, and of natural command that exists as a part of the personality, not requiring artificial titles or external support. Leo rules because he was born to rule.

Use this energy to take control of situations, to energize public opinion, to steer the direction of business operations, to maintain order over groups, to gain the support of an audience or a team, to cause others to follow your decisions, or to assume a leadership role.

Leo is traditionally assigned to the rear portions of the heart region of the human body, which includes the upper spine but not the shoulders. Its energy can be used to treat problems with the heart, the back, and the spine, and also problems with anxiety and phobias.

In astrology, the Sun is the ruler of Leo. It is the Sun that defines the solar side of the wheel of the twelve signs of the zodiac. Unlike most of the other planets, the Sun rules only a single sign, Leo.

Cancer: Cardinal Water (Blue-Purple)

This sign has for its symbol in modern astrology the crab. In older illustrations, it is not always easy to tell what the exact species is, and sometimes the symbol is said to be a crayfish or lobster. For example, the creature that rises from the pool in the older Tarot designs of the Moon card looks more like some kind of crayfish than a crab.

Figure 6.9: Cancer, the Crab

The important point is that the creature is hard-shelled, has pincers, or claws, and lives beneath the surface of the water. These aspects of its nature define the energy of this sign. Its energy is to hold things together, to maintain the center, to stand its ground. The Water in this sign is modified by the Cardinal energy, which causes it to move in one direction, like a river.

This sign is linked to the home and the family in astrology. The crab gathers things and holds them within its claws, defending them fiercely against those who try to take them. The motives behind this purpose are often concealed from view, but they are deep and potent.

Call forth this energy in matters that relate to the home and family, to calm and set-tle disputes between siblings or between parents and children, teenage rebellions, and resentment and rivalry in domestic situations. Use it when seeking to acquire something for your house or living space and to deal with any issues that arise in whatever you think of as your space.

Cancer rules the front of the torso, which involves the breasts and also the stomach region. Its energy can help with problems relating to the breasts and can soothe heart-burn and stomach cramps.

In astrology, the Moon rules the sign of Cancer. This is the only sign ruled by the Moon, and the Moon's presence in this sign defines the lunar side of the zodiac.

Pisces: Mutable Water (Red-Orange)

The Age of Christianity that extends back two thousand years or so corresponds more or less with the astrological Age of Pisces. It is perhaps no coincidence that the pope wears a hat in the shape of a fish, or that in the Gospels the leader of the apostles is Peter, who was a fisherman. Fish appear sexless due to their lack of external genitalia. The priests of the Roman Catholic Church similarly strive to appear sexless by adopting long, feminine robes and denying themselves sexual union.

Figure 6.10: Pisces, the Fishes

The pervading features of Pisces are modesty and service to others. The energy here is the emotional energy of elemental Water, which is tender and caring, busying itself with small but necessary tasks. The best model of Mutable Water is the wave, which rolls onto the beach, slows, then rolls back, then comes in again and repeats this back and forth motion endlessly and tirelessly.

There is no arrogance in this sign. Its motive is to help others, with no thought of gain. It is service for its own sake. In excess, it can be too humble and modest.

The symbol of Pisces is two fish swimming in opposite directions. This is often referred to as the fishes, to indicate two different species of fish. However, the two fish are usually depicted in illustrations as identical, and therefore may also be conceived to be the same fish swimming back and forth, back and forth, in a Mutable motion.

The energy of this sign can be used to induce modest behavior and introspection. It can prompt acts of charity, kindness, and service to others without desire for notice or reward. Use it to induce a judge or jury to show mercy, to moderate the behavior of a tyrant, or to assist the humble and the weak.

On the human body, the traditional influence of Pisces is over the feet. In a more general sense, Pisces presides over the mechanism of fluid retention in the body. Its energy can be used to treat all problems of the feet, such as arthritis in the toes, gout, fungus, ingrown toenails, and swelling of the feet.

In astrology, the planet Jupiter rules the sign of Pisces on the lunar side of the zodiac.

Scorpio: Fixed Water (Yellow-Green)

What happens to water when it remains sitting in one place for a long time? It becomes corrupted and poisonous; it becomes undrinkable; it becomes so clouded and murky that its depths cannot be seen; it may even turn black. The life of water is motion, and when it is fixed into place, it dies.

Figure 6.11: Scorpio, the Scorpion

The symbol of this sign is the scorpion, an insect with a sting in its tail. No insect is more feared or hated. It is feared because it can cause great pain or death, and hated because it strikes unpredictably and with seeming malice.

What can the nature of the scorpion tell us about this sign? Its energy is potent yet concealed, held in reserve, hidden from sight. It tends toward harsh or even hateful actions, especially where revenge is a factor. Resentment is stored up, perhaps for years, before finally being released in a violent action, and the moment of that action is unpredictable. There is emotional control here—not a lack of emotions but the ability to control the expression of emotions. There is also strength of will, determination, and the ability to focus on a single purpose for prolonged periods, even for years.

This is not always a harmful or malicious energy, but it does have this tendency to a greater degree than any other sign of the zodiac. The emotional nature of elemental Water, when prevented from flowing freely, tends to become corrupted, and dark feelings may arise and be brooded upon in secret. At its best, this is the energy of those who pursue their goals in the face of all opposition and disappointment, undaunted by failure.

The energy of this sign may be called forth to exact vengeance for wrongs committed. It is not a sign of justice, however—it is a sign of retribution. It is the energy of a lynch mob, or of someone who believes they have been wronged striking back in a secret, underhanded manner at the person who wronged them. This is the sign of actions committed under the cover of darkness, whether they are justified or unjustified. It is lashing out in secret, and then drawing back to watch the result. It is the energy of those determined to get their way, by fair means or foul, and it enables the achievement of hidden purposes, especially violent purposes, that have been brooded over.

Scorpio rules the sexual parts of the body and the anus. In general, it presides over human sexuality and excretion. It can be used to treat physical problems with erectile dysfunction and difficulty with conceiving a child, as well as hemorrhoids, genital warts, and infections of the penis and vagina. It can also be used to lessen the severity of the symptoms of sexually transmitted diseases.

In astrology, the planet Mars rules the sign of Scorpio on the solar side of the zodiac.

Libra: Cardinal Air (Green)

The Cardinal quality of elemental Air causes it to expand and rise. Air is the element associated with intellectual activity, with ideas and plans and schemes. This is a clear, bright, clean energy, a fresh breeze blowing away smoke and fog.

Figure 6.12: Libra, the Scales

The symbol of this sign is a set of scales, the pans of which are empty and in perfect balance. Their emptiness suggests the air all about them, and their equality indicates balanced forces, evenness of intellectual judgment, fairness, and justice. The scales have long been the symbol of the goddess Justice.

The energy of this sign is harmonious and honest, seeking an outcome of events with fairness for all involved. It is also the love of intellectual activity, particularly that found in the order and harmony of the arts.

Use the energy of this sign in matters having to do with finding a true judgment, the fair division of property, legal judgments, in conducting debates fairly and openly, when seeking justice for others or yourself, or to escape an unfair or malicious decision or judgment. This energy cannot be used for deception or malice. It is too balanced and open for such abuse. Use it to find the truth, wherever it lies.

Libra presides over the kidneys, the lower back, and in general the skin. Its energy can be helpful in treating skin conditions, kidney stones and infection, and lower back pains.

In astrology, the planet Venus is the ruler of the sign of Libra, which is located on the solar side of the zodiac.

Gemini: Mutable Air (Purple)

The airy element of this sign gives it an intellectual aspect, but the Mutable quality causes that energy to be wayward and unpredictable, darting this way and that, vacillating in opinions and beliefs, pulled first by one pole and then by its opposite, with equal force.

Figure 6.13: Gemini, the Twins

The symbol of Gemini is that of two young twin boys. It has been associated with the mythical founders of Rome, the brothers Romulus and Remus, and also with the twin stars Castor and Pollux. Twins, in mythology at least, tend to be of opposite natures, or at least very different from each other. This is not so much true of reality, where twins often show very similar interests and behaviors, but the reality of the myth is what concerns us in magic. In myth, twins are opposite poles.

There is quickness of apprehension here, the ability to respond in a superficial way to any possible situation that may arise. There is quickness in finding solutions, quickness in coming up with explanations, and quickness of wit. This energy is very persuasive. It is warm and bright and clever, and easily charms others. It has enthusiasm for intellectual games and new ideas but may soon lose interest and turn to some other diversion.

In a practical sense, this is a useful sign for works involving speech giving, advertising, selling, and anything that requires persuasion of others, especially when persuading them to act on impulse. It is helpful to get a proposal accepted, to get hired for a job, to gain government or private grants and appointments, to achieve political office, or to win over others, especially for a social cause or project.

The twins of Gemini preside over the arms and the lungs. Use this energy to address smoking issues and cigarette addiction, diseases of the lungs, and asthma and other breathing problems, such as fluid in the lungs. It can be used to help clear the lungs during bouts of the flu, bad colds, or pneumonia, and also for any problems that afflict the shoulder joints, arms, and hands, such as shoulder separation, arthritis in the hands, numbness of the fingers, or elbow pain.

In astrology, the planet Mercury is the ruler of the sign of Gemini, located on the lunar side of the zodiac.

Aquarius: Fixed Air (Orange)

When Air is fixed motionless, it tends to become stifling and a bit oppressive. Air in a closed room is stuffy. Odors linger. Air naturally wants to expand, just as water wants to flow. This may cause this sign to express indolence or even laziness. However, Air is the intellectual element, and when held in place for a long time, the result can be deep thought and deep study.

Figure 6.14: Aquarius, the Waterbearer

The symbol of Aquarius is that of a person pouring water out of a large pot. This may seem odd for an Air sign, but the water represents emotions. The figure is emptying out his emotions, or purging himself of his passions. Water also represents cleansing, and by pouring out his water, the figure is cleansing himself of irrational impulses.

This is the most rational and the most intellectual of all the signs. There is a love for knowledge here, not so much for the uses it can be put to but for its own sake. This is the sign of philosophy and reasoned debate. Because Air is naturally expansive, even when fixed into place (for example, when it fills a balloon), the general energy here is honest and forthcoming, but it can be unpredictable in its expression.

This sign can be used in works connected with teaching, philosophy, ensuring fairness in debates and intellectual contests, schoolwork, and studies, or when seeking a position of trust or authority.

Traditionally, Aquarius is associated with the lower legs and with the circulatory system, except for the heart, which falls under Leo. The circulatory system was probably linked to this sign because problems with circulation often show up as swelling of the lower legs. Use this energy to address problems with ankle sprains, cramps in the calves, shin splints, and pain in the Achilles tendon, and also with swollen legs and varicose veins.

In astrology, the planet Saturn is the ruler of the sign of Aquarius, located on the lunar side of the zodiac.

Capricorn: Cardinal Earth (Yellow-Orange)

The Cardinal quality expressed through elemental Earth results in a climbing or ascending energy, such as mountain climbing or rock climbing. It is the tendency to rise above the horizon and seek out new vistas and new lands to explore. It is thinking outside the box, and acting to leave the box.

Figure 6.15: Capricorn, the Goat

The symbol of this sign is the mountain goat, which is the most able climber in all the animal kingdom. Goats can scale almost sheer cliffs, using only the tiniest footholds. Domestic goats climb trees and often find their way onto the roofs of houses. The climbing ability of this animal is almost miraculous.

The intellectual energy of this sign is devoted to practical goals, which are pursued step by step until achieved. There is great determination to surmount obstacles, no matter how daunting they may appear. Those motivated by the energy of this sign do not give up. They tend to be introspective and do not talk about their hopes and fears, but their determination to succeed can move mountains.

Use the energy of this sign in works of magic to overcome obstacles, recover from setbacks, to strengthen resolve, or to achieve difficult goals of a practical nature. Use it to counter and neutralize self-doubt or the doubt of others. It is also helpful when pursuing long-term career goals.

Capricorn is specifically associated with the knees, but more generally may be said to preside over the entire skeletal system of the body, including the teeth. Its energy may be used to address problems and pains with the knee joints, the teeth, and the jaw, and also with bruised, cracked, or broken bones, as well as weak or soft bones.

In astrology, the planet Saturn is the ruler of the sign of Capricorn, located on the solar side of the zodiac.

Virgo: Mutable Earth (Blue-Green)

This is a darting, back-and-forth energy on the surface of the Earth. It is quick and limited by the Mutable quality, but given weight and force by the Earth element. Those who possess this energy appear to be much more intelligent than they really are due to their excellent memory, which allows them to retain and call up obscure facts at a moment's notice. There is a broadness of interests here, but no great depth.

Figure 6.16: Virgo, the Virgin

The symbol of this sign is the goddess Virgo, a goddess of the harvest. She is often shown carrying a sheaf of ripe wheat, which she holds in the same way she would hold a newborn child. Grains are the bounty of the earth, but they spring from its surface, not its depths—plowing and planting never penetrate far into the ground, and in this sense express the superficial nature of this sign. Wheat has been called the staff of life, a reference to the shape of a stalk of wheat, which resembles a staff, and to the fact that wheat feeds and sustains the lives of a large portion of humanity, particularly in the West.

Planting and harvesting are cyclical activities and express the Mutable nature of this sign. In order to get life from the ground, it must be fertilized. Before you can take out, you must put in.

The energy of Virgo is analytical and precise. Each individual grain of wheat must be picked up and brought together to fulfill the harvest. There is precision here, attention to detail, and unflagging energy to tie up loose ends. Every t is crossed and every i dotted. This energy can become frustrated and angry when it encounters sloppiness or indifference to detail.

Use this energy when dealing with matters that are highly intricate, detailed, or complex to ensure accuracy and precision. Use it in the organization or storage of information and in sorting out confusing problems, as well as in dealing with libraries, computers, government bureaucracy, rules and regulations, permits, red tape, and delays in business.

Virgo is associated with the digestive system of the body, particularly the upper intestines, where nutrients are absorbed, and also the spleen. It is not so much concerned with the stomach in its function as the receiving container of food, which is ruled by Cancer, or the lower intestine in its function of excretion, which is presided over by Scorpio, but with the function of the digestive system to break down and absorb the nutritional value of foods. The energy of this sign can help with problems of food poisoning, indigestion, and food allergies.

In astrology, the planet Mercury rules the sign of Virgo, located on the solar side of the zodiac.

Taurus: Fixed Earth (Red-Purple)

When a bull plants its feet, it is hard to move, and when it gets moving, it is hard to stop. The traditional symbol for this sign of the zodiac is the bull. In ancient times, the bull represented brute force. Oxen were used for the hardest farm labors. The bull was known for its proverbial strength, stamina, and stubbornness.

Figure 6.17: Taurus, the Bull

The Fixed quality of elemental Earth is unmoving. It will stand its ground with a dogged determination that cannot be shaken, not even by common sense. This energy does not care greatly about logic or reason, and it does not even care much about right and justice, but it does care about keeping what it owns, and never retreating in the face of a challenge. The expression of this energy is fearless, but at times unwise.

There is patience here, and empathy for others provided they do not challenge the position of who or what embodies this energy. The Earth element makes this energy practical in seeking to achieve its purposes.

This energy can be used to resist those who seek to displace you or overthrow you. It is also useful for building up databases and accumulating practical information. It is not so much an energy for charging through barriers, like the energy of Aries, but more for standing up to and resisting the charge of others. Use it in dealing with teachers and other authority figures who try to intimidate you. Use it to prevent anyone from riding roughshod over a business or organization. Use it to stand your ground, or to help someone else stand their ground.

Taurus presides over the neck, the throat, and the upper shoulders, but not so much the shoulder joints, which are given over to Gemini. It also influences the thyroid gland. Its energy can be applied to cure problems with neck strain, shoulder cramps, and voice strain. It can soothe the throat of those suffering from colds or the flu.

In astrology, the planet Venus rules the sign of Taurus, which falls on the lunar side of the zodiac.

Workings: The Twelve Zodiac Signs

The following workings are designed to make you completely familiar with the nature of the zodiac signs, their component energies, their interrelationships with one another, and their occult correspondences. In particular, it is important to become familiar with the colors associated with the signs in kinesic magic, so that visualizing the color of a sign will help to evoke its power.

Working 1: Zodiac Glyphs

The purpose of this working is to associate in your mind on the subconscious level the signs of the zodiac with their astrological symbols.

Cut twelve squares of white paper, each about two inches (five centimeters) in size. With a black marker, draw the glyph of a different sign of the zodiac on one side of each slip of paper. You can also use blank, white file cards for this purpose—cut each file card into six parts that are roughly square. Mix up the squares of paper or cardboard and stack them into a pile on a table face down.

Adopt the sitting posture in front of the table. Take a few silent breaths to calm and focus your thoughts.

With your right hand, turn over the top square to expose its zodiac sign. If it is sideways or upside down, rotate it so that it is right-side up from your perspective. Return your hand to your right knee.

Gaze at the glyph of the sign for several slow breaths, then inhale deeply and vibrate the name of the sign audibly, drawing out its vowels to make your chest and throat resonate. If necessary for reasons of privacy, you may vibrate the name in a whisper without using your vocal cords. This will mute the sound, but you will still feel the vibration of the vowels.

Close your eyes and visualize the black glyph floating in space before you, its edges shimmering with white light to define it against your inner darkness. Contemplate the glyph for a minute or so with your eyes closed. Make it three-dimensional by giving it thickness and texture, as though it were carved from a plate of black stone.

Open your eyes, and with your right hand, turn over the second slip of paper to expose its symbol. Orient it so that it is upright from your perspective and return your hand to your knee.

Imprint it in your mind for several silent breaths, then vibrate the name of the sign. Close your eyes and visualize the glyph glowing around the edges against your inner darkness for a minute or so. Make it three-dimensional in your mind.

Do this for all twelve of the zodiac signs.

To end the exercise, relax your mind and take a few silent breaths, then stand up.

Working 2: The Glyphs on the Zodiac Wheel

Take the twelve squares of paper bearing the zodiac symbols that you made for the first working and mix them up. Place the pile on a table, face down.

Adopt the sitting posture in front of the table and draw a couple of silent breaths to prepare your mind.

Visualize a glowing circle of white light on the surface of the table with the pile of paper squares at its center. This circle should be around twelve inches (thirty centimeters) in diameter.

With your right hand, turn over the first square of paper. As you hold it in your hand, say aloud the name of the sign that is inscribed on it, and speak its quality and element. For example, for the glyph of the sign of Pisces you would say, "Pisces, Mutable Water."

Place the square on the imaginary circle of light in the position its sign has on the standard wheel of the zodiac. In the usual orientation of the zodiac, Aries is on the left, Libra on the right, Capricorn at the top, and Cancer at the bottom.

Go through all twelve slips of paper, turning each one over and speaking aloud the name of its sign as you place it in its proper position on the wheel of the zodiac. If you forget the location for any of the glyphs, refer briefly to one of the illustrations of the zodiac earlier in this chapter and then continue.

When all the glyphs have been correctly placed, return your right hand to your knee and spend several minutes silently contemplating the relationships of the signs to one another.

Draw a few slow, silent breaths and stand up to end the working.

Working 3: Zodiac Trines

Assume the sitting posture facing east, and take a few silent breaths to prepare. Close your eyes.

Visualize the wheel of the zodiac as it is usually represented, with Aries on the left side, Libra on the right, Capricorn at the top, and Cancer at the bottom. Move your focus of attention from one sign to another as you establish this visualization.

When you can clearly imagine the zodiac in your mind, draw an equilateral triangle starting with Aries and proceeding to Sagittarius, then down to Leo, and then back to Aries to complete the triangle. This triangle points to the left. Visualize the three line segments of this triangle in glowing red. This is the Fire triangle of the zodiac, which connects the three Fire signs.

Hold this triangle in your mind against the backdrop of the zodiac wheel for a minute or so, with the glyphs of the three Fire signs at its points glowing red. Do not worry about the colors of the individual glyphs; just imagine all three of them as red. Allow the triangle and the red coloring of the glyphs to fade, but continue to sustain the wheel of the zodiac in gray or black lines that are edged in silver.

Draw a second triangle beginning with Cancer and proceeding to Pisces, then to Scorpio, and then back to Cancer. This triangle points downward. Visualize its line segments glowing bright blue as you draw them. As its points touch the three signs, they also glow blue. This is the Water triangle, which links the three Water signs.

Sustain the blue triangle and the three blue Water signs, then let the triangle and the color fade, but continue to hold the wheel of the zodiac clearly in your imagination.

Draw a third triangle that begins at Libra, goes to Gemini, then to Aquarius, and then back to Libra, and color it bright yellow as you draw it. This triangle points to the right. As it touches each sign, the glyph of the sign glows bright yellow as well. This is the Air triangle of the zodiac, which links the three Air signs.

Contemplate this yellow triangle and its three yellow signs for a minute or so, then allow the triangle and the color to fade away, but sustain the wheel of the zodiac.

Draw a fourth triangle beginning at Capricorn and going to Virgo, then to Taurus, and back to Capricorn. Visualize its line segments and its signs glowing a deep green color. This triangle points upward. It is the Earth triangle of the zodiac, which links the three Earth signs.

Contemplate the Earth triangle and its signs for a minute or so, then allow the triangle and the green to fade away. Continue to visualize the gray or black wheel of the zodiac edged in glowing silver for a few seconds.

Open your eyes, take several silent breaths, and stand up to end.

Working 4: Zodiac Squares

This is similar to the third working, but it involves the three squares of the qualities on the wheel of the zodiac.

Begin in the same way by adopting the sitting posture facing the east. Take a few silent breaths to prepare, and close your eyes.

In your mind, create the wheel of the zodiac against a black backdrop. It is best to imagine it in a neutral gray or black but edged with silver radiance so that it is visible. Establish the glyphs of the twelve signs upon this wheel by moving your attention from sign to sign to reinforce each glyph in your imagination.

When you have the zodiac clearly established, draw a square with line segments that begin at Aries and go to Capricorn, then to Libra, then to Cancer, and back to Aries. As you draw this square, color it bright red, and as it touches each sign, color the glyph of that sign red as well. This is the Cardinal square of the zodiac, which joins the four Cardinal signs.

Sustain this square for a minute or so in your imagination, then allow it and the red color to fade but continue to visualize the zodiac.

Draw a second square with line segments that begin at Sagittarius and move to Virgo, then to Gemini, then to Pisces, and back to Sagittarius. Color its segments bright yellow, and the glyph of each sign it touches yellow as well. This is the Mutable square of the zodiac, which joins the four Mutable signs.

Contemplate this yellow square and its signs for a minute or so, then allow it to fade.

Draw a third square with line segments that start at Leo and move to Taurus, then to Aquarius, then to Scorpio, and back to Leo. Color this square bright blue as you draw it, and as it touches each sign, make the glyph of the sign bright blue as well. This is the Fixed square of the zodiac, which joins the four Fixed signs.

Hold this blue square and its signs clearly in your mind for a minute or so, then allow it to fade away.

Open your eyes, take a few silent breaths to relax, and stand up to end.

Working 5: Zodiac Colors

For this working you will need a set of colored pencils, colored markers, or crayons in the following six colors: red, yellow, blue, green, purple, and orange. Set them on a table with a blank sheet of white paper and a pencil.

Adopt the sitting posture in front of the table and take a few silent breaths to compose your mind.

From memory, use the pencil to draw the wheel of the zodiac on the paper. Make two concentric circles with about three-quarters of an inch (two centimeters) between them, and divide the space between the circles into twelve equal segments. Mark all twelve signs in their proper places inside these segments.

Also working from memory, use the colored pencils, markers, or crayons to lightly shade in each sign with its proper color. Begin with the primary colors: Aries (red), Sagittarius (yellow), and Leo (blue). Go on to the secondary colors: Libra (green), Gemini (purple), and Aquarius (orange). Finally, shade in the tertiary colors by combining the primaries with the secondaries: Cancer (blue-purple), Pisces (red-orange), Scorpio (yellow-green); Capricorn (yellow-orange), Virgo (blue-green), Taurus (red-purple).

Resume the sitting posture, close your eyes, and visualize the colored zodiac you just made for several minutes.

Open your eyes, take a few silent breaths, and stand to end.

Working 6: Ruling Planets

Face east in the standing posture. Take a few silent breaths to focus your mind.

Shift into the prayer posture. Visualize a large glyph of Leo floating in the air on your right side, and a large glyph of Cancer floating on your left. Mentally color these glyphs with their zodiac colors, blue for Leo and blue-purple for Cancer.

Change to the ankh posture, and as you do so, form your right hand in the gesture of the Sun and your left hand in the gesture of the Moon. Speak these words:

> Sun in Leo rules the day;
> Moon in Cancer rules the night.

Resume the prayer posture. Allow the glyphs of Leo and Cancer to fade, and visualize in their zodiac colors the glyph of Virgo (blue-green) on your right and the glyph of Gemini (purple) on your left.

Change to the ankh posture and make the gesture of Mercury with both hands. Speak these words:

> Mercury in Virgo rules beneath the Sun;
> Mercury in Gemini rules beneath the Moon.

Go back to the prayer posture and visualize Libra (green) on your right and Taurus (red-purple) on your left.

Change to the ankh posture, with both hands in the gesture of Venus. Speak these words:

> Venus in Libra rules beneath the Sun;
> Venus in Taurus rules beneath the Moon.

Resume the prayer posture and visualize the glyph of Scorpio (yellow-green) on your right and the glyph of Aries (red) on your left.

Go to the ankh posture, with both hands in the gesture of Mars, and speak these words:

> Mars in Scorpio rules beneath the Sun;
> Mars in Aries rules beneath the Moon.

Resume the prayer posture and visualize the glyph of Sagittarius (yellow) on your right side and the glyph of Pisces (red-orange) on your left.

Change to the ankh posture, with both hands in the Jupiter gesture, and say these words:

Jupiter in Sagittarius rules beneath the Sun;
Jupiter in Pisces rules beneath the Moon.

Return to the prayer posture and visualize the glyph of Capricorn (yellow-orange) on your right and the glyph of Aquarius (orange) on your left.

Shift to the ankh posture, with both hands in the gesture of Saturn, and say these words:

Saturn in Capricorn rules beneath the Sun;
Saturn in Aquarius rules beneath the Moon.

Move into the closing posture, with your forearms crossed, your hands closed into fists, and your eyes shut. Spend a minute visualizing the wheel of the zodiac with the ruling planets on the solar and lunar sides of the wheel. Starting with Leo and Cancer, visualize each pair of signs in succession upward from the bottom of the zodiac.

Shift into the standing posture and take a few silent breaths to relax and end.

Working 7: Drawing Down the Zodiac

The purpose of this working is to draw the zodiac down from the heavens and manifest it on the surface of the Earth. Of course, the zodiac can never be brought down from the sphere of the fixed stars, but a material expression of it can be reflected and impressed on the floor or ground around you as a magic circle.

Bear in mind that when the zodiac is brought down from the heavens to the Earth, it is inverted or reflected. This means the signs proceed in the opposite direction around the zodiac wheel when you stand above it, looking down at it.

Adopt the standing posture facing east in an open space where you can move in all directions unobstructed. Take a few silent breaths to focus your thoughts.

Change to the invoking posture and draw down the energy of the Cardinal sign Aries into the space where you are working.

Shift into the scrying posture and visualize the red glyph of Aries through the window of the scrying triangle you have formed between your hands.

Take a step forward to the east, then shift into the manifesting posture by taking a step with your right foot and extending your arms, with the triangle between your hands turned flat. Use your will to transfer the glyph of Aries in the triangle down onto the floor in front of you, and visualize it glowing there.

Step back into the prayer posture and contemplate the glyph of Aries on the floor for a minute or so. Take a full step backward into your original starting position and resume the standing posture.

Rotate on your own axis a quarter turn clockwise so that you face south. Change to the invoking posture and draw down the energy of Cancer. Shift to the scrying posture and visualize the glyph of Cancer through the scrying triangle between your hands.

Take one step forward to the south. Change to the manifesting posture as you step forward again on your right leg and extend your hands. Project the glyph of Cancer downward from the triangle between them onto the floor.

Step back into the prayer posture to contemplate the glyph of Cancer on the floor for a minute or so. Take a full step backward to your starting position and resume the standing posture.

Rotate a quarter turn clockwise to face west. Change to the invoking posture and draw down the energy of Libra. Shift to the scrying posture and scry the glyph of Libra through the triangle between your hands.

Take one full step forward toward the west. Step forward again on your right leg into the manifesting posture as you project the glyph of Libra onto the floor. Step back into the prayer posture and contemplate the glyph of Libra for a minute, then take a full step backward and resume the standing posture.

Rotate clockwise to face the north. Change to the invoking posture and draw down the energy of Capricorn. Shift into the scrying posture and visualize the glyph of Capricorn through the scrying triangle. Take a full step forward toward the north while still holding the scrying triangle with your hands. Step forward on your right leg as you shift into the manifesting posture, and project the glyph of Capricorn from the triangle down onto the floor. Step back into the prayer posture and contemplate the glyph for a minute. Take a full step backward to your original position and assume the standing posture.

Rotate clockwise to face the east once again. Assume the ankh posture and visualize the complete reflected circle of the zodiac around you on the floor. Bear in mind that the sequence of the signs will be inverted. Contemplate the complete zodiac as a magic circle around you for a minute or so.

Change into the macrocosm posture, and as you do so, release the glyphs of the zodiac from the floor to rise upward into the heavens around you. See their energies streaming upward to the stars.

Shift to the closing posture and contemplate your inner stillness for a minute.

To end the working, adopt the standing posture and take a few silent breaths to relax.

Working 8: Planets in the Signs

This is a mental working designed to give an understanding of the planets in the signs of the zodiac. You should focus on only one planet at a time on its day of the week, but you can work successively with all seven planets on their own days. It is good practice to perform this working over the span of a week, focusing on a different planet on each of the seven days.

Assume the standing posture facing east, and take a few silent breaths to focus your mind on what you are about to do. Make the gesture of the planet that corresponds to the day of the week with both hands while in the standing posture.

Visualize the glyph of Aries in the air before you in its red color, and mentally draw the glyph of the planet in front of it in its color while holding the standing posture. The glyph of the planet is superimposed on the glyph of the sign in the same way the actual planets in the heavens move in front of the signs of the zodiac. Consider the qualities of the sign Aries in combination with the qualities of the planet, and formulate three words that best express these combined energies. Say the words out loud when you have decided on them.

For example, suppose you are working with the Moon on a Monday. The active energy of the Moon is cool and veiled. It works beneath the surface. However, the backdrop energy of Aries is fiery and direct. How can these energies be reconciled? The cool energy of the Moon cannot actually become hot, but the action of the lunar energy can take on a more frenetic, aggressive expression. You might choose words such as "delirious, fevered, obsessive" to describe these combined energies.

Do the same for all twelve of the signs of the zodiac in succession. As you perform this working over a period of weeks and months, your understanding of the planets in the signs will become more precise and refined, and the three words you choose to describe each pairing will evolve.

To end, open your hands to release the planetary gesture and take a few silent breaths to relax your mind.

Working 9: Invoking the Birth Sign

This working is a useful way to reset yourself in much the same way you would reset a computer that has become slow or nonfunctional due to coding conflicts. It is a way to reconnect with who you are in an astrological sense.

Start by facing the east in the standing posture and take a few silent breaths to focus your mind.

Shift into the prayer posture and visualize the glyph of your birth sign floating in the air in front of you. It should be colored with the color of its sign. You may find it useful to close your eyes as you contemplate your birth sign for a minute or so.

Change to the invoking posture, and use the power of your will to draw down the energy of your birth sign through the top of your head so that if fills your body. Imagine that your body is hollow, and that the energy of the sign swirls like colored smoke to every part of it, even to the tips of your fingers and toes.

When you are filled with the energy of your birth sign, shift to the closing posture and contemplate the nature of this energy for a minute or so.

Resume the standing posture and take a few silent breaths to end. The energy of your birth sign will gradually fade away over the next several hours until it has returned to a normal level within you.

Working 10: Zodiac Color Breathing

Face east in the standing posture and take several silent breaths to focus your mind on the work ahead. It is best to do this exercise with your eyes closed.

Change to the prayer posture. Visualize your transparent aura lying in its normal position an inch or two away from your skin all around your body. Your aura will be colored by your emotions, but for this exercise visualize it as colorless.

Breathe in silently through your nose to fill your lungs, then exhale through your mouth using a slow, audible breath while shifting smoothly into the opening posture. Remember to expand your stance from a narrow to a medium distance as you change postures. Use the sound of the controlled release of your breath to help expand your aura outward into a sphere about your body. The inner surface of this transparent sphere should be visualized about a foot (thirty centimeters) away from the palms of your hands when your arms are fully extended to the sides.

Move back into the prayer posture with a silent inhalation through your nose. As you silently exhale through your nose, visualize the bright red glyph of Aries floating in the darkness in front of you. Imagine it about three feet (ninety centimeters) away and about a foot in height.

Inhale slowly through your mouth with an audible breath, and as you do so, draw in the red color of the sign to fill your lungs with Aries energy. Continue to visualize the glyph of Aries in the darkness in front of you.

Shift back to the opening posture as you slowly exhale through your mouth with an audible breath, and use this sound to push the red energy of Aries out from your lungs through your hands so that it fills your aura and changes it to a transparent red. Continue to visualize the red glyph of Aries as you do so.

Change back to the prayer posture with a slow, silent inhalation through your nose, and let the color fade from your aura and the glyph of Aries fade from your mental field of view. As you silently exhale through your nose, visualize the glyph of Taurus floating in the darkness in front of you. It is colored red-purple.

Inhale with a slow, audible breath through your mouth, and as you do so, fill your lungs with the red-purple color of Taurus. Be aware of it filling your chest as you continue to visualize the glyph of Taurus.

Move smoothly into the opening posture as you exhale with an audible breath through your mouth. As you do so, use your flat palms to push the red-purple energy of Taurus out of your lungs and into your aura, which changes to a transparent red-purple color.

Continue in this way through all twelve signs of the zodiac, alternating audible cycles of breath through your mouth with silent cycles through your nose. The silent inhalations clear your aura of color, and the silent exhalations focus your mind on the glyphs of the zodiac signs. The audible inhalations pull the color of the glyph into your lungs, and the audible exhalations push this color out through your palms to fill your aura.

This alternation of audible and silent breath cycles should be slow and rhythmic. You should strive for a kind of slow breaststroke motion with your arms, as though swimming. As you audibly exhale, extend your hands outward in front of you, back to back, and open them to the sides, palms turned outward. As you audibly inhale, bring your hands directly inward in front of your chest to make the prayer gesture, with palms pressed together.

If you have difficulty breathing through your nose, or your nose is completely obstructed, you can draw silent breaths through you mouth by breathing slowly and keeping your lips and throat open.

You may become lightheaded. If you find yourself becoming dizzy, pause the exercise, open your eyes, and stand in the prayer posture, breathing normally until you regain your balance, or if necessary abandon the exercise and sit down.

When you have filled your aura with the red-orange energy of Pisces, allow the color to fade as you inhale a silent breath and resume the prayer posture. Exhale silently and shift into the opening posture one final time while visualizing your colorless expanded aura.

Shift into the closing posture, and as you do so, pull your aura back down close to your body into its normal resting position. Contemplate your transparent aura in its normal state for a minute or so, with eyes closed and forearms crossed, hands closed into fists.

Change to the standing posture and take a few silent breaths to relax your mind and end.

CHAPTER 7
ZODIAC HAND GESTURES

ALL OF THE HAND GESTURES OF THE zodiac signs can be made with either hand. Usually, when made with the left hand, which is the hand of reception, they attract the occult energies of the signs, and when made with the right hand, which is the hand of projection, they project these energies. But when using the general invocation posture, the energies are attracted with both hands, and when using the general banishing posture, they are banished with both hands. This applies to the elements and planets as well.

It is easiest to learn how to form the hand gestures by holding up your hand in front of you so you can see its palm. You should practice the gestures with both hands until they become second nature. Remember not to strain your hands when making these gestures. They should be almost effortless. If your fingers want to bend, allow them to bend rather than trying to force them straight. Refer to the accompanying illustrations.

When you manipulate the occult energies of the twelve signs, you use the same general procedures that have already been described for the five elements and seven planets. The gesture of the sign you are working with will usually be made with both hands, unless you are alchemically transmuting the energy of one sign into the energy of another. Then you make the sign that is the source of the energy with the left hand and the sign the energy is to be transmuted into with the right hand.

The energy of one sign may be changed by spiritual alchemy into the energy of another sign, the energy of one planet into another planet, and the energy of one element into another element, but you should not try to transmute the energy of an element into that of a planet or sign, or the energy of a planet into that of an element or sign, or the energy of a sign into that of a planet or element. The difference between the qualities of the energies from one occult set to another is too great to allow a natural transmutation between sets.

The postures you adopt determine the flow of the energy that has been attracted into the left hand. The general procedures when working with occult energies are invoking, banishing, receiving, projecting, channeling, and balancing. Since they have already been described in great detail in previous chapters, I will not say much about them here.

The signs have always been associated with different parts of the human body in astrology. For this reason, the occult energies of the zodiac are especially beneficial when seeking to treat or cure sickness, pain, or infirmity in a particular organ or location in the body. This is done by projecting the energy into the painful or sick place through the right hand, ideally by laying the right hand directly against the skin over the ailing place. If necessary, the energy can be projected a short distance through the air by means of a ray, which takes the astral form of a twisting stream of energy, but it is more effective for healing if the hand is actually laid on the sick part of the body.

The signs of the zodiac move in a circle around the heavens along the celestial equator, occupying at various times of the year all directions, so there is no definite single point of the compass to assign to a sign. Like the planets, the signs are above the spheres of the elements, and do not have a fixed direction on the surface of the Earth, as do the four lower elements. It is possible to arbitrarily assign directions of the compass to the signs, as I did in the seventh working of the previous chapter, but I do not believe it is really necessary in kinesic magic.

Aries

Hand Gesture of Aries

Extend your index finger, with your other fingers folded down against your palm, and fold your thumb over the tops of your middle and ring fingers.

Figure 7.1: Hand Gesture of Aries

Element: Fire

Quality: Cardinal

Polarity: Positive

Sect: Lunar

Color: Red

Body: Head

Meditation on Aries

Begin in the standing posture. It does not matter which way you face, but for general practice you can face east, if it is convenient. Take a few deep breaths to clear your mind.

Bring your feet together and spread your arms wide in the ankh posture, with both hands formed in the gesture of Aries. Speak the following incantation:

Noble Aries, come to me,
Reveal yourself that I may see.

Expand your stance to a medium distance and bring your hands together in the scrying posture. Gaze through the upright triangle you have formed between your thumbs and index fingers. Visualize the traditional figure of Aries, the white ram with curling horns, as though seeing it through the astral window of the scrying triangle. Hold this image in your mind for a minute or two, then recite this incantation:

The thrusting ram parts the way,
His potent horns win the day.

Narrow your stance as you shift into the prayer posture, with hands pressed flat together in front of your breast and gaze lowered. Visualize trapped between your palms the bright red astrological symbol of Aries, as though you were holding it flat between your hands. Be aware of the heat and active thrusting energy of this fiery Cardinal sign on your palms. Feel its courage and self-confidence, its optimism and determination. Hold this posture for a minute or two.

Widen your stance and change to the loosing posture. As you raise your hands above your head and part your palms, release the sign to expand and vanish upward. Speak this incantation:

Noble Aries, from me fly;
Return above into the sky.

Adopt the closing posture and hold it for a minute, with feet together, eyes shut, forearms crossed at the wrists in front of your chest, and hands closed into fists. Be aware of your inner stillness.

Shift to the standing posture and take a few silent breaths to end the meditation on Aries.

Sagittarius

Hand Gesture of Sagittarius

Extend your index and middle fingers together, with your ring and small fingers folded down to your palm. Cross the end of your thumb over your ring finger.

Figure 7.2: Hand Gesture of Sagittarius

Element: Fire

Quality: Mutable

Polarity: Positive

Sect: Solar

Color: Yellow

Body: Thighs

Meditation on Sagittarius

Begin in the standing posture and take a few silent breaths to clear your mind.

Shift into the ankh posture, with both hands in the gesture of Sagittarius. Speak the following incantation:

Noble Sagittarius, come to me,
Reveal yourself that I may see.

Widen your stance and bring your hands together in the scrying posture. Gaze through the upright triangle and visualize the traditional figure of Sagittarius, the bearded centaur drawing back his bow to release his arrow. Hold this image in your mind for a minute, then speak the following incantation:

The archer draws his bow of yew,
His eye is keen, his aim is true.

Shift into the prayer posture and visualize between your palms the bright yellow astrological symbol of Sagittarius. Be aware of the hot vibrating energy of this fiery Mutable sign on your palms. Feel its openness and love of freedom, its curiosity and optimism. Hold this posture for a minute.

Change to the loosing posture and release the sign to expand and vanish upward. Speak this incantation:

Noble Sagittarius, from me fly;
Return above into the sky.

Adopt the closing posture and hold it for a minute with your mind empty.

Shift to the standing posture and take a few silent breaths to end the meditation on Sagittarius.

Leo

Hand Gesture of Leo

Extend your index, middle, and ring fingers together, touching each other, and fold your small finger down. Place the tip of your thumb on the nail of your small finger. Your small finger and thumb do not need to touch your palm when making this gesture. Allow your hand to bend slightly to avoid strain.

Figure 7.3: Hand Gesture of Leo

Element: Fire

Quality: Fixed

Polarity: Positive

Sect: Solar

Color: Blue

Body: Heart

Meditation on Leo

Begin in the standing posture. Take a few silent breaths to clear your mind.

Spread your arms wide in the ankh posture, with both hands in the gesture of Leo. Speak the following incantation:

Noble Leo, come to me,
Reveal yourself that I may see.

Bring your hands together in the scrying posture and visualize through the upright triangle you have formed between your thumbs and index fingers the traditional figure of Leo, a golden male lion with his head surrounded by a tawny mane. Hold this image in your mind for a minute, then recite this incantation:

The lion is king of all the land,
Against his wrath no foe can stand.

Shift into the prayer posture, with hands pressed flat together in front of your breast and gaze lowered. Visualize between your palms the bright blue astrological symbol of Leo, as though you were holding it flat between your hands. Be aware of the steady, constant heat and deep reserves of energy of this fiery Fixed sign on your palms. Feel its generosity, its good cheer, its creativity and steady passion. Hold this posture for a minute.

Shift into the loosing posture and release the sign to expand and vanish upward. Speak this incantation:

Noble Leo, from me fly;
Return above into the sky.

Adopt the closing posture and hold it for a minute, with eyes shut and arms crossed at the wrists in front of your chest, your hands closed into fists.

Shift to the standing posture and take a few silent breaths to end the meditation on Leo.

Cancer

Hand Gesture of Cancer

Extend your small finger and fold down your index, middle, and ring fingers, holding them gently in place, with your thumb across the end segments of all three. Again, do not strain your fingers. You must be able to maintain these gestures for extended periods of time.

Figure 7.4: Hand Gesture of Cancer

Element: Water

Quality: Cardinal

Polarity: Negative

Sect: Lunar

Color: Blue-purple

Body: Breast and stomach

Meditation on Cancer

Begin in the standing posture. It does not matter which way you face, but for general practice you can face east, if it is convenient. Take a few silent breaths to clear your mind.

Spread your arms wide in the ankh posture, with both hands in the gesture of Cancer. Speak the following incantation:

Noble Cancer, come to me,
Reveal yourself that I may see.

Bring your hands together in the scrying posture and gaze through the upright triangle you have formed between your thumbs and index fingers. Visualize the traditional figure of Cancer, the green crab with upraised pincers emerging from the water, as though seeing it through the astral window of the scrying triangle. Hold this image in your mind for a minute or two, then recite this incantation:

The grasping crab grabs hold to keep,
Loss of loved ones makes her weep.

Shift into the prayer posture, with hands pressed flat together in front of your breast and gaze lowered. Visualize between your palms the blue-purple astrological symbol of Cancer, as though you were holding it flat between your hands. Be aware of the coolness and deep stillness of this watery Cardinal sign on your palms. Feel its deep emotions, its loyalty, its sympathy, and its empathy for others, but also its tenacious ability to endure. Hold this posture for a minute or two.

Move into the loosing posture and release the sign to expand and vanish upward. Speak this incantation:

Noble Cancer, from me fly;
Return above into the sky.

Adopt the closing posture and hold it for a minute, with eyes shut and arms crossed at the wrists in front of your chest, your hands closed into fists.

Shift to the standing posture and take a few silent breaths to end the meditation on Cancer.

Pisces

Hand Gesture of Pisces
Extend your small and ring fingers together and touching while folding down your index and middle fingers, with your thumb pressed across their end segments. Your hand will be slightly bent, which is fine—don't strain to make it flat.

Figure 7.5: Hand Gesture of Pisces

Element: Water
Quality: Mutable

Polarity: Negative

Sect: Lunar

Color: Red-orange

Body: Feet

Meditation on Pisces

Begin in the standing posture and draw a couple of slow, silent breaths to clear your mind.

Spread your arms wide in the ankh posture, with both hands in the gesture of Pisces. Speak the following incantation:

> Noble Pisces, come to me,
> Reveal yourself that I may see.

Bring your hands together in the scrying posture and gaze through the upright triangle between your thumbs and index fingers. Visualize the traditional figure of Pisces—two fishes of different species, one above the other, facing in opposite directions—as though seeing it through the astral window of the triangle. Hold this image in your mind for a minute, then recite this incantation:

> The fishes swim both left and right,
> They serve by day and watch by night.

Shift into the prayer posture, with hands pressed flat together in front of your breast and gaze lowered. Visualize between your palms the red-orange astrological symbol of Pisces, as though you were holding it flat between your hands. Be aware of the cool, eddying currents of this watery Mutable sign on your palms. Feel its gentleness, its compassion, its trust, its intuition and selfless dedication to serving others. Hold this posture for a minute or so.

Move into the loosing posture and release the sign to expand and vanish upward. Speak this incantation:

> Noble Pisces, from me fly;
> Return above into the sky.

Adopt the closing posture and hold it for a minute.

Shift to the standing posture and take a few silent breaths to end the meditation on Pisces.

Scorpio

Hand Gesture of Scorpio

Fold down your index finger and put your thumb across its last segment. Extend your middle, ring, and small fingers together and touching each other.

Figure 7.6: Hand Gesture of Scorpio

Element: Water

Quality: Fixed

Polarity: Negative

Sect: Solar

Color: Yellow-green

Body: Reproductive organs

Meditation on Scorpio

Begin in the standing posture and draw a few silent breaths to prepare.

Spread your arms wide in the ankh posture, with both hands formed in the gesture of Scorpio. Speak the following incantation:

Noble Scorpio, come to me,
Reveal yourself that I may see.

Bring your hands together in the scrying posture and gaze through the upright triangle you have formed between your thumbs and index fingers. Visualize the traditional figure of Scorpio, a large black scorpion with its tail raised, as though seeing it through the astral window of the scrying triangle. Hold this image in your mind for a minute, then recite this incantation:

> The scorpion broods upon his foe
> Until he strikes the killing blow.

Shift into the prayer posture, with hands pressed flat together in front of your breast and gaze lowered. Visualize between your palms the yellow-green astrological symbol of Scorpio, as though you were holding it flat between your hands. Be aware of the motionless pool of energy of this watery Fixed sign on your palms. Feel its depth, its secretiveness, its hidden passion that can become violent if corrupted by jealousy or suspicion. Hold this posture for a minute or so.

Move into the loosing posture and release the sign to expand and vanish upward. Speak this incantation:

> Noble Scorpio, from me fly;
> Return above into the sky.

Adopt the closing posture and hold it for a minute, with eyes shut and arms crossed at the wrists in front of your chest, hands closed into fists.

Shift to the standing posture and take a few silent breaths to end the meditation on Scorpio.

Libra

Hand Gesture of Libra

Extend your fingers together, then fold the middle finger downward toward your palm and hold it in place with the end of your thumb. Do not strain your hand—your middle finger does not need to touch your palm. Your three extended fingers should be parallel to each other.

Figure 7.7: Hand Gesture of Libra

Element: Air

Quality: Cardinal

Polarity: Positive

Sect: Solar

Color: Green

Body: Hips and kidneys

Meditation on Libra

Begin in the standing posture. Take a few silent breaths to clear and focus your mind.

Spread your arms wide in the ankh posture, with both hands in the gesture of Libra. Speak the following incantation:

Noble Libra, come to me,
Reveal yourself that I may see.

Bring your hands together in the scrying posture and visualize through the upright triangle you have formed between your thumbs and index fingers the traditional figure of Libra, a woman in a white gown who holds a set of scales in her hand, as though seeing this figure through the astral window of the scrying triangle. Maintain this image in your mind for a minute or so, then recite the following incantation:

The balance weighs both truth and lies,
The goddess sees with open eyes.

Shift into the prayer posture, with hands pressed flat together in front of your breast and gaze lowered. Visualize between your palms the bright green astrological symbol of Libra, as though you were holding it flat between your hands. Be aware of the fresh, purifying energy of this airy Cardinal sign on your palms. Feel it blow away injustice and impose in its place order, fairness, and balance. Hold this posture for a minute or so.

Move into the loosing posture and release the sign to expand and vanish upward. Speak this incantation:

> **Noble Libra, from me fly;**
> **Return above into the sky.**

Adopt the closing posture and hold it for a minute, with eyes shut and arms crossed at the wrists in front of your chest, your hands closed into fists.

Shift to the standing posture and take a few silent breaths to end the meditation on Libra.

Gemini

Hand Gesture of Gemini

Extend all four fingers together and fold the ring finger down toward your palm. Hold it in place by pressing the end of your thumb over its nail. The other extended fingers should be parallel to each other. Do not strain your hand.

Figure 7.8: Hand Gesture of Gemini

Element: Air

Quality: Mutable

Polarity: Positive

Sect: Lunar

Color: Purple

Body: Lungs and arms

Meditation on Gemini

Begin in the standing posture. Take a few silent breaths to focus your mind.

Bring your feet together and spread your arms wide in the ankh posture, with both hands making the gesture of Gemini. Speak the following incantation:

> Noble Gemini, come to me,
> Reveal yourself that I may see.

Open your feet to a medium stance and bring your hands together in the scrying posture. Gaze through the upright triangle you have formed between your thumbs and index fingers. Visualize the traditional figures of Gemini, young twin brothers standing side by side, as though seeing them through the astral window of the scrying triangle. Hold this image in your mind for a minute, then recite this incantation:

> The gentle twins are wise and kind;
> Shown the truth, they change their mind.

Shift into the prayer posture, with hands pressed flat together in front of your breast and gaze lowered. Visualize between your palms the purple astrological symbol of Gemini, as though you were holding it flat between your hands. Be aware of changeable breezes blowing this way and that from this airy Mutable sign between your palms. Feel its interchange of ideas, its quick communication, the breath of its words, its movement from place to place, its adaptability to circumstances, its ability to access and respond to change. Hold this posture for a minute or so.

Move into the loosing posture and release the sign to expand and vanish upward. Speak this incantation:

> Noble Gemini, from me fly;
> Return above into the sky.

Adopt the closing posture and hold it for a minute, with eyes shut and arms crossed at the wrists in front of your chest, your hands closed into fists.

Shift to the standing posture and take a few silent breaths to end the meditation on Gemini.

Aquarius

Hand Gesture of Aquarius

Extend the four fingers together and fold your middle and ring fingers down toward your palm. Hold these fingers in this position with your thumb across their end segments. Do not worry about them touching your palm. Just keep your hand relaxed and your extended index and small fingers parallel to each other.

Figure 7.9: Hand Gesture of Aquarius

Element: Air

Quality: Fixed

Polarity: Positive

Sect: Lunar

Color: Orange

Body: Shins and ankles

Meditation on Aquarius

Begin in the standing posture. Take a few silent breaths to clear and focus your mind.

Bring your feet together and spread your arms wide in the ankh posture, with both hands making the gesture of Aquarius. Speak the following incantation:

Noble Aquarius, come to me,
Reveal yourself that I may see.

Widen your stance and bring your hands together in the scrying posture. Gaze through the upright triangle you have formed between your thumbs and index fingers. Visualize the traditional figure of Aquarius, a man who pours water onto the ground from a large pitcher, as though seeing it through the astral window of the scrying triangle. Hold this image in your mind for a minute or so, then recite this incantation:

The waterbearer takes his stand,
He pours his wisdom on the land.

Shift into the prayer posture, with hands pressed flat together in front of your breast and gaze lowered. Visualize between your palms the orange astrological symbol of Aquarius, as though you were holding it flat between your hands. Be aware of the cooling swirl of this airy Fixed sign around your palms. Feel its intellectual energy and ability to solve problems without emotion, its originality and independence of thought and action, its impulse to debate and educate. Hold this posture for a minute or so.

Move into the loosing posture and release the sign to expand and vanish upward. Speak this incantation:

Noble Aquarius, from me fly;
Return above into the sky.

Adopt the closing posture and hold it for a minute, with eyes shut and arms crossed at the wrists in front of your chest, your hands closed into fists.

Shift to the standing posture and take a few silent breaths to end the meditation on Aquarius.

Capricorn

Hand Gesture of Capricorn
Extend the four fingers together and fold your middle and small fingers down toward your palm. Hold these fingers in this position, with your thumb across their end segments. Do not worry about them touching your palm. Just keep your hand relaxed and your extended index and ring fingers parallel to each other.

Figure 7.10: Hand Gesture of Capricorn

Element: Earth

Quality: Cardinal

Polarity: Positive

Sect: Solar

Color: Yellow-orange

Body: Knees

Meditation on Capricorn

Begin in the standing posture. Take a few silent breaths to prepare yourself.

Bring your feet together and spread your arms wide in the ankh posture, with both hands in the gesture of Capricorn. Speak the following incantation:

Noble Capricorn, come to me,
Reveal yourself that I may see.

Widen your stance and bring your hands together in the scrying posture. Gaze through the upright triangle you have formed between your thumbs and index fingers. Visualize the traditional figure of Capricorn—the mountain goat with his long beard, standing upon a prominence—as though seeing it through the astral window of the scrying triangle. Hold this image in your mind for a minute, then recite this incantation:

The nimble goat can never stop;
Ambition drives him to the top.

Shift into the prayer posture, with hands pressed flat together in front of your breast and gaze lowered. Visualize between your palms the yellow-orange astrological symbol of Capricorn, as though you were holding it flat between your hands. Be aware of the rich, dark soil ready to burst forth with dormant life in this earthy Cardinal sign on your palms. Feel its ambition, self-discipline, practical judgment, determination, and ability to realize ideas on the material level. Hold this posture for a minute or two.

Move into the loosing posture and release the sign to expand and vanish upward. Speak this incantation:

Noble Capricorn, from me fly;
Return above into the sky.

Adopt the closing posture and hold it for a minute, with eyes shut and arms crossed at the wrists in front of your chest, your hands closed into fists.

Shift to the standing posture and take a few silent breaths to end the meditation on Capricorn.

Virgo

Hand Gesture of Virgo

Extend the four fingers together and fold your index and ring fingers down toward your palm. Hold these fingers in this position, with your thumb across their end segments. Do not worry about them touching your palm; just keep your hand relaxed and your extended middle and small finger parallel to each other.

Figure 7.11: Hand Gesture of Virgo

Element: Earth
Quality: Mutable

Polarity: Negative

Sect: Solar

Color: Blue-green

Body: Bowels

Meditation on Virgo

Begin in the standing posture and draw a few silent breaths to clear your mind.

Close your stance and spread your arms wide in the ankh posture, with both hands formed in the gesture of Virgo. Speak the following incantation:

> Noble Virgo, come to me,
> Reveal yourself that I may see.

Widen your stance and bring your hands together in the scrying posture. Gaze through the upright triangle you have formed between your thumbs and index fingers. Visualize the traditional figure of Virgo, a young virgin in a flowing white gown who carries a sheaf of ripe wheat, as though seeing it through the astral window of the scrying triangle. Hold this image in your mind for a minute or so, then recite this incantation:

> The modest virgin sifts the soil
> And sows her seeds with honest toil.

Shift into the prayer posture, with hands pressed flat together in front of your breast and gaze lowered. Visualize between your palms the blue-green astrological symbol of Virgo, as though you were holding it flat between your hands. Be aware of the fine, dry dust of this earthy Mutable sign on your palms. Feel its meticulous and analytical nature, its attention to fine detail, its ability to sift through the chaff to find the grain. Hold this posture for a minute or so.

Move into the loosing posture and release the sign to expand and vanish upward. Speak this incantation:

> Noble Virgo, from me fly;
> Return above into the sky.

Adopt the closing posture and hold it for a minute, with eyes shut and arms crossed at the wrists in front of your chest, your hands closed into fists.

Shift to the standing posture and take a few silent breaths to end the meditation on Virgo.

Taurus

Hand Gesture of Taurus

Extend your four fingers, then fold your index and small fingers near your palm, holding them down with your thumb across their end segments. Your extended middle and ring fingers should be touching each other. Do not try to fully straighten your hand. The gesture must be effortless so that it can be held for extended periods of time without cramping.

Figure 7.12: Hand Gesture of Taurus

Element: Earth

Quality: Fixed

Polarity: Negative

Sect: Lunar

Color: Red-purple

Body: Neck and throat

Meditation on Taurus

Begin in the standing posture. Take a few silent breaths to clear your mind.

Spread your arms wide as you adopt the ankh posture, with both hands formed in the gesture of Taurus. Speak the following incantation:

Noble Taurus, come to me,
Reveal yourself that I may see.

Bring your hands together in the scrying posture and gaze through the upright triangle you have formed between your thumbs and index fingers. Visualize the traditional
figure of Taurus, a powerful black bull, as though seeing it through the astral window
of the scrying triangle. Hold this image in your mind for a minute or so, then recite this
incantation:

The brave bull stands before the gate,
He will not yield for love or hate.

Shift into the prayer posture, with hands pressed flat together in front of your breast
and gaze lowered. Visualize between your palms the red-purple astrological symbol of
Taurus, as though you were holding it flat between your hands. Be aware of the weight
and hardness of this earthy Fixed sign on your palms. Feel its stable, reliable solidity, its
patience, practicality, and sense of responsibility, but also its possessiveness and stubborn
refusal to be moved. Hold this posture for about a minute.

Move into the loosing posture and release the sign to expand and vanish upward.
Speak this incantation:

Noble Taurus, from me fly;
Return above into the sky.

Adopt the closing posture and hold it for a minute, with eyes shut and arms crossed
at the wrists in front of your chest, your hands closed into fists.

Shift to the standing posture and take a few silent breaths to end the meditation on
Taurus.

Workings: Zodiac Hand Gestures

In the previous chapter you practiced gaining familiarity with the natures and interrelationships of the twelve signs of the zodiac. The set of workings below will give you
practice in using the hand gestures of the signs to concentrate and manipulate their
unique energies in useful ways, such as absorbing or expelling zodiacal energies from
the body, projecting these energies into materials or objects to infuse or charge them,

filling a space, coloring the aura, projecting the energies of the signs into another person, balancing opposite energies, invoking elemental trines, and associating the energies with the parts of the human body.

Working 1: Absorbing Energy

Sometimes the vitality in the area of the body ruled by a sign will be weak. It may feel tired. There may be a dull ache. There may be trembling in that region. You can strengthen that part of the body by absorbing into it the occult energy of the sign that rules over it.

Begin in the standing posture. It does not matter which way you face, but for purposes of practice, face the east. Take a few slow, silent breaths.

With both hands, form the gesture of the sign you wish to practice with. Adopt the spiral invoking posture, with your left hand raised and your right hand pressed over your heart-center. Use the force of your will to draw down the energy of the sign and send it in a contracting spiral through your upper body and into your heart-center. Visualize the energy flowing through you in a stream that is the color associated with the sign. Fill the sphere of your heart-center so that it turns from soft white to the color of the sign.

Shift to the closing posture to cut off this flow of energy once your heart-center is full, with hands closed into fists and crossed at the wrists, head bowed, and eyes shut. Hold this posture for a minute as you visualize the sphere of your heart-center spinning rapidly counterclockwise and deeply tinted with the sign's color.

Once again, make the gesture of the sign with both hands. Adopt the ankh posture, opening your arms out to the sides, with palms turned forward. Mentally draw the energy from your heart-center and send it either down your left side to the lower regions of your body or up your right side to the higher regions, depending on where the region of the sign is located.

For example, the red energy of Aries would be drawn up the right side to your head, the red-orange energy of Pisces would be sent down the left side to your feet, and the blue energy of Leo would be expanded in a counterclockwise-turning circle (when viewed from the back) in the central region of your torso.

Shift into the prayer posture and visualize that part of your body you have charged with zodiacal energy filled with that energy and glowing with its color. It should feel energized, refreshed, and cleansed. Recite the following incantation:

Twelve signs are in the zodiac wheel,
With the power of _____ (name of zodiac sign), my _____ (part of body) I heal.

Insert in the blank spaces the name of the zodiac sign and the name of the part of your body corresponding with the sign. For example, if you are infusing into yourself the energy of Capricorn, you would say, "With the power of Capricorn, my knees I heal."

Shift into the standing posture and take a few silent breaths to end.

Working 2: Purging Energy

It sometimes may happen that a region of your body that is ruled by a sign of the zodiac becomes supercharged with the energy of that sign. This can occur if you've been brooding over the health of that part of your body or over the activities and attitudes of life associated with the sign. The part of your body associated with the sign will feel tense, charged, tight, and over-full, like your stomach when you eat too much. It may become visibly swollen.

For example, too much Aries energy will give you a pounding headache, too much Taurus will make your neck and shoulders stiff, too much Gemini will give you tightness in your breathing or cramps and aches in your arms or hands, and so on.

It can be helpful to purge from the part of your body afflicted in this way the excess zodiacal energy of the sign set over it. The process is somewhat similar to the medieval practice of blood-letting, which was designed to purge the body of excess humours, but there is no need to break the skin in this working.

Begin in the standing posture facing east, and take a few silent breaths to calm and focus your mind.

Make the gesture of the sign you wish to purge from your body with both hands and shift into the ankh posture. Visualize that part of your body that feels tight or hot or that aches. Use your will to send the excess energy of the sign ruling that part of your body to your heart-center in a stream that is the color associated with the sign.

If the area is above your heart-center, send it down your left side, but if the area is below your heart-center, send it up your right side. Visualize the sphere of your heart-center spinning more rapidly and turning the color of the sign. If it happens that the excess of energy is in your heart region (the region of Leo), concentrate it into the sphere of your heart-center and visualize the sphere changing from soft white to blue.

Change to the prayer posture, with palms pressed together in front of your chest, head bowed, and gaze lowered. Speak the following incantation:

The wheel of the zodiac has no end,

From my _____ (part of body), the power of _____ (name of zodiac sign) I send.

For example, if you were purging the energy of Virgo from your bowel region to relieve constipation, the second line of the incantation would be, "From my bowels, the power of Virgo I send."

Form the gesture of the sign with both hands. Shift into the spiral banishing posture, with your left hand pressed to the center of your chest and your right hand directed downward at your side. Draw the energy of the sign into your left hand by the power of your will and send it through your upper body in an expanding spiral so that it exits downward in a stream from your right hand and flows into the ground below you.

When your heart-center has returned to its normal state, adopt the closing posture, with hands closed in fists, forearms crossed at the wrists, and eyes closed, to cut off the flow of energy from your body. Contemplate the energy balance in the region of your body you have just purged.

Shift to the standing posture and take a few slow, silent breaths to end.

Working 3: Infusing Water

At times it may be useful to infuse water with the occult energy of a sign of the zodiac, so that the energy will be transferred into the body of the person who drinks the water, or upon whom the water is sprinkled or wiped. In this way, the energy of a sign can be intensified in a person who is sick and may benefit from an increase of that energy. It is a process similar in purpose to the blessing of water in the Catholic Church, but by using this magic technique, water may be charged with the energy of any sign of the zodiac (or any element or planet, for that matter) to achieve a more specific result.

Wash your hands before beginning. The water you seek to infuse with zodiacal energy must be fresh and clean. It should be placed in an open basin or other vessel on your right side. It is best if you are able to actually dip your right hand into the water, but you can project the energy into the water over a short distance if necessary.

Begin as usual in the standing posture and calm yourself with a few slow, silent breaths.

Adopt the prayer posture and speak the following incantation:

_____ (Name of sign) turns about the pole,
As above, so below.

In the blank space, speak the name of the sign whose energy you will infuse into the water. For example, if you were infusing the water with the energy of Libra to use it to reduce the pain of a kidney stone or help expel the stone from the body, you would say, "Libra turns about the pole." The reference is, of course, to the celestial pole that is marked by Polaris, the North Star.

Make the gesture of the sign with both hands and adopt the magician posture, with your left hand raised above your head and your right hand touching the water in the basin or at least pointing down at the water. Gaze directly forward, and concentrate on the nature of the sign and its energy. Use the force of your will to pull down the energy of the sign and pass it through your body without charging any of your body centers.

The flow of energy should be visualized in the color associated with the sign. It enters your left hand and traces a contracting spiral to your heart-center, which it circles counterclockwise. Then it flows in an expanding spiral down your right arm and out your right hand into the water. Visualize the water changing to the color of the sign.

When the water is charged with as much zodiacal energy as possible, make the closing posture to cut off the flow. Hold this pose for a minute or so with your eyes shut while visualizing the charged water in the basin.

Move to the standing posture and take a few silent breaths to end.

Pour the water into a clean vessel that can be closed tightly and place it in a cool, dark place until you use it. It will hold the infusion of zodiacal energy for several days.

Working 4: Charging a Stone

Charging a stone with zodiacal energy is done in much the same manner as infusing water. Select a stone to contain the energy of the sign you wish to concentrate within it. Rounded, flat beach stones work well, but any shape will do. To practice this exercise, you may wish to select twelve stones, one for each zodiac sign.

It is easiest if the stone you use is in harmony with the nature of the sign. You can match the stone to the sign it represents by its color—the true color of a stone can be determined by wetting it. Or you can gather twelve stones of the same type and paint the astronomical glyphs of the signs on the stones in their colors. Bear in mind that this color matching is merely a helpful aid—any stone can be charged with any of the twelve signs.

The stone should be chosen for its intended task. Stone holds an occult charge for a very long time. That is why it was used by the ancients for their altars and statues of their gods, and why there are stone circles, and why a stone that fell from the heavens is venerated today by Muslims at Mecca.

You may intend to give the charged stone to someone to carry, so that person will have the benefit of its occult energy. In this case, it must be small enough to hold in the hand and put into a pocket. Or you may wish to bury the charged stone beneath the threshold of a house or set it inside a fireplace within a house, in which case the stone may be larger.

Place the stone you will charge on your right side, either on the floor beside your right foot or on a table so that you can touch it with your right hand.

Begin in the standing posture facing east and take a few silent breaths to calm and focus your mind.

Shift into the prayer posture to recite the following brief incantation. Speak the name of the sign in the blank space.

> **This stone lay long beneath your light,**
> _____ (Name of sign), **charge it with your might.**

Form both hands in the gesture of the sign with which you will charge the stone, and adopt the magician posture. Concentrate on the nature of the sign, and with the force of your will, draw the energy of the sign down into your left hand and send it circling your heart-center and out your right hand into the stone. Visualize the energy that flows through your body and out your right hand as a twisting stream in the color associated with the sign. The charge will be stronger if you actually touch your right hand to the stone.

Adopt the closing posture to cut off the flow of energy through your body, and spend a minute or so visualizing the energy of the sign that fills the stone, with your wrists crossed and eyes closed.

Shift to the standing posture and take a few silent breaths to end.

Wrap the stone in a white cloth of linen or cotton, such as a clean napkin or hand-kerchief, and put it away in a dark place until you make use of it. The stone will remain charged indefinitely, although over time the intensity of the charge will diminish.

Working 5: Coloring a Space

To infuse a space, location, or building with zodiacal energy, stand in the middle of the place in the standing posture and take a few slow, silent breaths.

Concentrate on the nature of the sign. When you have filled your mind with its characteristics, form the gesture of the sign with both hands and shift into the general invoking posture, with both arms raised above your head in a V-shape. Gaze heavenward.

Use the force of your will to draw down the energy of the sign, so that it swirls down all around you in an expanding vortex and fills the place you seek to charge. This vortex turns counterclockwise, when viewed from above. Visualize it tinting the air around you with the color of the sign, so that the color fills every corner of the space you charge.

Move into the prayer posture and speak this incantation, putting the name of the sign in the blank space of the second line.

> Starlight falls upon this place;
> Noble _____ (name of sign) fills this space.

Make the closing posture and contemplate the charged space for a minute or so with your eyes shut.

Move into the standing posture and take a few deep, slow breaths to end.

The zodiacal charge with which you have filled the space or building will remain dominant for a day and a night, after which the location will gradually regain its normal balance of occult energies.

Working 6: Coloring the Aura

At times it may be useful to infuse your aura with the energy of one of the zodiac signs. That energy will predominate within you while it fills your aura and will influence your thoughts, emotions, visions, and dreams, coloring them with the nature of the sign.

Begin in the standing posture facing east, and take a few silent breaths to calm and focus your mind.

Move into the prayer posture and recite this invocation. Put the name of the sign in the blank space.

The stars reflected in the sea,
The light of _____ (name of sign) covers me.

Make the gesture of the sign with which you will color your aura with both hands and shift into the macrocosm posture, with your hands together just above your head. Your eyes are rolled upward while you continue to face straight forward, and your feet and legs are together to form a single column.

Concentrate on the nature of the sign, and use your will to draw its energy down from the starry sphere of the heavens into your hands. Visualize this energy as a transparent ball about twelve inches in diameter that surrounds your hands just above your head. The ball is colored with the energy of the sign.

Shift into the microcosm posture, spreading wide your arms and legs while holding the gesture of the sign with your hands. Gaze forward. Allow the sphere of energy above your head to spread itself over the entire surface of your aura. It flows and spreads over your head, shoulders, and torso, down your arms to your hands, and down your legs to your feet. Visualize your entire aura tinted with the color of the sign.

Change to the closing posture and contemplate your tinted aura with your eyes shut and forearms crossed, your hands closed into fists, for a minute or so.

Move into the standing posture and take a few slow, silent breaths to end.

Your aura will remain tinted with the energy of the sign for several hours. If you perform this exercise just prior to meditation or going to bed, it will tend to provoke visions or dreams colored by the nature of the sign. If you do it just before giving a speech, participating in a competition or debate, or undertaking some other task, the energy of the sign will influence how well you perform that task.

Working 7: Infusing a Person

It may be useful to draw down the energy of a zodiac sign and infuse it directly into another human being, if that person is deficient in that occult energy and out of balance as a result.

Begin in the standing posture, with the person into whom you will channel the energy of the sign on your right side. Take a few slow, silent breaths to prepare.

Shift to the prayer posture and recite this brief incantation, which expresses your purpose:

Great _____ (name of sign) of the starry band,
Infuse this _____ (man/woman/child + person's name) by my right hand.

The name of the sign goes in the blank space in the first line, and you speak "man" or "woman" or "child" in the second line, depending on who you are treating. You can also include the name of the person in the second line if you know the name—for example, "Infuse this man John Smith by my right hand," or "Infuse this child Ellen Jones by my right hand."

Make the gesture of the sign with both hands and adopt the magician posture, with your receptive left hand raised high above your head and your projective right hand pointed at the person or actually touching the person. It is best to point at the part of the body ruled by the sign you will draw down from the heavens. For example, if you are dealing with Aries, you would point at or touch the head; if dealing with Taurus, the neck; and so on.

Because you are not pointing directly downward with your right hand, the magician posture is somewhat modified from its ideal form, but its function is the same.

Use the power of your will to draw down from the sphere of the fixed stars the energy of the sign indicated by your hand gesture, and send it flowing through your body and into the person you are infusing with that energy. Continue to channel the energy into the person until you sense that it is sufficient for your purpose.

Move to the closing posture to cut off the flow of energy through your body, and stand for a minute or so with forearms crossed at the wrists, hands closed into fists, and eyes shut as you visualize the energy of the sign inside the body of the person into whom you have projected it.

Adopt the standing pose and take a few silent breaths to end.

Working 8: Balancing Opposite Signs

The purpose of this exercise is to balance and integrate the energies of opposite signs on the wheel of the zodiac. Balance is vital to our lives. Without balance, we fall over, in both a literal and a figurative sense. Without balance, there is no power, a truth that every boxer, wrestler, and martial artist knows from experience.

Select a sign to work with on the solar side of the zodiac, and its opposite sign on the lunar side. For example, if you choose Capricorn on the solar side, the opposite sign is Cancer on the lunar side. The pairs of opposites are Leo/Aquarius, Virgo/Pisces, Libra/Aries, Scorpio/Taurus, Sagittarius/Gemini, and Capricorn/Cancer.

Begin in the standing posture facing east, and take a few slow, silent breaths to compose yourself.

Make the gesture of the solar sign with your right hand and the gesture of the lunar sign with your left hand, and as you do so, shift into the general invoking posture. Visualize around your right hand a sphere of energy that is colored with the color of the solar sign, and a similar sphere of energy around your left hand colored with the color of the lunar sign. For example, if the solar sign was Libra, the sphere around your right hand would be colored green. The opposite sign to Libra is Aries, so the color of this lunar sign around your left hand would be red.

Recite this incantation. Insert the sign on the solar side of the zodiac in the space on the first line, and the opposite sign on the lunar side of the zodiac in the space on the second line.

On my right hand, _____ (name of sign on solar side) of the Sun,
_____ (name of sign on lunar side) of the Moon to my left is come;
Above my head whirls the starry keep,
Below my feet roots of earth run deep.

Shift into the microcosm posture, with your arms and legs spread wide, and hold the gestures of the two signs with your hands. Visualize the energy of the sign on the solar side of the zodiac flowing from your right hand down your right arm and spreading itself through the right side of your body. At the same time, visualize the energy of the sign on the lunar side spreading through the left side of your body, so that a line drawn vertically through your head and torso divides these two energies.

Move into the macrocosm posture by bringing your feet together and pressing your palms flat together above the top of your head, with your fingers pointing upward. Visualize the energies of the two signs mingling and merging in your body. The color of their merged energies becomes a uniform cool blue-white. Recite this incantation:

Above, the left and right are one,
The Moon is married to the Sun.

With your will, draw the combined energy of both signs upward to your hands and send it streaming heavenward in a twisting blue-white ray from your fingertips, like the vertical beam from a searchlight.

To cut off this ray, sweep your arms out and down to the sides and bring your hands around into the closing posture, with your forearms crossed at the wrists in front of your chest, your hands clenched in fists, and your eyes shut. Hold this for a minute or so while you contemplate your inner balance.

Conclude the working by shifting to the standing posture and taking a few slow, silent breaths.

Working 9: Invoking the Trines

This complex working is both time-consuming and tiring. As a practice, it should be performed on its own, and you should rest after doing it. You will find it useful as a preliminary ritual to energize and balance the space in which you intend to do a work of magic associated with the zodiac. It is also good for cleansing and balancing your own aura.

Begin in the standing posture facing east, and take a few slow, silent breaths to focus your mind.

Make the opening posture to expand your aura away from the surface of your skin so that it forms a perfect transparent sphere seven to nine feet (approximately two to three meters) in diameter.

Move into the spiral invoking posture, with your left hand raised above your head and your right hand pressed flat over your heart-center. With the force of your will, draw down the pure blue-white light of the stars into your left hand, and send it through your body in a contracting spiral into your heart-center. Fill the spinning sphere of your heart-center with this frosty radiance so that its soft-white sphere glows blue-white.

This white energy is, of course, the energy of Spirit, but the neutral white of pure Spirit becomes colder when associated with the remote sphere of the fixed stars, where the constellations reside. This coolness is indicated by its slight bluish tint.

When your heart-center is filled with this energy of the stars, which underlies and sustains the twelve energies of the signs of the zodiac, shift to the closing posture to cut off its flow through your body, and stand with your forearms crossed at the wrists and eyes shut for a minute or so to contemplate your heart-center.

Shift into the general invoking posture, arms raised above your head in a V-shape, with both your hands formed in the gesture of elemental Air. Speak the following incantation:

Into the east I invoke the starry signs of Air.

Step forward with your right foot into a modified version of the projecting posture, with your hands formed in the gesture of the Mutable Air sign, Gemini. Instead of pointing to your right side with your right hand, point directly forward to the east at the level of your heart while pressing your left hand over your chest. Your right hand is turned downward in this posture.

Draw the energy that fills your heart-center into your left hand and send it through your upper body and out your right hand in a twisting stream. As you do so, use this stream to inscribe upon the air of the east the astrological glyph of the sign Gemini, as though painting it on the inside surface of your expanded aura with a stream of paint.

As the energy enters your left hand from your heart-center, it turns from blue-white to purple, the color of Gemini. The stream of energy leaving your right hand should be visualized as purple in color. Make the glyph of Gemini around twelve inches in height.

Step back with your right foot and shift to the closing posture to terminate the flow of energy from your heart-center. Contemplate the glyph of Gemini with your eyes closed for a minute or so.

Turn very slightly to the right and adopt the modified projecting posture again, but this time form your hands into the gesture of the Cardinal Air sign, Libra. Draw the energy from your heart-center into your left hand. As it leaves your heart-center, it turns from blue-white to green, the color of Libra. Project it out your right hand in a green stream, and use the stream to inscribe the green glyph of Libra in the east to the right side of the purple glyph of Gemini.

Shift to the closing posture to cut off the flow of energy, and with eyes closed, contemplate the purple sign of Gemini and the green sign of Libra floating at heart level upon the inner surface of your expanded aura.

Turn slightly to the left and step forward into the modified projecting posture, with your right arm extended toward the east. Form both hands in the gesture of the Fixed

Air sign, Aquarius. Draw energy into your left hand from your heart-center and send it streaming out your right hand. As the energy leaves your heart-center, it changes from blue-white to orange. With the orange stream flowing from your extended right hand, inscribe the orange glyph of Aquarius to the left side of the purple glyph of Gemini.

Make the closing posture to cut off the flow of energy through your body, and with your eyes shut, contemplate the three glyphs that float at heart level in the east—purple Gemini in the center, green Libra on its right side, and orange Aquarius on its left side.

Open your eyes and relax your hands at your sides as you assume the standing posture. Turn on your own body axis half a circle in a clockwise direction to face the west. Make the general invoking posture, with your arms raised above your head, and form both your hands into the gesture of elemental Water. Speak this incantation:

Into the west I invoke the starry signs of Water.

Step forward in the modified projecting posture, with your right arm extended to the west in front of you, and form the gesture of the Mutable Water sign, Pisces, with both hands. Draw energy from your charged heart-center. As it flows into your left hand and through your upper body in an expanding spiral, it becomes by spiritual alchemy red-orange, the color of Pisces. With your right hand, use this energy stream to inscribe the red-orange glyph of Pisces on the inner surface of your expanded aura at heart level in the west.

Make the closing posture and contemplate with your eyes shut the red-orange sign of Pisces for a minute or so.

Turn slightly to the right and adopt the modified projecting posture. Form both hands in the gesture of the Cardinal Water sign, Cancer. Draw energy from your heart-center, transmute it into the blue-purple energy of Cancer, and use the stream flowing from your right hand to inscribe the blue-purple glyph of Cancer to the right of the red-orange glyph of Pisces.

Shift to the closing posture to cut off the flow of energy through your body, and contemplate with your eyes shut the red-orange glyph of Pisces and the blue-purple glyph of Cancer floating at heart level on the inner surface of your expanded aura.

Turn slightly to the left and adopt the projecting posture, with both hands formed in the gesture of the Fixed Water sign, Scorpio. Draw energy from your heart-center and inscribe the yellow-green glyph of Scorpio just to the left side of the glyph of Pisces.

Make the closing posture, and contemplate the red-orange glyph of Pisces in the center, the blue-purple glyph of Cancer to its right side, and the yellow-green glyph of Scorpio to the left side of Pisces.

Open your eyes and relax your hands at your sides in the standing posture. Rotate your body clockwise on your own axis three-quarters of a circle until you face the south. Make the general invoking posture, with your hands shaped in the gesture of elemental Fire. Speak this incantation:

Into the south I invoke the starry signs of Fire.

Adopt the modified projecting posture, right arm directed toward the south, with both hands formed in the gesture of the Mutable Fire sign, Sagittarius. Draw energy from your heart-center and project it in a yellow stream from your right hand to inscribe the yellow glyph of Sagittarius in the south at heart level.

Step back into the closing posture to cut off the flow of energy, and contemplate the yellow glyph of Sagittarius for a minute or so.

Turn slightly to the right and step forward with your right foot into the modified projecting posture, with your hands formed in the gesture of the Cardinal Fire sign, Aries. Draw energy from your heart-center, transmute it into the red energy of Aries, and use it to inscribe the red glyph of Aries just to the right side of the yellow glyph of Sagittarius.

Make the closing posture to cut off the energy flow and contemplate briefly the glyphs of Sagittarius and Aries.

Turn slightly to the left and adopt the projecting pose, with both hands formed in the gesture of the Fixed Fire sign, Leo. Draw energy from your heart-center and use it to inscribe the blue glyph of Leo to the left of the glyph of Sagittarius.

Make the closing posture and contemplate the yellow glyph of Sagittarius, with the red glyph of Aries on its right and the blue glyph of Leo on its left.

Open your eyes and relax your hands at your sides in the standing posture. Rotate your body clockwise half a circle until you face the north. Make the general invoking posture, with both hands formed in the gesture of elemental Earth. Speak this incantation:

Into the north I invoke the starry signs of Earth.

Adopt the modified projecting posture, with both hands formed in the gesture of the Mutable Earth sign, Virgo. Draw energy from your heart-center and use it to inscribe the blue-green glyph of Virgo upon the inner surface of your aura in the north.

Shift to the closing posture and contemplate the blue-green glyph of Virgo.

Turn slightly to the right. Again make the modified projecting posture, but with both hands formed in the gesture of the Cardinal Earth sign, Capricorn. Draw energy from your heart-center and use it to inscribe the yellow-orange glyph of Capricorn to the right of the blue-green glyph of Virgo.

Shift to the closing posture and contemplate the glyphs of Virgo and Capricorn.

Turn slightly to the left. Make the modified projecting posture, with both hands formed in the gesture of the Fixed Earth sign, Taurus. Draw energy from your heart-center and use it to inscribe the red-purple glyph of Taurus to the left of the glyph of Virgo.

Shift to the closing posture and contemplate with closed eyes the blue-green glyph of Virgo, with the yellow-orange glyph of Capricorn on its right and the red-purple glyph of Taurus on its left.

Adopt the standing posture, with your eyes open and hands relaxed at your sides, and rotate clockwise on your own body axis until you face east. Be aware of the twelve glyphs of the zodiac around your expanded aura.

Shift to the ankh posture, with your arms spread wide to your sides and your palms turned forward to the east. Speak the following incantation:

Before me, the signs of Air,
Behind me, the signs of Water,
On my right hand, the signs of Fire,
On my left hand, the signs of Earth.

At this point, you may wish to do some work of magic connected with the energies or spirits of the zodiac. The signs will pin your expanded aura in place at the four quarters, so that you can turn in different directions inside it without having your expanded aura turn with you.

If you are merely doing the working as a practice, or when you finish the main work of magic, shift smoothly from the ankh posture into the closing posture, and as you do so, draw your expanded aura back to its normal distance away from your body. Contemplate your contracted aura for a minute or so.

Shift to the standing posture and take a few slow, silent breaths to end.

Working 10: The Zodiac in the Body

This working is used to draw down the energies of the twelve signs of the zodiac into the twelve parts of your body that those signs rule and influence. You should memorize the twelve lines of the poem that form the twelve incantations in this working, but in the beginning of your practice, you can print them out on a sheet of paper and tape them to the wall in front of you if you need an aid to your memory. Or, if you wish, you may compose your own original incantations.

Begin as usual in the standing posture facing the east, and draw a few long, silent breaths to calm and focus your thoughts.

Form both hands in the gesture of Aries and raise both arms above your head in a V-shape in the general invoking posture. Incline your face upward. Visualize the red astrological glyph of Aries in the air above you as you gaze upward at an angle. Be aware of the Cardinal Fire energy of this sign. Speak the following incantation to the starry heavens:

At my head, the white ram, fire of my will.

Bring both your hands down, touch them together, and press them to the top of your head while holding the Aries gesture with your hands.

Raise them again in the invoking posture, but form your hands in the gesture of Taurus as you raise them. Visualize the red-purple glyph of Taurus floating in the air above you, and be aware of the Fixed Earth energy of this sign. Speak these words:

At my neck, the black bull, furrows to till.

Lower your hands to press on both sides of your neck where it joins your shoulders while holding them in the Taurus gesture.

Raise your arms again in the invoking posture, but with your hands formed in the Gemini gesture. Visualize the purple glyph of Gemini above your head, and become aware of the nature of the Mutable Air energy of this sign. Speak these words:

At my arms, twin brothers who sow and reap.

Lower your hands, cross your forearms, and press your hands against your upper arms while holding them in the Gemini gesture.

Raise your arms in the invoking posture, with both hands formed in the Cancer gesture. Visualize the blue-purple glyph of Cancer in the air above you, and become conscious of the Cardinal Water energy of this sign. Speak these words:

At my breast, crab's pincers that grasp and keep.

Lower your hands and press them against both sides of your chest just above your nipples while holding them in the Cancer gesture.

Raise your arms in the invoking posture, with your hands formed in the Leo gesture. Visualize the blue glyph of Leo above you upon the air, and fill your mind with the Fixed Fire energy of this sign. Speak these words:

At my heart, noble lion, to love under will.

Lower your hands and touch them together while pressing them to the center of your chest just below the level of your nipples. Hold the Leo gesture with both hands as you do this.

Raise your arms in the invoking posture, with your hands in the Virgo gesture. Visualize the blue-green glyph of Virgo floating in the air above you, and concentrate on the Mutable Earth energy of this sign. Speak these words:

At my gut, patient virgin, to grind and to mill.

Lower your hands and touch them together while pressing them to the center of your abdomen just below your solar plexus at the base of your sternum. Keep them in the gesture of Virgo as you do so.

Raise your arms in the invoking posture, with your hands in the Libra gesture. Visualize the green glyph of Libra above you in the air, and think of the Cardinal Air energy of this sign. Speak these words:

At my reins, the balance, joy against strife.

Lower your hands to the sides of your body just above your hips, at the level of your kidneys, and press them into your sides while holding the gesture of Libra with both hands.

Raise your arms in the invoking posture, with your hands in the Scorpio gesture. Visualize the yellow-green glyph of Scorpio floating in the air above you while concentrating on the energy of this Fixed Water sign. Speak these words:

At my loins, the scorpion brings death or life.

Lower your hands, touch them together, and press them into your groin while holding them in the gesture of Scorpio.

Raise your arms in the invoking posture, with both hands in the Sagittarius gesture. Visualize the yellow glyph of Sagittarius while focusing your mind on the Mutable Fire energy of this sign. Speak these words:

At my thighs, the sharp arrows, straight and long.

Lower your hands and press them against the fronts of your upper thighs while holding both hands in the Sagittarius gesture.

Raise your arms in the invoking posture, with both hands formed in the Capricorn gesture. Visualize the yellow-orange glyph of Capricorn in the air above you, and focus your thoughts on the Cardinal Earth energy of this sign. Speak these words:

At my knees, the horned goat, climbing and strong.

Lower your hands and bend forward to press them against the fronts of your knees while holding them in the Capricorn gesture.

Straighten your back and raise your arms in the invoking posture, with both hands shaped in the gesture of Aquarius. Visualize the orange glyph of Aquarius floating above you, and concentrate your thoughts on the Fixed Air energy of this sign. Speak these words:

At my shins, the waterman who walks the land.

Lower your hands and bend forward to press them against the fronts of your shins while holding them in the gesture of Aquarius.

Straighten and raise your arms in the invoking posture, with your hands held in the gesture of Pisces. Visualize the red-orange glyph of Pisces in the air above you while concentrating on the Mutable Water energy of this sign. Speak these words.

At my feet, the two fishes, on which I stand.

Lower your hands and bend forward to press them to the tops of your feet while keeping them in the gesture of Pisces. Take care not to lose your balance.

Straighten your back and assume the standing posture. Hold it for a minute or so to rest your arms and contemplate the twelve zodiac zones of your body. Then draw a few silent breaths to end.

If your balance is not good enough to do this working from the standing posture, you may use the sitting posture.

CHAPTER 8
LAYING ON OF HANDS

THE LAYING ON OF HANDS IS ONE OF the most ancient forms of healing. It has been used since the beginning of recorded history. Shamans relied on the power of their touch to stop the bleeding of open wounds, to cure skin ulcers, to reduce fever, and even to perform operations within the body. The same practices that took place around open campfires ten thousand years ago still go on today, although they are dismissed by modern medicine as superstitious nonsense.

In China, Japan, Korea, and other Eastern nations, the healer is believed to draw upon the power of a universal occult energy known to the Chinese as *chi*, as we discussed earlier in the book. This is a kind of potent force that pervades all things and can be manipulated by magic to either heal or kill. The word the Polynesians use to describe this concept is *mana*. It has been called *vrill, Odic energy, kundalini,* and other names. George Lucas used the same concept in his Star Wars movies, calling it simply *the Force.*

In Eastern magic, chi is a blind force. That is to say, it has no morality or intelligence. It is like electricity and can be manipulated to heal or harm by anyone who understands how to handle it.

In the West, the power of healing was usually understood to be divine and spiritual in nature. The power came from God either directly or through the mediation of one of his angels. In order to harness this power, the healer had to be in communication with his spiritual center. He was not necessarily a kind or good man, in the conventional sense, but he was a man to whom God paid attention. He was marked or selected by

God for his role as healer, or at least that was the belief. The Russian monk Rasputin was such a healer.

There is really no difference in the way Eastern mystics and Western holy men heal. The two ways of looking at the healing process are looking at the same thing from different angles. The healing energy is indeed an occult force, as is understood in the East, but it requires spiritual awareness before it can be effectively used, as is believed in the West.

The twenty-four types of occult energies described in this book are various differentiated aspects of the single magical essence known as *mana* or *chi*. Think of the underlying potential itself as pure white light, and think of the various forces described here—those of the elements, the planets, and the signs of the zodiac—as white light that has passed through different colored filters. This is a useful way to understand that although these forces are all distinct, at their root they are only one thing—the essential power of magic itself.

By limiting the scope of this universal magical potential in a certain way, we make it more applicable to a specific use. The element Fire, for example, is vitalizing and energizing. It can be used to heighten enthusiasm, to overcome doubt and fear, and to power through obstacles and burn through illusions. The same universal energy of magic, when limited or filtered in another way, becomes the element Earth. This can be used to ground and center the mind, to provide stability to the emotions, to resist those who would move you from your purpose, to realize ideas, and to bring things conceived and planned into physical reality.

The method of healing described in this chapter relies on either the infusion and concentration of a particularized occult force in an afflicted part of the body that is deficient in that force, or the withdrawal and banishing of a portion of that force when it is present to an excessive degree.

First, Do No Harm

Before you attempt to perform any act of occult healing, you must understand the illness. Before you try to balance esoteric forces within your body or the body of another person, you must perceive where those forces are out of balance. The ancient motto of Hippocrates applies: *First, do no harm*. It is better to do nothing at all than to apply occult energies wrongly, in a way that will only make the problem worse.

It is always best to rely on conventional medicine for serious illnesses or disorders where conventional medicine can be applied. The practices of modern medicine are effective, reliable, and predictable. Magic, by its very nature, is unpredictable. An expected effect cannot always be relied upon to follow a specific action. Sometimes the working of magic takes unexpected and extraordinary directions. Always resort to conventional medicine first to treat life-threatening, debilitating, or incapacitating disorders. Only when it fails, or cannot treat such disorders of the body and mind, should you consider occult healing.

Modern medicine has very little to say about spiritual disorders, and here occult healing can be quite beneficial, since there is often no recourse except prayer, which of course is itself a magical action.

The Placebo Effect

Most people have heard about the placebo effect. This is the rather contemptuous name given for the phenomenon that takes place when a person suffering from some complaint cures himself with only his own conviction that he will be cured. In its simplest form, it occurs when a doctor gives a patient a pill that contains only powdered sugar but which the patient believes is a strong medicine that will make him better. Because he believes the pill will help him, the pill does indeed help him, even though it contains nothing that could help him in any physical way.

The placebo effect is powerful, so much so that physicians have always relied on it in various ways to assist their treatment of those who are sick or injured. It is the power of the subconscious mind, the influence of a deep and unquestioned belief over the body. Doctors are reluctant to tell a patient that there is no hope, because in their practices they have seen extraordinary cures, and they have also seen people who are sick wither and die for no physical reason. They use belief in the mind of the patient to cure, not to harm. If they cannot promise a cure, they can at least ensure that the patient retains the hope of a cure, and they do so.

It is the placebo effect working in reverse that causes indigenous people in Australia, South America, and Africa to sicken and die after receiving a sentence of death from their local practitioner of black magic, who always makes sure that the victim knows he has been cursed. Many cases of these mysterious deaths were recorded by European colonials living in Africa during the nineteenth century, and such malicious death magic still takes place today. The evil shaman turns the power of the victim's own mind against him. The medical name for this practice is *psychogenic death* or *psychosomatic death*, but more colloquially it is known as *Voodoo death* or *bone-pointing*.

When we seek to use magic to lessen suffering or cure others who are injured, ill, or infirm, we should always enlist the aid of their own power of belief. We use it ourselves when we work magic alone—our belief in the efficacy of our magic causes it to realize itself in the world. It is much easier to treat others when we rely upon the same power of belief in them to heal or help themselves.

One way to enlist belief in our laying on of hands is to tell the person being treated what is being done and what will be the result. This can be accomplished through incantations that state the purpose of the work, and also by explaining to the sufferer what will happen before the treatment begins, as a way of preparing the person's mind and making it a fertile ground in which the magic can work.

Another occult effect that is treated contemptuously in the modern world but that possesses immense power is trance. In the eighteenth century it was called *mesmerism*, and science today knows it as *hypnosis*, but it is the same trance induction that has existed since the beginning of recorded history. Trance works in unison with belief. A person who is in a trance state can believe much more strongly, free from the weakening effect of self-doubt.

Trance is used for crass purposes much more widely than you might imagine. When a charismatic Christian preacher stirs his flock into religious enthusiasm, he is employing trance induction through the use of his voice and hand gestures. Most powerful orators have the ability to induce a receptive state of trance in their listeners. Adolf Hitler is the most obvious example. He was famed for his ability to stir massive crowds into a heightened emotional state with only his words and his presence on a stage.

Trance induction is also employed by television producers to make their audience receptive to suggestion. The flicker of the old-style cathode ray tube television screen by itself helped to induce a trance state in viewers. Those who control television rely on trance induction not only to sell their advertised products but also to promote their preferred ideologies.

It is possible to enlist the aid of trance induction during healing through the use of words and gestures. The same suggestions, repeated over and over in different forms, will seat themselves in the deep mind of the person being treated, and will help to activate that person's belief in the efficacy of the treatment. I have provided an example of trance induction in the tenth working at the end of this chapter.

Slow, rhythmic, repeated motions of the hands over the head, torso, and limbs of a person will also aid in the induction of a receptive trance state that will allow the person's own mind to assist in the treatment. This was discovered by Franz Anton Mesmer by accident in the eighteenth century, but it has been know about and used in magic for thousands of years. The Egyptian priests used it to treat the sick in ancient Egypt. It is instructive to study the hand and body postures depicted in Egyptian tomb paintings and papyrus scrolls.

Rhythmic hand motions can assist the magician in moving energies through the body of a sufferer, and can also encourage that person to lapse into a receptive mental state in which they activate their own power of belief to aid the flow and circulation of those same occult energies.

Sometimes it is not possible to use the placebo effect or trance induction when laying on the hands for the purpose of healing. The person you treat may be unconscious, for example, or too weak and delirious to concentrate on what you are saying and doing. In these cases you must rely entirely on your own power of will, your own visualization, and your own strength of belief in the efficacy of your magic. But in the cases where you can induce a receptive mind state in which to plant positive beliefs, you should do so, because it will greatly aid in the efficacy of your healing.

Direct Healing

In order to use your control over occult energies to help or heal others by direct laying on of the hands, with the knowledge and consent of the other person, it is important to inform them that you will need to touch their body, sometimes in places that are usually not touched outside of intimacy. By this I mean the breasts, buttocks, thighs, and groin. If a touch in these regions becomes necessary, you should tell the other person very clearly what you need to do and why, and get the explicit consent of that person before you treat them.

If you have any reason to believe a person might misinterpret your healing touch on a part of their body, it is better not to touch them in that place, but instead to hold your hand over that part of their body at a distance of several inches and project energy from your hand into their body. When done with proper focus, this technique can be effective.

When treating others with their knowledge and consent, it is important that the person treated have confidence in you, or at least an open mind. Doubt or an expectation of failure on the person's part will usually destroy all hope for a successful healing. This is a negative placebo effect, where the certainty in the mind of the patient that a procedure will fail actually causes it to fail.

Be positive when you establish a personal communication with the individual you are going to treat. Project an air of complete confidence and avoid saying or doing anything that might arouse doubt or nervousness in their mind. You do not need to say anything that is untrue or deceive the person in any way—just take care not to undermine your own magic before you even begin your work. Doubt is fatal in the mind of the magician when magic is worked, but it can also be fatal to success when harbored in the mind of the person toward whom the magic is directed.

This is why one of the traditional defenses against the evil eye is laughter and ridicule. Contempt for the person casting the evil eye destroys its effectiveness. Conversely, a strong belief on the part of the person to whom a work of magic is directed greatly enhances the success of the magic, which is why shamans always tell those they intend to kill by black magic the day on which they are going to die. The growing apprehension in the mind of the victim helps to make it so.

Covert Healing

At times you may wish to speed the healing or reduce the suffering of another person without being able to inform the person about what you are doing. They may be hostile toward you or may harbor contempt for your abilities as a healer, for example. Or they may not believe in magic.

Covert healing can be done by brief and seemingly casual touches. If you first load your right hand with an energy sphere, the compressed energy can be transferred to an afflicted part of the body of another individual by the lightest contact, even through clothing. It will jump from your hand into the person you touch the way static electricity jumps from person to person.

First charge your right hand with whatever energy you judge is best suited to help the other person. You can pull the energy directly from the elemental, planetary, or zodiacal sphere with your left hand and guide it through your body into your right hand by using the magician posture, or you can first charge your heart-center with the energy and then draw it out into your right hand with the projecting posture when you have need for it.

It is possible to banish an excess of elemental energy from someone without that person ever becoming aware of what you are doing. If you detect that they are suffering from an excess of Air, for example—they may be chattering incessantly, or laughing hysterically for no reason, or fidgeting with their hands—make the Air gesture with both your hands and casually lay your left hand on their shoulder or arm while talking to them. Point your right hand to the ground. This is a modified form of the channeling posture. Allow the excess of esoteric Air energy to flow in a double spiral through your upper body, around your heart-center, and out your right hand into the ground, or into a large, dense object such as a boulder or tree. This will relieve the elemental pressure inside them and give them relief from their nervous fidgeting, and they will remain none the wiser that you have done it.

An excess of Fire will generally cause flushing, sweating, aggression, loud talking, irritation, anger, and impatience. Too much Water results in dreaminess, listlessness, vagueness, languor, moving in slow motion, slurred or soft speech, tears, excess empathy, heightened sensitivity, and excessive sensuality. Too much Earth will cause dullness, stubbornness, blunt speech, vulgarity, lack of tact, gluttony, lack of imagination, boorishness, and body obsession. All of these elemental excesses can be helped by draining away the superabundance of elemental energy with the channeling posture.

Using the channeling posture, it is also possible to transfer an excess of elemental energy from one person to another person, if you can manage to touch the person suffering from the excess with your left hand and the other individual with your right hand. Both your hands should be formed in the gesture of the element you are dealing with. You can do this without physical touch, drawing in the excess energy with your left hand and projecting it through the air with your right hand, but it requires a more intense concentration and a vivid visualization of the energy stream.

Compensation for Healing Work

In my opinion, you should not ask for money or any other reward when you do occult healing. Healing others is its own reward, and if you do not believe this, then you should not be doing it at all. Healing by the laying on of hands is a selfless calling that is spiritual in nature. Unless you feel called, do not make healing a part of your magical work. The desire to make money will corrupt and ultimately destroy the effectiveness of your healing, because it will disturb the tranquility of mind and the lack of a lust for result that are essential to the success of any form of magic.

If you find that you have a natural talent for laying on of hands, after experimenting with it to cure minor complaints such as headaches, bruises, small cuts, muscle aches, and so on, you should not refuse to try to help those who come to you for help. Your natural talent for this branch of magic is a clear indicator that you are intended to use it to help others. It is an aspect of your True Will in the sense that Aleister Crowley used the term—an expression of your highest fulfillment as a magician. However, you should never force your healing on others against their wishes. If they indicate that they do not want your help, respect their wishes.

Healing others covertly, when they are not even aware of what you are doing, is a gray area in a moral sense. This should be done rarely and only when it is impossible to directly ask the ailing person if they want your help. For example, you may find someone unconscious at the scene of an accident. Your first response should be to call for professional medical assistance. Your second response, if you are trained in first aid, should be to give the injured person whatever physical first aid you can. Only after this has been done should you consider resorting to magical healing.

Even when you do not ask for any compensation for your healing work, those you help may from time to time press a gift upon you. The gracious thing to do is accept the gift with humility and thanks. Do not take any gift that might cause hardship to those who give it, and never imply that you would be willing to accept a gift. If a gift is given, it must be completely spontaneous and voluntary.

Workings: Laying On of Hands

The healing of others, both in body and in mind, is the highest purpose for which magic can be used. It was this power of healing that caused Jesus to be so beloved by the common people. Not everyone is called upon to heal others, and no one should try to use magic to heal unless it feels completely right and natural to do so on a spiritual level. It is a great gift. If you possess this gift latently within you, these workings will help to awaken and develop it. Experiment with them to gain an awareness of what using the forces of magic to heal feels like, by applying them both to yourself and to others, and then decide whether the role of a healer is right for you. If it is not your path, do not be discouraged. The uses of magic are as manifold and diverse as the stars in the heavens. You will find those you are meant to find and make them your own.

Working 1: Elemental Warming

The lower elements, Fire and Air, are the warm elements. Fire is warm and dry; Air is warm and moist. Their energies can be combined to apply a therapeutic warmth to a region of the body that can be benefited by it. It acts in much the same way as a hot compress or hot water bottle, except that the elemental warmth penetrates deeply to the root of the problem rather than lying on the surface of the skin.

You can practice this working by yourself. When you do so, send the elemental warmth into some inanimate object, such as a pillow or a chair. Here, I will describe how to use it to treat another person.

Assume the standing posture, with the person you intend to help standing in front of you. If that person is too ill to stand, they can sit or lie down. It is best to avoid the distraction of eye contact. Stand behind the person, or at least avoid meeting their gaze. The part of the body you intend to treat should be within easy reach of your hands. Take a few silent breaths to focus your mind.

Move into the general invoking posture, with your left hand formed in the gesture of Fire and your right hand in the gesture of Air. Draw down a sphere of red energy around your left hand and a sphere of yellow energy around your right hand. Visualize these spheres, the blazing, prickly, dry heat of Fire around your left hand and the whirling, moist heat of Air around your right hand.

Approach the sufferer and lay your hands directly on the part of the body that requires warmth. Press your left palm flat against the area and place your right palm over your left hand. Mentally combine the two energy spheres into a single orange sphere, and cause this to sink from your hands into the flesh of the person you are treating. Allow all of the elemental heat to flow from your hands into the other person. Visualize a gentle warmth spreading through the area.

Step back and assume the closing posture. Hold it for a minute or so in silent contemplation of the area of the person's body you have just treated.

Move into the standing posture and take a few silent breaths to end.

Working 2: Elemental Cooling

The two cool elements are Water, which is cool and wet, and Earth, which is cool and dry. They can be used to induce coolness in a part of the body that is inflamed or swollen and to soothe sunburn or skin irritations.

Begin in the standing posture, with the person you intend to treat standing or sitting in front of you and the part of the body to which you will apply the cooling energy within easy reach. Take a few silent breaths to prepare yourself.

Raise your arms in the invoking posture, and form your left hand in the gesture of Water and your right hand in the gesture of Earth. With the force of your will, draw the energy of elemental Water into your left hand so that it is surrounded by a glowing blue sphere. At the same time, draw the energy of elemental Earth into your right hand and surround it with a glowing dark-green sphere. For this working, the color of the sphere of Earth is green, not black, because you are using the life-giving properties of this element.

Lay your left palm over the area of the body you intend to cool, and press your right hand on top of your left hand, so that the two energy spheres combine and their colors merge into a single blue-green sphere. Cause this sphere to sink into the body of the person you are treating, and visualize it flowing to the injured area with a soothing coolness that is like the sensation of cool, wet mud.

Step back and assume the closing posture. Maintain it for a minute or so while contemplating the healing action of the elemental energies you have invoked.

Shift into the standing posture and take a few silent breaths to end.

Working 3: Curing Headaches

Headaches lend themselves to treatment by a laying on of hands. The zone of the head falls under the influence of the zodiac sign Aries. This sign can be combined with a planet to soothe head pain, but that planet is not Mars, the ruling planet of Aries. Fiery Mars would only intensify the pounding pain. Instead, the power of the Moon may be combined with that of Aries. The cooling, narcotic lunar properties suppress the heat of a headache and bring relief.

Assume the standing posture behind the person who is suffering from a headache, and take a few silent breaths to focus your mind. The person can be standing or sitting and should face away from you. If the pain is debilitating, the person may even lie down, and in this case you should stand at the head of the bed or couch on which they lie.

Move into the general invoking posture and form the gesture of the Moon with your left hand and the gesture of Aries with your right hand. Draw the energy of the Moon down into your left hand and visualize a purple sphere around it. Draw the energy of Aries into your right hand and visualize a red sphere around it.

Lower your arms and gently press your left hand against the left temple of the person you are treating. At the same time, press your right hand to their right temple. Continue to hold the gestures of the Moon and Aries.

Visualize the energy spheres flowing together inside the head of the sufferer and mingling in a sphere of red-purple energy that is serene and cooling, like a basin of cool, clear water. When all the energy has flowed from your hands into the head of the sufferer, relax your hands and gently massage the temples of the person with your fingertips as you sustain this visualization of the mingled energy spheres for a minute or so.

Step back and move into the closing posture. Contemplate the soothed head of the person with your eyes shut for a minute.

Shift into the standing posture and take a few silent breaths to end.

Working 4: Lifting Depression

Depression is often described as a feeling of weight upon the body—sometimes as a weight upon the head or on the shoulders, and sometimes as a weight on the heart or chest, accompanied by a difficulty in breathing. The antidotes to depression are courage, vigor, lightness, and expansion. A good combination of energies for this purpose is the sign of Leo coupled with the planet Jupiter.

Those who are depressed often avoid speaking about it or seeking treatment for it, but you may be able to help them without their knowledge by transferring energy to them covertly. You must make the decision whether the need of the person suffering from depression outweighs your obligation to ask their permission before treating them.

First you must charge your heart-center with the mingled energies of Jupiter and Leo. Begin in the standing posture in a private place where you will not be observed, and take a few silent breaths to focus your thoughts.

Adopt the general invoking posture, with your left hand raised in the gesture of Jupiter and your right hand raised in the gesture of Leo. Draw down the orange energy of Jupiter into your left hand, and at the same time conceive the blue energy of Leo entering your right hand. Visualize these energies as glowing, translucent spheres that surround your hands.

Shift into the spiral invoking posture while maintaining these gestures with both hands, and continue to draw down the energy of Jupiter with your left hand. The energy of this planet is the primary energy. It is filtered through the gesture of the sign and modified by it as it flows in a contracting spiral through your right hand and into your heart-center. Fill the spinning sphere of your heart-center with the combined energies of Jupiter and Leo so that it glows a bright orange edged with blue.

Move to the closing posture to cut off the flow of these energies. End this part of the working by adopting the standing posture and drawing several silent breaths.

You can carry the mingled energies of Leo and Jupiter within your heart-center for a period of hours before they begin to fade. Within that time, find occasion to approach the person suffering from depression and make physical contact with that person. During this contact, the energy in your heart-center must be transferred into the body of the other person.

A hug or an embrace is a good method for transferring this occult potency. Also effective is to hold the person's left hand with your right hand. Failing these methods, you can brush against the person, pretend to stumble and fall against them, or lay your right hand on their chest, back, left shoulder, or left arm. Any of these contacts will make an effective transfer of energy if the focus of your will is strong.

Feel the energy leave your heart-center as you touch the person. Visualize strongly the vitalizing, expansive energy rushing into their body and filling them.

When you break the contact, turn your thoughts away from that person and make your mind tranquil. Think of common, everyday things. Have no concern about the person you just treated, other than a quiet assurance in the back of your mind that the person is content and feeling well.

Working 5: Relieving Indigestion

Stomach pain or discomfort, queasiness, acid reflux, and bloating can all be addressed by applying the cooling, condensing influence of Saturn modified by the energy of Virgo, which rules the region of the stomach.

Begin in the standing posture and take a few silent breaths to relax and focus your mind on what you are about to do.

Shift to the invoking posture and make the gesture of Saturn with your left hand and the gesture of Virgo with your right hand.

Draw the energy of Saturn into your left hand and imagine a sphere of blue light forming around it. At the same time, draw the energy of Virgo into your right hand and visualize a glowing sphere of blue-green light around it. Feel the coolness and weight of Saturn (cross over crescent) in your left hand and the dryness and weight of Virgo (Mutable Earth) in your right hand.

Change to the spiral invoking posture, with your left hand raised above your head and your right hand pressed to the center of your chest, but maintain the two hand gestures.

Using the force of your will, send the blue energy of Saturn from your left hand in a contracting spiral through your body to your right hand, where it mingles with the blue-green energy of Virgo and enters your heart-center. Fill your heart-center and charge it with these mingled energies.

Shift to the closing posture and spend a minute contemplating your heart-center, filled with the mingled energies of Saturn and Virgo. Visualize it as a spinning blue sphere edged with green.

Move to the standing posture and take a few silent breaths to end this part of the working.

The charge in your heart-center will not fade away for several hours, but you should treat the person suffering from stomach complaints as soon after this charging as possible for the greatest effectiveness. When you are ready to infuse these energies into the sufferer, have them stand, sit, or lie in front of you.

Adopt a modified form of the projecting posture, with your left hand pressed to your chest in the gesture of Saturn and your extended right hand in the gesture of Virgo. Step forward on your right foot and press your right hand firmly over the upper part of the stomach of the person with indigestion, but not so firmly that it causes pain. Use your will to direct the mingled energies of Virgo and Saturn out of your heart-center, along your left arm, across your shoulders, down your right arm to your right hand, and into the abdomen of the person you are treating. Hold the posture until all the energy you have added to your heart-center has been expelled into the body of the other person and your heart-center has returned to its normal soft-white color.

Step away from the other person and make the closing gesture to cut off the flow of energy through your body. Hold it with your eyes shut for a minute and empty your mind of all lust for result.

Move into the standing posture and take a few silent breaths to end.

Working 6: Treating Constipation

It is not absolutely necessary to charge yourself with energy in order to use energy to heal others. Your own body centers hold constant charges, and a portion of these charges can be projected directly to another person. Since this depletes your own natural energy state, it will tire you, and you will need some time to regain your usual energy level, but it is not dangerous. Your own natural defenses will not allow you to project so much energy that it becomes a serious danger to your health.

Constipation falls under the zone of Scorpio, which rules over the sex organs, the lower bowel, the anus, and the function of excretion. It is also under the influence of the watery Moon, because in kinesic magic the root-center of the body is assigned to the Moon. When these energies are weak in the body, problems can arise.

Adopt the standing posture and take a few deep, silent breaths to focus and prepare your mind.

Approach the person you intend to treat for constipation, who should be standing or lying down—the seated position is not convenient for this exercise. Shift into a modified projecting posture, with your left hand in the gesture of the Moon pressed to your lower belly below your navel and your extended right hand in the gesture of Scorpio.

Press your right hand firmly against the lower belly of the person you are treating, just below their navel. Use the power of your will to draw the energy of Scorpio and also the energy of the Moon from your lower abdomen. Direct these two mingled energy streams up your left arm, across your shoulders, and down your right arm into the belly of the person you are treating.

Continue in this way until you feel a distinct hollowness or weakness in your own lower belly. When you feel this, step back and make the closing posture to cut off the outflow of energies from your body. Hold the posture for a minute or so with your mind tranquil and empty.

Shift into the standing posture and take a few silent breaths to end.

Working 7: Banishing Fatigue

The person who is tired should sit with eyes closed and hands on knees on a plain kitchen chair placed so that you can stand behind the chair.

Begin in the standing posture and take a few silent breaths to prepare yourself for what you are about to do.

Shift into the general invoking posture and form both hands in the gesture of elemental Fire. Use the power of your will to draw down Fire energy into your hands, and visualize this energy as transparent red spheres around your hands. Feel the heat of the Fire—it should feel like the tingling radiance of a blazing fireplace when you hold your hand in front of the fireplace opening.

Approach the fatigued person from behind and relax your hands. Gently massage both temples of the person, making circular motions with the inner sides of your fingertips. Let some of the Fire energy flow into the head of the fatigued person.

Move your hands to the shoulders of the person on either side of the neck and begin to gently massage their neck and shoulders, forcing Fire energy into the muscles of the neck and shoulders as you do so.

Lay your palms flat against the sides of the person's neck so that your fingers wrap partway around the neck, and allow the remainder of the Fire energy to flow into the person's neck. Send this energy down into the fatigued person's body, and visualize it flowing in a red stream from your hands down each side of the person's body to their feet.

Step back and assume the closing posture to cut off the flow of Fire energy from your hands. Hold this posture silently for a minute or so.

Shift into the standing posture and take a few silent breaths to end.

Working 8: Reducing Chronic Pain

The purpose of this working is to lessen the severity of chronic pain in another individual. Have the person suffering from chronic pain lie down, with the part of the body that hurts uppermost. It should be within easy reach of your hands. For example, if it is lower back pain, have the person lie on their stomach if they are able, or on their side.

Begin in the standing posture, with the person on your right side, and prepare your mind by drawing a few silent breaths.

Shift into the magician posture and form both hands in the gesture of the Moon. Raise your left hand high above your head and gently press your right hand to the part of the body of the other person that is hurting.

Draw soothing, cooling lunar energy down from the sphere of the Moon, and direct it through your upper body in a double spiral, so that it flows down your left arm and loops once around your heart-center in a contracting spiral, then moves from your heart-center down your right arm in an expanding spiral and out your right hand.

As you feel this lunar energy begin to course through your body, press a little more firmly with your right hand against the place that hurts, and move this hand in a slow circular motion, massaging the energy of the Moon into the area where there is pain. If the place is very sensitive, do this gently. Visualize the energy flowing into the person's body from your fingertips like cooling mist and settling into the part that hurts.

Step back and make the closing posture to cut off the flow of lunar energy through your body. Hold the posture for a minute or so in silence, with your eyes shut and your mind tranquil and empty. If the person you have treated happens to speak, ask them to please be silent for a minute.

Shift into the standing posture, with your hands relaxed and open at your sides, and take a few silent breaths to end.

Working 9: Accelerated Healing

This quick technique should be used for minor injuries such as cuts, boils, scrapes, sunburn, bruises, and so on. Mercury energy is ideal for transferring vitality into an injured part of the body to increase the rate of healing. The person you are treating may stand, sit, or lie down, but whatever position they adopt, the injured part of their body must be within easy reach.

Begin in the standing posture and take a few silent breaths to focus your mind.

Make both hands in the gesture of Mercury and shift into a modified version of the projecting posture. Press your left hand flat over your heart-center. Step forward on your right foot and press your right hand over the injured place of the other person so that your palm covers it.

Draw the soft-white energy of Mercury from the sphere of your heart-center into your left hand, and send it in an expanding spiral through your upper body and out your right hand, so that it floods into the injured area of the person you are treating. Visualize this as a rush of energy through your body.

Don't worry, you are not going to draw so much Mercury energy from your heart-center that it will harm your own health. Your body has natural fail-safes that prevent this from occurring. But you can draw enough of your own Mercury energy to increase the rate of healing of the minor injury you are treating.

When you feel you have projected enough Mercury energy into the injured place, step back and assume the closing posture to cut off the flow of energy. Hold it for a minute without speaking.

Change to the standing pose and take a few silent breaths to end.

Working 10: Balancing the Zodiac Zones of the Body

This somewhat involved exercise should be regarded as a general tune-up for the entire body of the person to whom you apply it. It balances internal energies, cleans out physical, emotional, and mental toxins, energizes and improves the circulation of the blood, and produces a mild euphoria and feeling of well-being.

The words spoken to the person being treated are a general guideline only. You can make up your own words on the spot as you do the exercise. Their purpose is to cause the person you are treating to participate in the treatment. You want to engage the person's powers of visualization to assist in the transfer of zodiacal energies.

I have given short forms of the words here, but in performing this healing, you should extend each talk for at least a minute or two, repeating key phrases a number of times, to give the person being treated ample opportunity to visualize the energies you are describing.

Be aware that you are inducing a form of trance in the mind of the person you are treating that will increase the efficacy of the treatment. Speak in a gentle, regular, soothing voice and maintain complete confidence in what you are saying. Repetition is the key, so repeat the same phrases multiple times.

Have the person remove their shoes and lie on their back on a couch or bed, with their eyes closed, legs together, and arms at their sides.

Stand at the side of the couch. Begin as usual in the standing posture, and take a few silent breaths to clear and focus your mind.

Make both your hands into the gesture of Aries and shift to the spiral invoking posture. Draw the red energy of Aries into the sphere of your heart-center until it is bright red and spinning rapidly.

Shift into the projecting posture and press your right hand to the top of the head of the person you are treating. Continue to hold the Aries gesture with both hands. Let the energy of Aries flow from your heart-center into the person's head, and as you do so, say the following to the person, or words to the same effect:

> Your head is filling with the tingling, fiery energy of Aries. It flows from my hand into your head and soothes your head, filling your head with a warm red glow. It is a pleasant sensation. Feel its comforting warmth.

Continue speaking on this theme for a minute or so in a gentle, pleasant voice until your heart-center has returned to a soft white.

Change into the spiral invoking posture, with your hands formed in the gesture of Taurus, and draw down the red-purple energy of Taurus from the heavens into your heart-center until it is filled with this energy.

Shift into the projecting posture and lay your right hand on the throat of the person you are treating. Let the red-purple energy of Taurus flood from your right hand into the neck and upper shoulders of the person. Speak the following words, or words of the same general meaning:

> Your neck is filling with the cool, refreshing energy of Taurus. It flows outward from your neck into your shoulders and makes them feel relaxed. All the tension has gone from your neck and shoulders. Your neck and shoulders glow with this soothing energy.

Repeat these and similar words for a minute or so.

Adopt the spiral invoking posture, with both hands in the gesture of Gemini. Fill your heart-center with the purple energy of this sign.

Shift to the projecting posture and lay your right hand upon the upper chest of the person you are treating. Infuse the energy of Gemini into the upper chest, lungs, and arms of the person you are treating. Speak the following, or words to the same effect:

Your lungs are expanding and opening with fresh, clean air that is filled with the tingling energy of Gemini. It fills your lungs with a health-giving purple mist each time you breathe in. Inhale and feel it fill your lungs. The mist soaks into your chest and carries away all tiredness. It expands down your arms to your fingertips. Feel them tingle.

Continue with these and similar words for a minute.

Change back to the spiral invoking posture, with both your hands formed in the gesture of Cancer. Draw the blue-purple energy of Cancer down into your left hand and send it into the sphere of your heart-center.

Move into the projecting posture and lay your right hand between the nipples of the person you are treating. Send the energy of Cancer deep into the breast and stomach of the person. Speak these or similar words:

Your breasts and the front of your chest are filling with the cool, soothing blue-purple energy of Cancer. Feel the muscles over your ribs and breastbone relax. The blue-purple energy flows deep into your stomach and washes away all tension and discomfort.

Continue in this way for a minute or so as you empty your heart-center of the energy of Cancer.

Step back and once more adopt the spiral invoking posture, this time with your hands formed in the gesture of Leo. Draw down the rich blue energy of Leo and fill your heart-center with it.

Change to the projecting posture and place your right hand over the solar plexus of the person who lies before you. Send the energy deep into the body of the person you are treating as you flood their spine and heart with the blue energy of Leo and speak the following words:

Your heart fills with the vitalizing blue energy of Leo, which causes it to beat more regularly and more strongly. This energy flows downward into your spine and fills it from the top, where it joins your skull, to your tailbone at its base, making your entire spine tingle and feel refreshed.

Speak in this vein for a minute or so.

Revert to the spiral invoking posture, with both hands in the gesture of Virgo. Draw the blue-green energy of Virgo into your heart-center.

While you maintain the hand gesture, shift to the projecting posture and press your right hand upon the person's abdomen just above the navel. Visualize blue-green energy flowing from your heart-center in an expanding spiral down your right arm and into the small intestine of the person. Speak these or similar words:

> Strengthening, life-giving blue-green energy of Virgo floods into your intestines and into your spleen, making them active and strong, filling your abdomen with health and well-being. Feel the healthy energy within them, carrying away all tension and invigorating them.

Continue to speak in this way for a minute.

Straighten up and adopt the spiral invoking posture, with your hands in the gesture of Libra. Draw the green energy of Libra into your left hand and send it in a contracting spiral into your heart-center.

Change to the projecting posture and press your right hand upon the navel of the person you are treating. Release the energy of Libra to flow down your right arm and into the kidneys, lower back muscles, and buttocks of the person. Speak these or similar words:

> Active, expansive green energy of Libra floods through your abdomen and into both your kidneys in your lower back. It fills your lower back muscles and the muscles of your buttocks, making them feel light and relaxed, carrying away all tension and fatigue.

Adopt the spiral invoking posture, with your hands in the gesture of Scorpio, and draw down the yellow-green energy of this sign into your heart-center.

Change to the projecting posture and press your right hand gently to the abdomen of the person you are treating just below the navel, if you previously obtained explicit permission from the person you are treating to apply this touch. For obvious reasons of social propriety, you cannot press your hand to the groin of the person unless you know that person intimately, but that is where most of the energy needs to be sent. Speak these words:

Potent yellow-green energy of Scorpio flows into your groin, expanding into the region of your sexual organs and invigorating all of them. They feel energized and healthy, washed clean of all weakness and renewed.

Continue speaking in this manner for a minute or so.

Step back into the spiral invoking posture, with both hands in the gesture of Sagittarius, and draw down the yellow energy of this sign into your heart-center.

Change into the projecting posture and lay your right hand across both upper thighs of the person you are treating. Flood the thighs, hips, and liver of the person with the yellow energy of Sagittarius as you speak the following words or words of the same import:

Fiery yellow energy of Sagittarius floods down into your thighs and sends a gentle warmth upward to fill your hips and your liver with radiant, life-giving vitality. It drives away any discomfort or tension that might have accumulated there.

Continue speaking in this way in a soothing voice for a minute or so.

Adopt the spiral invoking posture, with both hands in the gesture of Capricorn, and draw the yellow-orange energy of this sign into your heart-center.

Change to the projecting posture and lay your right hand across both knees of the person you are treating. Flood their knee joints with the yellow-orange energy of Capricorn. Say these or similar words:

As I touch your knees, they are flooded with the earthy, strengthening yellow-orange energy of Capricorn. It fills both knee joints and drives away fatigue and soreness. It spreads through your bones, up and down your legs, making them strong and healthy.

Keep speaking in this way for a minute or so.

Move back into the spiral invoking posture and make your hands into the gesture of Aquarius. Draw down the orange energy of this sign and fill your heart-center with it.

Change to the projecting posture and press your right hand over both shins of the person you are treating. Flood the shins with the airy orange energy of Aquarius. Speak these words or similar words:

Your shins and the muscles of your calves and ankles are filling with the airy orange energy of Aquarius. It makes them feel lighter and drives away tiredness and aches while at the same time strengthening them.

Talk this way for a minute as you empty the Aquarius energy from your heart-center into the shins under your right hand.

Adopt the spiral invoking posture, with your hands in the gesture of Pisces, and draw into your heart-center the red-orange energy of this sign.

Shift into the projecting posture and press your right hand across both insteps of the person being treated. Send the energy of Pisces into the person's feet through your right hand, and speak these or similar words:

Into both your feet flows the gentle red-orange energy of Pisces. It fills your insteps, your toes, your heels, and the soles of your feet, making all their muscles and joints tingle with a pleasant, relaxed sensation that banishes tiredness from them.

Continue to speak in this soothing way for a minute.

Step back and adopt the manifesting posture, with both arms extended over the body of the person lying before you, palms turned downward, the fingers of your hands forming a triangle between your thumbs and forefingers. Speak these words or something like them of your own composition:

The twelve zones of your body are filled with the twelve healing, vitalizing, strengthening powers of the zodiac. Lie still with your eyes closed for a minute or two and be aware of these powers soothing and energizing your entire body.

Continue to stand in this posture for a minute or two as you visualize along with the person the twelve energies filling the person's body. There must be a strong visualization on your part.

Shift into the closing posture and hold it for a minute silently, with your mind relaxed and tranquil. Release any expectation of result from your thoughts.

Change to the standing posture and draw a few silent breaths to end the exercise. If the person lying before you has not opened their eyes, tell them to open them and to stand up, if they are well enough to stand. Assure them that the treatment is complete and was successful. It is important that both you and the person you have treated have confidence in the working of the twelve zodiacal energies.

APPENDIX
QUICK REFERENCE GUIDES

THE FOLLOWING THREE FIGURES ARE intended as quick visual guides to the twenty-four postures, the twenty-four hand gestures, and the occult correspondences on the wheel of the zodiac used in kinesic magic. You may find it useful to photocopy them, enlarge them, and put them on your wall, where you can look at them while you are practicing.

In the first figure, the zodiac signs have been applied to the twelve pairs of postures in their elemental trines: first the three Earth signs, then the Air signs, then the Water signs, and finally the Fire signs. If you study the relationship between each pair of postures and the zodiac sign, you will find many symbolic links.

In the illustrations of the twenty-four hand gestures, the hand shown is a right hand viewed from the palm. You should not strive to imitate these hand positions exactly, but should make each gesture with your hand relaxed. Your fingers will often be slightly bent, but this is not important so long as the gestures are distinct.

In the final illustration, the occult correspondences used in kinesic magic are gathered together on the wheel of the zodiac for convenience. This figure shows the order of the zodiac signs; the solar and lunar sects; the element, quality, and ruling planet of each sign; and the color associated with each sign.

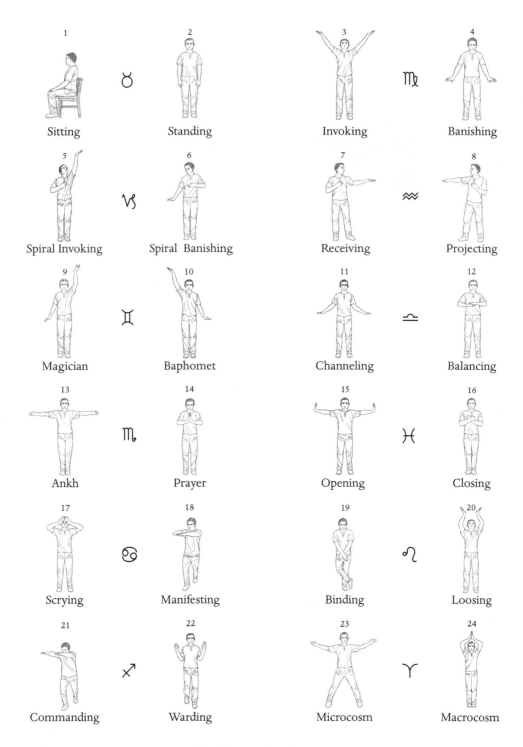

The Twenty-Four Postures

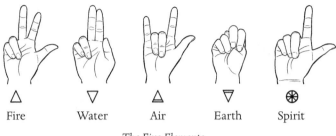

Fire   Water   Air   Earth   Spirit

The Five Elements

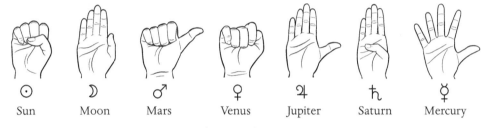

Sun   Moon   Mars   Venus   Jupiter   Saturn   Mercury

The Seven Planets

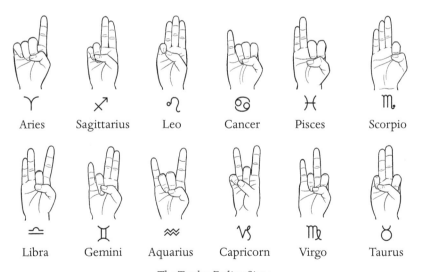

Aries   Sagittarius   Leo   Cancer   Pisces   Scorpio

Libra   Gemini   Aquarius   Capricorn   Virgo   Taurus

The Twelve Zodiac Signs

The Twenty-Four Hand Gestures

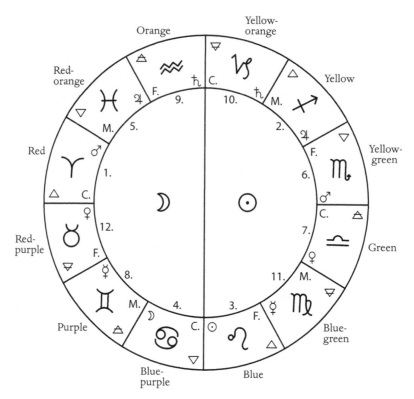

Occult Correspondences on the Wheel of the Zodiac

To Write to the Author

If you wish to contact the author or would like more information about this book, please write to the author in care of Llewellyn Worldwide Ltd. and we will forward your request. Both the author and the publisher appreciate hearing from you and learning of your enjoyment of this book and how it has helped you. Llewellyn Worldwide Ltd. cannot guarantee that every letter written to the author can be answered, but all will be forwarded. Please write to:

Donald Tyson
℅ Llewellyn Worldwide
2143 Wooddale Drive
Woodbury, MN 55125-2989
Please enclose a self-addressed stamped envelope for reply,
or $1.00 to cover costs. If outside the U.S.A., enclose
an international postal reply coupon.

Many of Llewellyn's authors have websites with additional information and resources. For more information, please visit our website at http://www.llewellyn.com.